Advance praise for *An Intelligent Career*:

"A clear and comprehensive exploration of the fundamentals that underlie career success."
—Larry Smith, Associate Professor, University of Waterloo and author of *No Fears, No Excuses: What You Need to Do to Have a Great Career*

"Carefully researched and easily accessible, *An Intelligent Career* will help you think about and manage your career in immensely practical ways. Chock full of interesting stories with deep insights, this book should be required reading not just for millennials but for anyone looking to reassert ownership of their own career."
—Sydney Finkelstein, Professor, Dartmouth College and author of *Superbosses: How Exceptional Leaders Master the Flow of Talent*

"*An Intelligent Career* takes readers beyond a psychological approach to career consulting into emphasizing the value of your own experience integrated into the real world, including emerging technology. Your career decisions are now in context, so you can approach your career future with greater conviction."
—Pam Lassiter, Principal, Lassiter Consulting and author of *CareerJournal.com's Editor's Choice, The New Job Security*

"The digital age makes continued learning and conscious career decision-making a number one priority in order to stay relevant in today's workforce. *An Intelligent Career* is a compelling and stimulating read which provides readers with invaluable insights and practical advice on how to manage your career in the 21st century. A must-read for everybody who cares about their careers."
—Nick van Dam, Global CLO at McKinsey & Company and Professor, Nyenrode Business University

"Written by three of the most eminent people studying careers today, this book helps you find your personal answers to some of the most pressing questions about you and your career, such as: What am I good at? What drives me? How do I work best? and Who can help me thrive? This book is a rich, concise, and beautifully written distillation of years of research and thinking (by the authors and others, such as Ellen Langer, Edgar Schein, and Mary Catherine Bateson) about the different types of career intelligence. It provides clear, concise steps for taking stock (growing your self-awareness) and taking action (achieving success.) The final chapter, 'Building Your World' is beautifully written and provides enough wisdom and inspiration to make it alone worth the price of the book! You or someone you love should definitely have a copy of *An Intelligent Career*!"
—Douglas (Tim) Hall, Professor, Boston University and author of *Careers Around the World* and *Careers In and Out of Organizations*

"*An Intelligent Career* provides insight and inspiration for how to use work to become the person you want to be, rather than be used by work and left behind as the digital revolution changes the landscape of careers. This splendid book will greatly increase your knowledge of why, how, and when to make your next career move."
—Mark Savickas, Professor, Northeastern Ohio Universities College of Medicine and author of *Life Design Counseling Manual* and *Career Counseling*

"An appealing wake-up call, with academically supported practical advice, structured storytelling, cutting-edge approaches and historical best practices. An inspiring guide to life and career, to be put into the hands of every ambitious information worker. A real treasure."
—Wolfgang Hennen, CFO and Chief HR Officer at Lidl Belgium

"Modern careers take place in conditions of uncertainty, disruption, and emergence. While most of us can't *control* our careers, we can create *propensity for success* by becoming more aware of current and potential change and adapting ourselves so that we can take advantage of emergent opportunities. If career self-management is about creating an adaptive mindset, then *An Intelligent Career* provides a practical toolkit for survival in this environment."
—David Clutterbuck, Principal, David Clutterbuck Partnership and author of *The Talent Wave: Why Succession Planning Fails and What to Do About It*

An Intelligent Career

Taking Ownership of Your Work and Your Life

MICHAEL B. ARTHUR

SVETLANA N. KHAPOVA

AND

JULIA RICHARDSON

Oxford University Press is a department of the University of Oxford. It furthers the University's objective of excellence in research, scholarship, and education by publishing worldwide. Oxford is a registered trade mark of Oxford University Press in the UK and certain other countries.

Published in the United States of America by Oxford University Press
198 Madison Avenue, New York, NY 10016, United States of America.

Library of Congress Cataloging-in-Publication Data
Names: Arthur, Michael B. (Michael Bernard), 1945– author. | Khapova, Svetlana N., author. | Richardson, Julia, 1964- author.
Title: An intelligent career : taking ownership of your work and your life / Michael B. Arthur, Svetlana N. Khapova, Julia Richardson.
Description: Oxford ; New York : Oxford University Press, [2017] | Includes bibliographical references and index.
Identifiers: LCCN 2016012100 | ISBN 9780190494131 (hardback : alk. paper)
Subjects: LCSH: Career development. | Career changes. | Quality of work life.
Classification: LCC HF5549.5.C35 A779 2017 | DDC 650.1—dc23
LC record available at https://lccn.loc.gov/2016012100

9 8 7 6 5 4 3 2 1

Printed by Sheridan Books, Inc., United States of America

To intelligent career owners everywhere.

CONTENTS

I keep six honest serving-men
(They taught me all I knew);
Their names are What and Why and When
And How and Where and Who.

—Rudyard Kipling

Your boss applauds your performance but promotes someone else into a job you covet. A colleague urges you to go along with the group rather than express your own values. A reading on motivation contradicts what you are witnessing at work. An appeal to your expertise from a complete outsider catches you unaware. What is going on? Why is it happening to you? When can you respond? How can you take greater control over your situation?

If you have thought about these kinds of questions, this book is for you. *An Intelligent Career* will help you make sense of your employment situation—including self-employment and unemployment—and to make positive changes. Ultimately, our goal is to help you learn to work on your own terms, to assume ownership of your career, and to understand what that can mean for your life as a whole.

WHAT IS AN INTELLIGENT CAREER?

An intelligent career involves using your intelligence to pursue your career. The *Oxford English Dictionary* defines "intelligence" as understanding, knowledge, or comprehension of something.[1] In this straightforward sense, intelligence can also be applied to learning new things, so that intelligence can feed on itself. For example, you choose to reuse tools that worked well and stop using ineffective ones. You learn about how other people work and become more selective about those you want to work with again or about how you will work with them.

We define "career" as the evolving sequence of a person's work experiences over time: *evolving* because nobody knows what the future will bring; concerning both *work* and time because it is over time that someone can change the way they work or it can be changed for them by outside forces.[2] We also use the term "intelligent career" in this book to emphasize your opportunity to claim *ownership* of your career. How are you applying your intelligence to your career? In what direction are you *going*? What is preventing you from moving ahead? How can you clear the way? Owning your career calls for you to be in control of, and take action over, questions like these.[3]

For most of human history, our primary economic concern has been with physical work. People were needed to work in the fields, mine coal, build railroads, or work in factories that manufactured industrial goods. However, as technology has advanced, physical strength or agility has become less important, and work has become increasingly driven by a new principle. This new principle is what the late Dartmouth business professor James Brian Quinn defined as "the development and deployment of intellectual resources, rather than . . . the management of physical assets."[4] This includes the application of intellectual resources to physical work, for example in the health professions, or a wide variety of skills and crafts, or the delivery of computer-assisted production and operations work.

We are living in an information age, when managing big data in areas such as finance, healthcare, and marketing is a field unto itself. Never before have we had so much information about so many subjects. Professions have been specialized to the extent that we need specialists to manage groups of specialists who would otherwise not be able to talk to one another. This exponential growth in information has spawned a knowledge economy. It is an economy in which we can expect technology to take over more and more tasks as we become freer to do what we do best: think, learn, synthesize, analyze, imagine, invent, and most of all—work together.

WHAT ABOUT YOUR CAREER?

You don't need to join any diploma-seeking paper chase to have an intelligent career. However, the proportion of people advancing to higher education provides one indicator of where things are going. That proportion has exceeded 40% in some countries, and is still rising.[5] Another indicator is the rapid growth of connections to the World Wide Web, especially in supposedly less "developed" countries. In classrooms and through on-the-job learning, people are being trained to work in a knowledge-driven world and to contribute to its insatiable thirst for intellectual resources.[6] Physical space is interwoven with virtual space, and we all use goods and services from far-flung places. Intelligent careers are the lifeblood of this world.

Intelligent careers contribute to wider collective efforts and invite you to apply your intelligence to a range of underlying challenges. These challenges call on both your rational and relational skills: to grapple with a compelling problem on your own, to understand and communicate effectively with other people, to collaborate effectively in a high-performing team, and more. They call on your capabilities to take care of yourself and care about other people, and to adapt to changing circumstances. By combining these capabilities, an intelligent career can encompass making an individual contribution, working effectively with other people, and contributing to both the generation and transfer of knowledge.

Intelligent careers also involve more than seeking an education or topping up your skills. They call for an understanding of the changing nature of work and employment and of the processes through which knowledge is generated, transferred, and applied. That means appreciating new career possibilities, more dynamic work arrangements, and the growing demand for knowledge work around the globe. It means navigating your work life with an authenticity that replaces any straightforward loyalty to a single employer. It calls for better understanding of yourself, your collaborators, the employers and customers for whom you work, and the world you live in.

WHAT ABOUT RIGHT NOW?

- Do you know enough about the potential opportunities open to you?
- Is anyone helping you identify and understand those opportunities?
- Do you have your own talent agent—literally or figuratively?
- Are you working with an employment agency, a headhunter, or a career coach that understands you and is helping you look ahead to your next move?
- Do you have a group of former colleagues, occupational peers, fellow alums, friends, or family performing a similar function?
- Who are the people that appreciate what you can do and stand ready to recommend you for new work?
- Would you like to better support a client, friend, or loved one as they pursue their intelligent career?
- How do you get noticed and included in an employer's search for talent?
- How do you respond to a search when you are contacted?
- How can you think about your response, gather more information, and stay in the running for other searches?

If you are wondering about any of these questions, this book can help. It can help anyone seeking to take greater control over their own lives: professionals ready to plan their next move, people stuck or unhappy with where they are right now, students making the transition to the work world, people who are presently unemployed, midlife career changers, dual-career couples, and more. This book is also for prospective advisors—managers, teachers, consultants, and coaches—who seek to better understand and work with others. If you are such an advisor, we still address you directly, in anticipation that you may want to test the ideas in this book on yourself before applying them to other people.

Just as the knowledge economy is global, so is the intended audience for this book. Intelligent careers are a global phenomenon calling for shared understanding across and between nations and cultures. Our goal is to help you find common ground with other readers wherever they may live. It's in your and their interests to use available technology to talk with and learn from one another. And it's in your and their interests to build the knowledge economy together.

WHAT'S IN THIS BOOK?

An Intelligent Career will help you make informed choices in today's changing world of work. It's not going to give you direct answers, but it will signpost the landscape and point out significant landmarks. It will help you examine a range of issues, both personal and environmental, and allow you to take a dynamic, multifaceted, view of your life's work. It will help you identify and work on the most significant questions that you face. Along the way, you will also discover that the most effective intelligent career owners create personal paths to success. These may or may not gel with the paths anticipated by your present or future employer.

We deliver our message in two parts: one to help you make fuller sense of the present, and one to help you take action in the future. The first part encourages you to reflect, through a series of questions presented in the chapter titles. These questions echo the "six wise men" cited in the Kipling verse at the beginning of this introduction, and invite you to pursue a deeper understanding of your life and work experiences to this point. The second part anticipates your further participation in the knowledge economy. There, chapter titles employ action verbs pointing you to how you can influence the way your future life and work develop. We also call on you to both recognize and act on the opportunities available to you, and invite you to contribute to the overall health (and not just the financial health) of our interdependent world.

Why three authors? Writing this book called for the exploration and reconciliation of a wide range of approaches, and we quickly determined that a collaborative approach would produce a clearer and more timely guide. In writing for a global audience, we also took advantage of our separate locations, across three continents and three countries. We further reached out to our separate networks in other parts of the globe in seeking ideas, examples, and insights to complement our own. As a result, the examples in this book come from far and wide. They involve people who have been influenced by different social backgrounds, passed through varied educational systems, are young, old, middle-aged; single, married, and parents of small children and grown children.

All our examples are real—concerning people we have interviewed directly or who have been interviewed by a colleague or featured in a respected periodical, newspaper, or website. Most examples are about people who have expanded their opportunities. Some, though, report where people have stumbled. For better or worse, the examples are all about how people have applied their intelligence in some way: to make sense of the world, to keep up with a changing job, to stay employable for other jobs, and—for many—to build a satisfying career.

WHAT'S NOT IN THIS BOOK?

This is not a book that pursues any formal approach to intelligence, such as your intelligence quotient (IQ) or emotional intelligence (EQ), although we provide relevant background information on those concepts. More broadly, this is not a scholarly treatise. Rather, it directly addresses the lay reader on whose career we focus.

Also, this is not a book that seeks to impose any restricted view of what you should do with your career. For example, we cover interpersonal networking here, but not to the exclusion of your inner self. We cover technology, but in a way that seeks to help you see the advantages and the pitfalls. By the end, we are writing about the "world" in which you are building your intelligent career. However, it is a personal world, shaped by your own experiences and relationships.

Moreover, this is not a book with self-tests and quizzes to puzzle out whether you are more suited for training gorillas or designing robots. It will not directly teach you how to manage your emotions, evaluate your transferable skills, dress for success, or take on new technology (although we will show you where some of these topics fit into the wider learning landscape). We do not promise you will become rich—although you might.

ARE YOU READY?

Living an intelligent career involves, in the words of our subtitle, taking ownership of your life and your world. Wherever you live—from the Russian Federation, across Europe to North and South America, around the Southern Hemisphere and back to Asia and Africa, we are all participants in the same economic system. In one sense we all compete for work, but in another sense we want that competition to be productive. We want a system that links effort to rewards, recognizes the importance of taking responsibility, and provides opportunities to learn. This being the case, how can we help create these outcomes for ourselves—rather than expect governments or employers to create them for us?

The second part of our subtitle refers to your world. This is the social world you are building as you pursue your career. It is a world that calls for collaborative work—with other people; within and between organizations, regions, and countries; between alliance partners; or within and between professional communities—directed toward a global marketplace. Your own and other people's social worlds are the glue that holds everything together. Developing and deepening your relationships with other people on your own terms, face-to-face or over the Web, are fundamental to a successful intelligent career.

Understanding yourself, making money, and improving the social world around you are not contradictory ideas. You just need to do the work to bring them together—to take ownership of your intelligent career!

Taking Stock

I n this first part of the book we help you take stock of your present situation. That is, we help you reflect on the education, relationships, and experiences you have accrued, and how they can contribute to your intelligent career. We do so through six chapters that ask successive questions about what an intelligent career means, or can mean, to you. Those questions are: "What does an intelligent career involve?" "Where do intelligent careers happen?" "Why do you work?" "How do you work?" "With whom do you work?" and "When do you change?" The sections in each chapter offer alternative responses to the chapter title, each helping you better appreciate how intelligent careers come about.

Whatever your present situation, you will have been exposed to a range of thorny debates about the future of work. These concern such topics as the distribution of wealth, the future of global trade, the fate of the middle class, the returns to capital versus labor, the relevance of trade unionism, and the benefits versus costs of technology.[1] History tells us there have been similar debates before—about, for example, the introduction of the printed word, the factory system, the delivery of goods versus services, and most recently the emergence of the World Wide Web. It's important to know about these debates, but it's also important to keep things in perspective.

In this part of the book we invite you to take ownership of your own intelligent career. Doing so does not necessarily mean pursuing greater wealth, prestige, or power. It means taking ownership on your own terms and being ready to navigate your future life's journey. Our proposition is straightforward. The better prepared you are to succeed in your intelligent career, the better prepared you will be to make a difference in the world—and to contribute to those debates from your own experience.

What Does an Intelligent Career Involve?

Not I, nor anyone else can travel that road for you,
You must travel it for yourself.
It is not far,
It is within reach.

—Walt Whitman

Dominique Browning seemed to do everything right. She studied at two prestigious universities and then began a career in publishing from the ground up. She held positions at *Savvy*, *American Photographer*, and *Esquire* magazines, building experience before taking the job of executive editor at *Texas Monthly*. She went on to break an industry-wide glass ceiling at *Newsweek*, where she was the first woman to be appointed as an assistant managing editor. After her success at *Newsweek*, she stepped out of the publishing industry to serve as a founding partner at Edison Schools, seeking to bring more efficient private management to struggling publicly funded schools. Along the way she married and had two sons. A few years later she returned to publishing, this time as editor-in-chief at *Mirabella* magazine.

With her distinctive combination of writing, editing, publishing, and business experience she was next recruited to take the helm of the re-launched magazine *House & Garden*. She served in that role for twelve years as the magazine was passed among five publishers, ending up with the prestigious Condé Nast publishing group. By that time, she had become a respected and leading editor in New York's highly competitive publishing industry. She had an office to go to, appointments to keep, and a title. She was divorced now, but that suited her. She enjoyed the inter-action with her fellow workers, always had things to do, and liked being busy. She had what she wanted.[1]

Then one Monday in late 2007 she went to her corporate headquarters for an anticipated regular meeting. Instead, she was told that the maga-zine was to be discontinued, and everyone had to pack up and leave by Friday. Security guards were assigned to watch employees' every move. In public, she sustained her leadership role, asserting her team "had a great run," "took a magazine from zero to 950,000 readers in 10 years," won multiple awards, and published six books. "We were the gold standard. We published great design and we always held out for the great project." In private, she was in a tailspin:

> Without work, who was I? I do not mean that my title defined me. What did define me was the simple act of working. The loss of my job triggered a cascade of self-doubt and depression. I felt like a fail-ure. Not that the magazine had failed—that I had. . . . I didn't want time to think things over, things like feeling guilty about spend-ing more time with my office mates than with my children; feeling sad that those children were leaving home; or feeling disappointed in love or frightened by terrible illness. . . . With the closing of the magazine, my beloved family of colleagues was obliterated. And so was the structure of my life.[2]

With the end of her former life at *House & Garden*, Browning lurched into self-doubt and depression. She had lunch with every person in her field that she knew, but couldn't find comparable work. Finally, she decided to get out of debt by selling her New York home. She retreated to a run-down house in Rhode Island she had bought after her divorce, and began to reread classic books and play the piano again. She wrote that she had a different kind of work to do now, to grow into what she called "a new season." Walking along the beach, she found inspiration in the shifting tides.

> I am not old and not young; not betrothed and not alone; not broken and yet not quite whole; thinking back, looking forward. But present. These are my intertidal years.[3]

In time, she recovered, taking writing and consulting assignments that kept her active and provided a source of income. In 2010 she published a book about her experiences and started a companion website. In 2011 she founded Moms' Clean Air Force, committed to helping busy parents lobby politicians to provide clean air for their children. Instead of fulfilling just one job, she was now applying and developing her talents across a range of jobs. She was free from the constant pressure of publishing deadlines, and her livelihood no longer depended on the decisions of any single employer.[4]

What can we make of the Dominique Browning story? Was she let down by her publisher, or did she let herself down? Was she simply a random casualty of changing industry circumstances, as print magazines came under pressure from alternative reading material on the World Wide Web? Had she anticipated the changes the Web would bring to her industry, or had she assumed that publishing would stay much the same? Did she respond to visible and highly flattering definitions of success, or was she really doing what she wanted to do? All of these questions relate to our main chapter title, "What Does an Intelligent Career Involve?" Let us examine that question through a series of alternative responses. For each response we invite you to think about how it applies to your own career, compare it with previous responses, and develop your awareness. By the end, you will have a deeper understanding of the chapter's underlying question and how it relates to your own situation.

CONDITIONAL LOYALTY

One way to respond to our chapter's opening question is to focus on traditional ideas about employee loyalty. For most of the twentieth century you were expected to spend your working life with one company, and be rewarded with a pension and a comfortable retirement. Proponents of career development, like Massachusetts Institute of Technology thought leader Edgar Schein, envisioned a "mutually profitable relationship" between the organization's human resource planning, on the one hand, and the individual's career, on the other. Recruitment, selection, job rotation, training, continuing education, job redesign, and even retirement were seen as "matching processes" that balanced organizational and individual needs, rather than as the sole prerogative of the organization. At the time of their publication in 1978, Schein's ideas were widely embraced by organizations and their employees.[5] Although Condé Nast wasn't Dominique Browning's first employer, it seems she had come to expect the kind of mutually profitable relationship that Schein described.

Yet, as her abrupt firing illustrates, for many of us the ideal of lifetime employment with a single employer has been relegated to the misty past. Today, few companies keep a salaried employee over the course of a lifetime. For example, IBM was once seen by many as the flagship of lifetime employment, claiming an ethos of "respect for the individual" that traced back to the early twentieth century. In 1984, an internal document proclaimed, "for more than four decades, not a single person has lost as much as an hour's work because of a layoff." Yet, by 1994 the company had used a series of early retirement programs to shed 100,000 workers, 25 percent of its global workforce. This collapse of IBM's longstanding no-layoff policy seemed like the final nail in the coffin of lifetime employment—at least in large, private sector corporations.[6]

Can anyone still aspire to lifetime employment? It may survive in the public sector, but even there it is controversial.[7] How about making partner in a large, well-established New York law firm? In dealing with the first major recession of the twenty-first century, the chairman of the venerable Wall Street law firm White & Case announced a second round of layoffs in which another 200 lawyers, including a number of partners, would lose their jobs. As one surviving partner commented:

> The loyalty of the institution to its people, and vice versa, isn't really there anymore—it's a different animal from what a lot of us were used to. It's much more of a business now and less of a true partnership. The problem is we're supposed to all be in this together. But at some point, you stop and think: 'Well, maybe we're not.'[8]

As the *New York Times* reported, the White & Case example is part of a larger picture of professional service providers that involves "a potential paradigm shift as fundamental as the one that has hit investment banks and the auto industry," namely that being big, as a business model, "seems bound for obsolescence."[9] Almost twenty years after pubishlishing his ideas about a mutually profitable employer-employee relationship, Edgar Schein saw a "normal evolution" in individuals taking responsibility for their own careers—"because the reality for organizations is that they cannot predict or control career paths in the way that they used to do."[10] The new loyalty, then, is more conditional, and as much on your own terms as your employer's terms. Today, you must cultivate those qualities that contribute to your intelligent career—among them making use of opportunity, adaptation, the Web, your talent, your knowledge, and your control over your own work—in order to stay employable.

OPPORTUNITY-TAKING

Another way to respond to our opening question is to focus on opportunity-taking. Take the example of Jeff Price, a one-time Hard Rock Café busboy, college disk jockey, independent rock band producer, and employee of online store eMusic. As he worked his way through those jobs, he saw inevitable changes taking hold in the music industry. He complained that digital distributors still worked under the old business model, developed when physical record production and distribution was standard practice. He believed the model had become exploitative, and founded TuneCore, the first music distributor to offer artists complete control over their work. Fueled by an investment from the recording equipment retailer Guitar Center, TuneCore grew to release "more songs in one day than a major record label releases in a year." The releases were exclusively digital, available for sale on iTunes and other online music stores. In a talk at the Australian Music Business Conference, he explained his motivation this way:

> I don't like bullies. I don't like scam artists or people that attempt to take advantage of others. I have a strong moral fiber that I try to emulate in my daily life—don't throw trash on the ground, help someone that is lost, stop for a crying child, give directions, provide information and advice when asked, get involved, help people. So I decided to do something about it and started a company that changed the music industry.[11]

Price was ready to seize an opportunity in a changing industry, and created an innovative business model that gave recording artists control over their work. He became one of an ascendant breed of people using the Web to practice *disintermediation*: bypassing traditional "middlemen" or gatekeepers to bring product or service providers and customers together.[12] Disintermediation has already dramatically changed, for example, the auction house, bookselling, and stockbroking industries. It is changing the broadcasting and entertainment industries, and all other industries where services can be delivered over the Web. It has changed the job search industry too, so that today people are taking the initiative to look for jobs themselves through social networking, rather than waiting for a recruiter to post an ad.[13] What opportunities can you take?

PERSISTENT ADAPTATION

Despite what Jeff Price observed, organizations *are* adapting. Under the old business model, an organization performed all of its major functions—manufacturing, service delivery, accounting, finance, information technology, marketing, public relations, research and development, and so on—in-house. Multistate and multinational organizations would then replicate these functions across different divisions or geographical locations concentrating on different product or service categories. This business strategy allowed time and space for people to explore new opportunities and to develop long-term careers. However, once organizations gave up on the lifetime employment model, the time, space, and opportunities within their boundaries began to diminish.

In the new world, adaptive organizations focus on an area of specialization, or their "core competencies." Organizations that had previously restricted themselves to local arrangements began looking further afield for supplies, services, and even workers. Well-known examples like Nike, outsourcing its shoe manufacturing to countries such as Indonesia and China, and Intel, making chips and switches but not personal computers, were widely imitated. For Nike, with core competencies in research and marketing, it felt comfortable to cut costs by outsourcing manufacturing. Over time, despite concern over the alleged use of "sweatshop" labor, the business argument that work should go to where the "value chain" is best served—that is, to where the work could be most economically or creatively performed—has held firm. As a result, "restructuring" and "outsourcing" initiatives have dismantled earlier arrangements in which employees expected to work together and stay together.

The late management guru Peter Drucker once compared a successful organization to an air base, where flyers, meteorologists, radio operators, doctors, armorers, photographers, and other specialists each exercised "decision-making skills and self-governing judgment." Despite their diversity, these separate specializations each contributed to the same purpose, the long-term well-being of the organization.[14] Today, the analogous contemporary organization is more like an independent filmmaking company. It also brings together diverse specialists—producers, directors, screenwriters, actors, technicians, and many more. However, their common purpose is to produce a single film. Once individual contributors have played their part, they are left to find their next "gig" on their own. How different is that from your own situation?

As the focus on organizational performance through restructuring continued, Drucker reversed his earlier position that organizations should take care of their employees' interests. The role of the organization as guardian of employees' careers, wrote Drucker, had failed.[15] In the foreseeable future, organizations and individuals would need to pursue separate agendas. You need to think about your own agenda and future employability, make sense of your organization's agenda, and adapt to it on your own terms.

YOUR OWN CONTRIBUTION

Drucker was on to something. He was one of the first management thinkers to focus on knowledge work, which he defined as a set of work roles requiring education, training, and "the ability to acquire and to apply theoretical and analytical knowledge." In doing so, he distinguished knowledge work from the mindlessly repetitive office and factory work that fueled the industrial age. Today, knowledge work is woven into the fabric of most skilled jobs in one way or another. Learning to use a new piece of software, teaching a class by applying the latest educational findings, or becoming comfortable with a new set of cultural assumptions for doing business in a foreign country are all examples of the knowledge work that is widely expected in the twenty-first century.

Statistics back up these claims. For example, the growth in higher education suggests that knowledge work in the United States and Canada has grown from around 20 percent to 35 percent of the national labor force, perhaps more if everyone in the broad US Bureau of Labor Statistics category of "managerial, professional and technical workers" is included. A report by McKinsey & Company suggested that 40 percent of the US labor force and 70 percent of jobs created since 1998 involved knowledge work.[16] Jobs with the fastest growth rates today require advanced knowledge or training in science and engineering; countries that excel today at educating young people in these fields will be the leaders of tomorrow.[17] Internet access is another way to estimate the number of people who are ready to contribute to the knowledge economy. Internet users in Asia (39%), South America (54%), and Africa (27%) are fast catching up to the more than 75% of the overall population in North America, western Europe, Australia, and New Zealand.[18]

In his landmark book *The World Is Flat, New York Times* journalist Thomas Friedman credits Nanda Nilekani, former CEO of Infosys, with providing the lesson that massive investments in technology and software have leveled the global playing field. Intellectual work can now be "disaggregated, delivered, distributed, produced, and put back together again," providing "a whole new degree of freedom" to the way people go about their work. Friedman concluded, "it is now possible for more people than ever to collaborate and compete in real time with more people on more different kinds of work from more different corners of the planet and on a more equal footing than at any previous time in the history of the world."[19] If you are reading this book, in all likelihood you are already one of those people. You are a contributor to the global knowledge-driven economy.

YOUR TALENT DEVELOPMENT

Instead of engaging in "matching processes," as Edgar Schein once suggested, organizations today focus on "recruiting, retaining and developing talent."[20] However, the specific focus is on pursuing the organization's own present and future business objectives. The language of *talent development* and creation of positions such as *talent development manager* plays well with senior managers and shareholders alike. A related idea is to join the so-called *war for talent*, where organizations vie to recruit and retain the best employees, but only because those employees are able to contribute to organizational goals.[21] How, though, does a company recruit and retain talent if its primary focus is what talented people can do for the company, rather than what the company might be able to do for those people?

The Dominique Browning story with which we opened this chapter offers a sharp lesson here. She was part of her employer's top talent pool, as long as the magazine she was editing served the organization's larger publishing strategy. At the time she was fired, it was also reported that her immediate boss, Condé Nast group's appointed publisher for *House & Garden*, had just resigned. Moreover, the group had three more magazines—*Architectural Digest*, and the recently launched *Domino* and *Vogue Living*—in the home design and furnishing field. There were also new magazines from other publishing houses getting in the way.[22] So Condé Nast took a simple choice to invest more in its three other magazines, rather than face an uncertain future with *House & Garden* in a crowded field. Given this choice, Browning and her staff became expendable. Their talent no longer mattered.

The problem with a talent-centered approach is that "inducing insiders with key knowledge to remain with the organization" is subject to the changing strategy of the organization.[23] Browning's reaction to being fired suggests she was very much induced to remain with Condé Nast. It's possible that employers may be becoming more sensitive to individual career agendas. Google has appealed to its managers to "Help employees with their career development."[24] UK management consultant David Clutterbuck has called for employers to "build an environment where honest, well-informed and continuous conversations about career opportunities can take place."[25] However, you need to exercise your own judgment. You can respect your organization's interest in retaining and developing talent while sustaining a separate interest—in pursuing and examining opportunities for yourself.

YOUR PATH TO PRODUCTIVITY

Popular author Daniel Pink has called the ubiquity of the personal computer "Karl Marx's revenge."[26] Pink was referring to Marx's argument about the industrial era, that the ruling class was able to wield their power over the working class because they owned the factories and the machinery—the "means of production." Pink's argument was that in the information age, the means of production—that is, the personal computer—had shifted from the factory or office to the worker's own home.[27] Moreover, the arrival of the personal computer was just the start of this shift. Today, there are faster and faster search engines and more and more voice- and video-conferencing services available without charge over the Web, while smart phones and tablets allow people to work anywhere and anytime and still maintain close connections with one another. All of these technologies favor intelligent careers acted out by people willing to take charge of their working lives on their own terms.

Technology does not facilitate intelligent careers by itself. End users—human beings—must be educated and trained for this shift in the means of production. The education innovators Bernie Trilling and Charles Fadel argue that the world has changed so fundamentally that "the roles of learning and education in day-to-day living have also changed forever." They envision a new balance between traditional and twenty-first-century education, as illustrated in Figure 1.1.[28]
The right-hand columns in Figure 1.1 are all components of intelligent careers. Instead of sitting at desks and receiving a fixed body of knowledge from a teacher at the front of the classroom, today's students will be better prepared for tomorrow's world by learning to collaborate with others in hands-on projects. In these, they can pose relevant questions, problem-solve, use Internet resources, and participate in a virtual community. In the global, knowledge-based economy, today's students need to be able to learn in new ways, and to interact productively with others very different from themselves.

Did you receive or are you receiving the kind of formal education that Trilling and Fadel propose—or anything like it? Do you take a learner-centered view of your own work arrangements? Can you interact with others, address questions and problems, and collaborate over shared goals with a sense of global community? How seriously do you take the call for lifelong learning in your own life? These are all questions worth asking for yourself, and—if you are a parent—for your children. Trends in technology and education suggest that today's intelligent career owners will have the wind at their backs. With new opportunities, however, come new obligations, to which we now turn.

Teacher-directed	Learner-centered
Direct instruction	Interactive exchange
Knowledge	Skills
Content	Process
Basic skills	Applied skills
Facts and principles	Questions and problems
Theory	Practice
Curriculum	Projects
Time-slotted	On-demand
One-size-fits-all	Personalized
Competitive	Collaborative
Classroom	Global community
Text-based	Web-based
Summative tests	Formative evaluations
Learning for school	Learning for life

A New   Balance

Figure 1.1   A "New Balance" Between Traditional and Twenty-First-Century Education

STAYING IN CONTROL

Let us turn to France for a troubling example. On a remarkable Sunday a few years ago, the French bank Société Générale (SocGen) stood to lose up to 50 billion euros in the futures market. It eliminated its exposure over the next three days, taking a loss of 6.4 billion euros, the biggest single reported trading loss in banking history. SocGen placed the entire blame on one of its traders, thirty-one-year-old Jérôme Kerviel. He was only supposed to work on "perfectly hedged" positions, where daily profits or losses were exactly offset against one another. However, he soon realized that he could game the system, buying and selling stock on the same day, or even on different days, to take advantage of price fluctuations. As a result he earned 43 million euros for the bank in the previous year, and an assigned (but unpaid) personal bonus of 300,000 euros. Along the way, by his reckoning, he generated a total of 93 "alertes"—warnings generated by SocGen's control system indicating that his trading was irregular.

Not surprisingly, Kerviel and his employer disagreed over who was to blame. SocGen presented him as an isolated case, but he claimed that what he did was common practice among other traders. He subsequently lost the argument in the courtroom. However, the *Financial Times* has observed that SocGen and many other investment banks were behaving like casinos, and that "no self-respecting casino would have made [SocGen's] mistake."[29] Despite receiving repeated warnings, neither the employee nor the employer placed any further check on the risk-taking involved. What can you learn from this?

Jérôme Kerviel's story coincided with the start of a four-year recession that has an enduring effect on the economic landscape. It parallels many other reports that CEOs, top management teams, or their subordinates took risks that lay beyond any public understanding of what their companies were about. In their greed, these wayward careerists—in Enron, Hollinger, Worldcom, and many other organizations—created grave consequences for others who could have reasonably expected greater stability in their lives.[30] Intelligent careers, with their emphasis on the individual talents and collaborative teamwork that make agile, innovative work possible, call for us to each manage our own ambitions. This includes supporting the kind of regulations that hold powerful individuals responsible for their actions, and taking personal responsibility to avoid getting into the kind of hole Kerviel dug for himself. Staying in control of your future is part of taking your career seriously.

BEING TRUE TO YOURSELF

"This above all: to thine own self be true." The often-repeated phrase from Shakespeare's character Polonius, in *Hamlet*, invites you to look to your inner self rather than being drawn by the kinds of temptations faced by Jerome Kerviel or the supervisors who seemed to condone his behavior. But just what is the self? One definition in the *Oxford English Dictionary* suggests that the self reflects who you really are, and is a permanent condition; another definition suggests that the self can respond to adult experience, and adapt over time. Recent evidence about the adaptability and learning capacity of the human brain suggests that we go with the second definition but acknowledge that self-development takes time. The best you can do is to be true to yourself right now, as you best understand it.

Polonius's advice continues: "And it must follow, as the night the day; Thou canst not then be false to any man."[31] This kind of advice concurs with what we say earlier—just do the best you can. The advice also has a strong social dimension, directed toward other people.[32] Job loss can highlight this. In a recent Canadian study, managers who had lost their jobs often reported becoming truer to their inner selves in their interactions with family and friends. Some also spoke about the need to find work that allowed them to more fully express themselves, to experience a greater sense of fulfillment, and to enjoy more positive relationships with others. Other studies have reported similar findings, emphasizing the need to be true to your inner self in order to promote more effective collaboration.[33]

A term related to the self is "authenticity," and in particular its contemporary *Oxford English Dictionary* definition as "a mode of existence arising from self-awareness, critical reflection on one's goals and values, and responsibility for one's own actions."[34] The philosopher and scholar Andrew Potter suggests that the demand for authenticity has become "one of the most powerful movements in contemporary life." Some suggest this stems from our collective disillusionment with corporate and government scandals—such as that involving the world soccer governing body Fédération Internationale de Football Association (FIFA).[35] Others suggest the movement reflects a broader malaise with the trappings of modern life, where authenticity is referenced in efforts to sell us products ranging from wine, tea, vacations, cosmetics, and even organic food. Yet, Potter suggests you can accept the market economy and still take on the need for an authentic, meaningful, ecologically sensible life. Authenticity and an intelligent career can be good for each other.[36]

A JOURNEY TO AUTHENTICITY

Authenticity is an important reference point for your intelligent career, because if you don't understand yourself, and what you want, it will be difficult to take charge of your own work. Participants in a study by researchers Lisa Mainero and Sherry Sullivan spoke about the need to be "genuine" and to "find one's true voice."[37] The emphasis is on personal choice and on making choices that are congruent with who you are. Others, such as Richard Peterson of Vanderbilt University, have suggested that the need for authenticity usually emerges when you didn't previously feel it—that is, when your instinctive sense of authenticity has been put in doubt or challenged.[38]

A further look at authenticity suggests it involves a four-stage journey, as the Copenhagen-based scholar Silvia Svejenova describes in her study of Spanish film director Pedro Almodovar. In the first stage, he began by personally funding and producing short films in his spare time and organizing viewings in friends' homes, bars, discothèques, or art galleries. In the second stage, he developed full-length feature films with support from established filmmaking companies and institutions, but was obligated to make films that satisfied his producers. In the third stage, Pedro and his brother Augustín registered their own production company, but coproduced their next two films in order to learn what was involved. The second film—*Women on the Verge of a Nervous Breakdown* (1987)—became an international hit but also exposed Pedro to a more mainstream group of gatekeepers (newspaper reviewers), and as a result he risked alienation from traditional supporters. In the fourth stage, he sought new levels of perfection. He built a wider production team and embarked on the expensive option of "sequential filming," following the logic of the action and allowing for character and plot development along the way.[39]

In keeping with Polonius's advice, Pedro Almodovar reflected, "Experience has taught me that the more honest and personal my work is, the more successful I am."[40] Svejenova suggests you can use his four-stage example to describe a journey toward authenticity, involving exploration, focus, independence, and professionalism, as described in Box 1.1, and that the four stages are applicable to a wide range of professional careers. The journey can take place within one or across different employers, including self-employment.

You can develop your own authenticity by recognizing the overlapping stages of exploration, focus, independence, and professionalism in your own work. When you do, authenticity can become both a motor and a

---

Box 1.1   STAGES IN THE DEVELOPMENT OF AUTHENTICITY

1. *Exploration*. At this first stage you practice authenticity by exploring a range of roles. You learn how to better express yourself, your talents, and your vision of the future. The wider the range of roles, the more agile you are likely to become. However, agility can be costly, as you will need to both practice multiple roles and appeal to different audiences.

2. *Focus*. At this next stage you focus on a particular work identity and pursue this in greater depth. You develop a signature style, which becomes your calling card or "personal brand." It not only indicates a professional skill set but also distinguishes your work from others in your field.

3. *Independence*. Members of professions value not only collective identity but also their autonomy. On the one hand you will seek to share common approaches, on the other hand you will want to build independence and enlarge your professional control and influence.

4. *Professionalism*. At this fourth stage, you direct your authenticity toward mastery of the work itself and the way in which you engage with your audiences. You seek to demonstrate continuity while exploring new areas of opportunity. You maintain relationships with valued colleagues, even though you may be unable to enjoy everyday interaction with them.

compass: a motor in driving you forward in the world, and a compass in guiding your interaction with that world. Being true to your self—developing a "path with the heart" as Svejenova puts it—can keep you going and keep you relevant in a complex and fragmented work environment. It can also lead you into deeper collaboration with others, but that's another story.[41]

In summary, developing an intelligent career means exercising conditional loyalty to your current employer, because their strategy and need for your services are always likely to change. It also means staying aware of the kind of opportunities available to you elsewhere, and seeing your career as the means through which you both adapt and contribute to the knowledge-driven world. Your intelligent career further involves focusing on your own talent development and leveraging information technology as your own means of production. It calls on you to be committed to a new vision of education across the life course, including collaborative learning with others. It means staying in control of your own career behavior regardless of the signals you may receive from other people. Not least, it involves being true to yourself and becoming authentic, in a broad sense, as you develop your career. A "path with a heart" is yours for the taking.

Where Do Intelligent Careers Happen?

I grew up in a company town
And I worked real hard 'til that company closed down
They gave my job to another man
On half my wages in some foreign land.

BILLY BRAGG

S amir Palnitkar grew up in a middle-class family in the Gujarat region on the west coast of India. His father worked in a state-owned oil refining company, and Palnitkar attended a company school run for employees' children. He went on to earn a place in the national university system, studying at the India Institute of Technology (IIT) campus in Kanpur, in the north. He performed well enough that on graduation he was offered a full scholarship to pursue graduate studies in electronic engineering in the United States at the University of Washington, Seattle. The scholarship included a $1,000 a month stipend as a teaching assistant but did not include travel expenses. Not wishing to see their son denied, his parents took out a bank loan to pay the airfare. Their support meant that he would be able to continue his career journey far away from home.

After finishing his master's degree in Seattle, he ventured south to Sun Microsystems, now part of Oracle Corporation, in California's Silicon Valley. He worked hard, both inside the company on microprocessor design and development and, in his spare time, writing what became a widely referenced book on chip design. Three years later, he cofounded his first company, I2P, a semiconductor design company based on his own software—which he had also written in his spare time. Moreover, he launched I2P without external funding because revenue was generated as soon as people subscribed to the service. The company grew to over 30 people before he sold it to the Oregon-based Lattice Semiconductor.

The success of I2P allowed him to launch two further companies, both of which received funding from Silicon Valley venture capital firms. The second company was Obongo, an electronic commerce software firm founded in 1999 with his former IIT classmate and Silicon Valley neighbor, Jai Rawat. This company was sold to America Online for a healthy profit in 2001. The third company was Ingot Systems, a semiconductor company specializing in high-speed memory controllers, which he sold to Virage Logic, another Silicon Valley company, in 2007. By then, he had long since paid back his parents' bank loan that had financed his first trip to the United States seventeen years earlier.

Palnitkar's success depended on more than hard work alone. *Where* he performed that work was highly relevant. He moved to another part of the Indian continent to pursue his first degree. Then he sought out and earned a scholarship to study in America. After that, he headed to Silicon Valley, which gave him inspiration to write his book, set up his first company, sell that company's product to another high technology firm, find partners for later ventures, and gain access to venture capital funding. In reflecting on his success, he stated:

Silicon Valley is a restless place. People are always talking about new ideas.

You go on a hike and hear people talking about how to improve the efficiency of CPU clusters. You go to a coffee shop and you hear new startup ideas all around you. This is a kind of experience you will not get anywhere else in the world.[1]

Samir Palnitkar made his first professional home in a location that nurtured his talents and gave him the opportunity to write his own programs and launch his own companies. How important is location in your career—to allow you to do the kind of work you do, meet others doing similar work, or find the encouragement to try new ideas? How important are particular private or public sector institutions to you? How important is the flexibility to work away from any traditional office by working from home, or from the nearest Web connection, to better accommodate your lifestyle? What about working for distant employers or collaborating within virtual communities—both more viable opportunities than they once were? Let us explore each of these considerations more deeply, again as a series of responses to our chapter title.

WHERE INDUSTRIES CLUSTER

For our first response, we draw on what economist Alfred Marshall wrote about the location of industries more than 125 years ago. Marshall's focus on the advantages that came from skilled tradespeople living close to one another foreshadowed the emergence of Silicon Valley:

> The mysteries of the trade become no mysteries; but are as it were in the air, and children learn many of them unconsciously. Good work is rightly appreciated, inventions and improvements in machinery, in processes and the general organization of the business have their merits promptly discussed: if one [person] starts a new idea, it is taken up by others and combined with suggestions of their own; and thus it becomes the source of further new ideas. And presently subsidiary trades grow up in the neighborhood, supplying it with implements and materials, organizing its traffic, and [thereby adding] to the [regional] economy.[2]

Over the next century, Marshall's words remained obvious to a modest cadre of economic geographers who studied such things. However, government and city planners, eager to attract existing industry participants, largely forgot the economic advantages of proximity. Then around the late 1970s the old lessons reemerged. Various reports asserted the significance of, for example, Grand Prix racing's Auto Alley around Oxford, England, the flower bulb industry around Lisse, The Netherlands, and the fireworks industry in Changsha, China.[3] The phenomenon has been further studied and confirmed across a wide range of industries where intelligent careers flourish—such as biotechnology, financial services, healthcare, mechanical engineering, medical devices, and many more. These industry *clusters* have been chronicled in the work of strategic management guru Michael Porter and his followers, who have claimed that almost all innovation stems from clusters of firms co-located in the same geographic region.[4]

Samir Palnitkar's story is testimony to the importance of clusters in one particular industry, that of high technology. In addition to Silicon Valley, his story includes the Puget Sound cluster around Seattle, in which the University of Washington and Microsoft participate, and the "Silicon Forest" cluster in Oregon, which includes Lattice Conductor, the buyer of his first company. Other high-technology clusters whose success has been dependent on ideas being "in the air," as Marshall put it, include London's Silicon Roundabout; North Carolina's Research Triangle; Boston's Route 128; Canada's High Technology Triangle in Waterloo, Ontario; the Grenoble region in France; and the Bangalore region in India. Similar observations can be made for many other clusters, across a wide range of industries, all around the globe.

Industry clusters also give rise to related service providers—such as consultants, educators, lawyers, and venture capitalists—to create a wider and more resilient "regional advantage." The University of California economist Anna Lee Saxenian has highlighted this term to signal how a mix of interdependent firms can gain mutual benefits from being in close proximity to one another.[5] It is important to know how regional advantage functions in and around your own home or in other places you may wish to call home. Do you work in an industry cluster, or are the customers for your work in an industry cluster? If so, what are the career benefits you gain from that cluster? If not, what are the challenges that you face?

WHERE ENTREPRENEURSHIP LEADS

However, geographic proximity can also become a liability. When entrepreneur Gavin Birer and his partner, Joel Heft, founded Canada's first legal process outsourcing company in 2006, they took aim at the fees levied by local law firms.[6] Their company, Legalwise OutSourcing Inc. of Toronto, quickly grew to have 25 full-time salaried lawyers working in two offices in Bangalore, India. In its early days, Legalwise performed routine tasks such as document reviewing, supporting e-discovery work, and standard form contracts. Yet, as clients became more at ease with the company's outsourcing process, they began to demand wider and more complex services. The economic benefits are clear: Indian lawyers cost as little as one-tenth of their Canadian counterparts and work complementary hours. As Canadian lawyers are leaving their offices at the end of the day, Indian lawyers are just arriving at their offices, ready to start work. That, says Birer, is "24/5 functionality." It is also part of a much wider trend in legal services outsourcing.[7]

In a contrasting example, serial entrepreneur Michael Enos pursued a new market opportunity when he created Fast Wrap—a shrink wrap company able to wrap buildings, bridges, boats, trains, cars, and everything in between, as well as provide shade tents for outdoor events and entertainment. Enos has grown the business to 64 centers around the United States and plans to expand internationally to Canada, Mexico, Turkey, and Dubai, opening a further 1,000 franchises over the next five years. Setting up a shrink-wrap franchise is a relatively low-tech operation; the initial investments are only plastic, vans, and tools. Yet, Enos will extend his horizons globally while keeping his corporate head office local in Reno, Nevada. He can do that by relying heavily on the Web for locating new customers, assisting in the delivery of products and services, and overall control of the business.[8]

Entrepreneurship—including launching or joining a start-up firm, and becoming a franchisor or franchisee—has become more attractive as the opportunities for long-term appointment have waned. Research data from 2016 suggest that between half and two-thirds of global working-age adults think that entrepreneurship is a good career choice for them.[9] Data from 2015 estimate around nine million workers are involved in the US franchising sector, contributing 900 billion dollars to the national economy.[10] Separate data confirm the importance of franchising to Europe and the rest of the world.[11] Where can you become an entrepreneur, either on your own or as part of a team, as you develop your intelligent career?

WHERE GOVERNMENTS LEAD

Governments also have an impact on where careers take place. Most obviously, they enact employment law and adopt trade policies that either encourage or discourage your participation in the emerging global marketplace. Seen in this light, governments have contributed to the widespread outsourcing of manufacturing work from high-wage to low-wage countries, and to the more recent outsourcing of services—including legal services, as described before. Across both manufacturing and services, governments also play a large part in providing the education systems that underlie their workers' readiness to participate in the knowledge economy and to take on more of the "value chain" before the final product—for example, a pair of sneakers, a laptop, a software program, or a legal document—is delivered to the eventual customer.

The Republic of Singapore provides an interesting example of a government actively seeking intelligent career opportunities for its workers. One program offers exceptional doctoral students generous grants to study overseas, regardless of nationality, as long as they commit to work in Singapore for a specific period of time after they receive their degrees. Another program encourages leading international scientists to relocate to Singapore. If those scientists—top biologists are a prominent example—do relocate, it is anticipated they will make greater use of the republic's established cadre of technicians, further adding to its economic success. From these and other efforts, the republic has posted an impressive growth in new employment opportunities. More recently, Singapore has sought to complement these efforts with additional investments in higher education and training for the incumbent Singaporean population.[12]

Government policy can also have a direct effect on the kind of intelligent career you can pursue. This may involve you directly as a public sector employee, or a member of the armed forces, in implementing that policy. Alternately it may involve you pursuing a career in the defense industry, working toward the development of military hardware and providing spinoff benefits for other industries. Other government initiatives concerned with entrepreneurship, innovation, corporate welfare, taxation, and intellectual property all have an influence over where and how work gets done. Behind all of these initiatives lies a political process that invites your input on how government policy is developed. You need to be aware of and somehow act on how those initiatives are affecting you.

WHERE INDUSTRY CLUSTERS INTERACT

Let us return to the information technology industry for a sequel to our earlier story of Samir Palnitkar. He went on to cofound a fourth company, Airtight Networks, specializing in security services for wireless networks. His collaborator was another ITT alumnus, Pravin Bhagwat, who had also left India to study and work in the United States. However, this company differed from previous companies in one crucial respect—it based its software development in India. The city of Pune was a fast-developing technology center, ranking third in national importance. It was just an overnight journey from Palnitkar's parents, close to his wife's parents, and an attractive place to raise his children, and its residents spoke the same Indian dialect as both sets of parents. A third founder already lived there, and Bhagwat was happy to join his two colleagues in their preferred location. As Palnitkar explained, "I was able to incubate a company, arrange financing, and then come back to India." He has since formed another company, Shop Socially, along similar lines.

A further answer, then, to this chapter's opening question about where intelligent careers happen is *between* industry clusters. A generation gap exists between the founders of Palnitkar's most recent companies and the cadre of Indian high-technology specialists subsequently recruited. The founders went overseas for higher education; most of the recruits did not. Younger graduates are less likely to have lived abroad or built cross-regional connections. Instead, sophisticated communications technologies and common use of the English language have facilitated collaboration between Indian and US clusters. The founders' early investments in studying abroad led to them becoming cross-regional entrepreneurs, with the knowledge, network connections, and cross-cultural skills to build bridges between countries. Pioneering intelligent career owners, no longer written off as part of a "brain drain," have instead come to be seen as agents of what Anna Lee Saxenian calls "brain circulation."[13]

Similar stories can be told about the emergence of high-technology regions in other countries, such as China, Israel, and Ireland, and about the interactions between other industry clusters such as those in biotechnology, education, filmmaking, healthcare, and many more. This is the way markets are supposed to work, with entrepreneurs crossing traditional boundaries, within or across nation-states, to open up opportunities for others. The classical economic argument is that India, the United States, and other trading nations all benefit from the arrangement, as clusters of intelligent career owners have extended their reach across regional and national boundaries. You need to be alert to, and ideally to anticipate, these changes. Paying greater attention to where professional opportunities are being created, instead of assuming your employer knows what's best for you, is a firm step in the right direction.

WHERE CITIES ATTRACT

Look for an industry cluster, and you will find one or more nearby cities: look for a city, and you will find one or more industry clusters. How, though, can you separate the relevance of each? Both cities and clusters appear to be driven by economic forces, but there are suggestions that those forces have different origins. Cities have commonly grown along traditional trade routes, as the "blue banana" in Figure 2.1 illustrates for trade across Europe, much of it originating in the Far East. In turn, shifts in patterns of trade can reverse a city's fortunes. For example, the relative shift of the UK toward trade with Europe, rather than the Americas, over the past 50 years has contributed to economic downturns for British west coast cities such as Liverpool and Manchester, and the revitalization of London. In contrast, America's increased trade with China has boosted the importance of its West

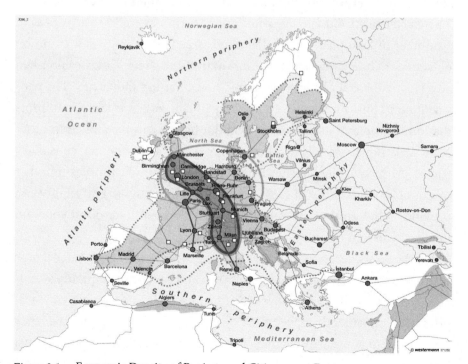

Figure 2.1   Economic Density of Regions and Cities across Europe

Coast cities, like Los Angeles and Seattle, over their East Coast counterparts.[14]

Cities are also meeting grounds for innovation. Some of this occurs within neatly aligned industry clusters, such as in San Jose's alignment with the Silicon Valley. However, innovation can also stem from the opportunity that physical closeness provides for cross-industry pollination. British social historian Peter Hall once described creative cities as "places of great social and intellectual turbulence."[15] More recently, Canadian scholar Richard Florida has argued that cities can give rise to a "creative class," which can be attracted by a "people climate" that exhibits tolerance, encourages diversity, and invests in lifestyle amenities—including simple things like bike lanes and running tracks—that are attractive to creative professionals.[16]

A straightforward example of innovation from physical proximity between industries can be seen in the success of Silicon Alley, a cluster of Internet and new media companies around Manhattan, New York City. The cluster hosts Google's second-largest office, as well as the offices of a number of European, Australian, and Israeli start-ups. Their common objective is to leverage the Alley's proximity to New York's established advertising, broadcasting, publishing, and retailing industries. The conversation in Silicon *Alley*, in contrast to Silicon *Valley*, is less about information technology itself and more about how it can be applied in other New York industries.[17] That Silicon Alley workers provide the "subsidiary trades" Alfred Marshall once wrote about is just one of a limitless number of examples of the kind of cross-fertilization that physical proximity can provide. What kind of cross-fertilization is happening around you, and how can you join in?

Further considerations for intelligent careers are that cities can become expensive for both people and employers, so that they commonly stimulate economic activity in other cities from which both people and supplies can conveniently travel. Cities, and the industry clusters that they host, are also subject to decline. That is seen around the globe in "rust belt" zones that have lost much of their former markets.[18] Economic hardship can be further triggered by the global economy, as established industries are more open to competitive goods and services from elsewhere.[19] What's happening in and around your city? How attractive is your regional economy right now? How much do you want to stay, and what are the alternatives?

FROM YOUR OWN HOME

The opportunity to communicate over the Web brings new flexibility to contemporary jobs. For example, Sandra, a single parent with a 13-year-old daughter, is a 45-year-old senior human resource manager working for a local council in the UK. She works from home one or two days each week, an arrangement that helps her to "reap the best from both worlds," in pursuing her career and engaging more fully with "the private side of life—family, friends, hobbies and so on." Michael, married with two small children, is a forty-year-old middle-level sales manager with a multinational in Canada. He works two or three days a week from home, has strong aspirations to be "a good dad" and a "good manager," and believes that working from home allows him to "have my cake and eat it."[20,21]

With growing calls for more work-life balance and flexible work arrangements, an increasing number of employers are providing employees like Sandra and Michael with opportunities to work from home. According to European Diversity Research and Consulting, telecommuting—the ability to work from home either full-time or part-time—is one of the most frequently implemented work-life balance programs in Europe.[22] Although working from home has disadvantages, the benefits to employees include avoiding long commutes, being able to attend to personal responsibilities—especially helpful for single parents or dual-career couples—and more control over individual work schedules. The benefits to employers have also been well documented, including reduction of real estate costs, increased retention, and employee satisfaction.[23] Can your company benefit—and can you?

You can also collaborate more extensively from your home. The widely reported example of the "open source" development of the Linux operating system portrays a global community of specialists committed to developing and maintaining the integrity of their work.[24] Open source initiatives have also been applied in a variety of applications such as reference works (witness *Wikipedia*), biotechnology, healthcare, agriculture, and even beer-making.[25] These communities can provide for skill development and reputation building as well as financial reward. What kind of virtual communities exist in your line of work, and how can you join in?

However, working from home can be problematic. US journalist Brigid Schulte has written a compelling account of going down "the rabbit hole of *busy*ness," trying to sustain high investments in both her professional life and her family when there is insufficient time for both.[26] The problems can vary by country and culture. Some countries assert workers' rights to family time in their employment legislation, while others prefer to leave any family accommodation to the employer's discretion. Relying on an employer's discretion can backfire, as it did for Yahoo workers when their new CEO insisted everyone working at home return to work in their offices.[27] Some cultures and religious sects are much more supportive of partners sharing work and family responsibilities than others. You need to put in the effort to understand your own situation, and frequently your partner's situation, to use your home effectively.

ON THE MOVE

According to the Fifth European Working Conditions Survey of employees in the European Union, more than twenty percent of them work in an outside location either at clients' premises, in a vehicle, or at an "outside site" such as a construction site, agricultural field, or city street. The proportion of individuals whose main workplace is not their employer's premises appears to increase after gaining early career experience, with male workers aged 35–49 accounting for the highest percentage (38%). Further research suggests that 50 percent of the US workforce holds a job in which they can work outside their office part of the time, and that 20–25 percent of the workforce does so frequently. Fortune 1000 companies around the globe are revamping their space around the fact that employees are already mobile, making it inefficient to provide them with permanent desks.[28]

UK scholars Donald Hislop and Carolyn Axtell have highlighted the implications of "mobile working" in a study of UK consultants. They found that 70 percent of those who traveled by car said that they worked from their car when it was parked. One consultant joked, "You sometimes get to the point where you know your car better than your wife or your friends!" Forty percent of car travelers said that they regularly worked from service stations or cafes. Others who were traveling longer distances reported working on planes or trains and in airport lounges and railway station waiting rooms. For these people, the idea of a permanent workspace is simply not viable.[29] In the words of Flavio Nunes, professor of geography at the University of Minho in Portugal, "[t]he workplace today can be found anywhere electronic networking is possible."[30]

What to think about being a business traveler working alone in your hotel room or ensconced in the corner of a coffee shop? On the one hand, you are away from home and using temporary workspaces for collaboration and cooperation. On the other hand, working on the move brings considerable drawbacks. Finnish researchers Matti Vartiainen and Ursula Hyrkkänen have observed a potential for increased stress, for example, because of cramped physical conditions, poor light or an unreliable Web connection. Meanwhile, back at the home office, tasks can pile up, lengthening the working day after traveling, while social relationships are disrupted. Asynchronous time zones can change the hours and rhythm of the work for one or more of the parties involved.[31] How much are you on the move? And how does that affect you?

WHERE INNOVATION CALLS

Wherever you may work, the end of the day is often a time to kick off your shoes, switch off from the rest of the world, and relax. However, for some people that's not the case. Giorgia Sgargetta works as a quality manager in a pesticide company near her hometown in the Abruzzo region of Italy. At the end of her day, she kisses her young daughter and husband good-night and heads off to her attic. There, she gets out her home chemistry kit, and draws on her PhD in detergent formulations, agrochemicals, and analytical chemistry to solve problems for the likes of Procter & Gamble, Dupont, and BASE. The arrangement seems to work well for her family as well as providing an opportunity to develop her expertise.[32]

What's going on here? Handing over puzzling problems to individuals outside an organization signals a shift from the research and development department toward "open innovation." Henry Chesbrough, an expert on the subject, describes it as a move away from the assumption that "all the smart people work for us" to the realization that "not all the smart people work for us." Rather than thinking that they can solve all of their problems using their own employees, an increasing number of organizations are recognizing the value of collaboration with outsiders who may be professionals, experts, or lone individuals who are interested in a particular field or product. In this way, they are tapping into knowledge that resides outside the organization's boundaries.[33]

There are various channels for people like Sgargetta to contribute to open innovation. Among them are brokers that commonly link innovation seekers to potential providers. A prominent example is InnoCentive, based in Waltham, Massachusetts, which links company requests to a global network of 140,000 scientists in more than 170 countries. Alternatively, user communities, such as the one encouraged by the toy-maker Lego, draw in customer ideas for the design and development of its products.[34] A growing number of Web postings from both private and public sector organizations specify the kind of innovation that they seek. You can either respond individually or collaborate in a group response, providing more specialized or more diversified expertise.

Although the organizational benefits of open innovation are clear, the individual benefits can also be substantial. For Sgargetta the financial rewards for solving postings on the InnoCentive website range anywhere from $10,000 to as high as $100,000 for the most complex or time-consuming projects. Moreover, despite working in her attic after a full day at her regular job, she is able to work from home in a way that allows for family time. How is she doing so far? Illustrative earnings include $30,000 for inventing a dye that turns dishwater blue after adding a specific amount of detergent, and $15,000 for helping to advance a biomarker for measuring the effects of a treatment for Lou Gehrig's disease. She lives in Italy, but open innovation allows her to do work for anyone.[35] What about you?

FROM WHERE YOU CHOOSE

In pursuing an intelligent career, you can take greater control over the jobs and learning you pursue and the employers you choose to work for. However, the emergence of the Web has radically changed old assumptions about where your work can be performed. In the past, people traveled across physical space—to relocate or emigrate—in search of work. Many people still do. However, there is a growing trend to let the Web do the walking and to contribute to the global economy from wherever you choose to be.

Automattic, a San Francisco–based developer of the popular blogging system WordPress, has a virtual hiring process. Their "work-with-us" web page invites applicants to "choose your own adventure," in which everyone works from "the location they choose", and employees are spread out "all over the world." If you get past your interview—commonly a virtual interview—you're invited to "do a project together," to "see how we work together". If you become a full-time employee you will meet up with the whole company in physical space once a year to "create bonds," and also join in project team meetings.[36]

Not everyone has the technical skills to be attractive to an employer like Automattic. However, the trends behind the company's human resources policy are clear. Intelligent careers are increasingly being performed away from any office—that is, from the house in which you live or from a location that allows you to do your work over the Web. Meeting with people in physical space is becoming more of a special event, and meeting with people in virtual space is becoming more common. The emergent flexibility about where you work is driving new business models, like that of Automattic, which supersede earlier assumptions about where you can work.

To recap, industry clusters have a long tradition as important locations for career opportunities. Entrepreneurs, governments, and—since the emergence of the Web—inter-cluster links between countries also influence where careers evolve. Cities have a long tradition of supporting high population densities, interdependent industries, and related opportunities for innovation. The Web has further influenced where and how your own career evolves: by working from home with your employer's agreement, or by working from temporary homes when you are traveling. The Web also allows you to respond to a large number of companies calling for open innovation, or to become a distant employee of an enterprising company that recruits in virtual rather than physical space. The opportunities for where you work can frequently stem from global, rather than local, employment initiatives.

Why Do You Work?

We must believe that we are gifted for something
and that this thing,
at whatever cost, must be attained.

—MARIE CURIE

Sarah Robinson had always wanted to teach. As a child in a middle-class Australian family, she spent hours playing school. When she went to school, she watched the teachers and dreamed of having her own classroom. She recalled her early school years as "a wonderful experience—secure, stable, supportive, and loving." It was no surprise when she embarked on a career as an early childhood educator, wanting to make sure other children would also have "happy memories," of their early learning experiences.

She trained for six years. She completed a Bachelor of Teaching in early childhood education, then enrolled in a follow-up "preservice" program. One professor described her as the most likely of all the participants "to enjoy a rewarding and enduring career as an early childhood educator." She saw her acceptance into the program as a "really exciting part of my life—a dream come true!"[1]

The preservice program followed a teaching method developed in Reggio Emilia, Italy, advocating that children contribute to their own curriculum decisions and collaborate in group learning. This was different from her own experience, and she wondered how she would respond. In one difficult practicum, several carefully planned classroom activities did not work. She wrote in a preservice journal that she had started to worry about her own future classroom, but was determined to "try to see what I can learn from things that don't go the way I want them to." By the end of the program, she was convinced the Reggio Emilia teaching methods she had learned were effective.

Her first appointment was as a teacher of six-to-seven-year-old children in a small elementary school in suburban Sydney. Aspiring to run an informal, project-based classroom, she was troubled that her colleagues stuck to more structured teaching practices. Encouraged to use metaphors in her journal, she wrote that she was walking into "a dark tunnel" where it was "up to me to find the light." However, she persevered with her dream of a flexible curriculum and built positive relationships with students and their parents. Beginning her second year, entering her classroom was like "walking in a beautiful, well-established garden." Yet, she still expressed frustration with her colleagues: "They get stuck in the one spot where they are treading on the flowers. They don't realize it, but they are ruining the garden."

In her third year, she described her work environment as a "theme park" rather than a garden. Teaching was like being on a "roller coaster with all its ups and downs." There was a "hall of mirrors" reflecting how "you see yourself as a teacher . . . but the reflection is often distorted by what is going on around us." By the following year, her sense of disconnection from her colleagues was almost unbearable. She found a job at another school, but again got little support from her fellow teachers. In despair, she resigned from her job and left the teaching profession.

What can we make of Robinson's early career experiences? One point of view would be she was following her true "vocation," another would be she simply needed to work to support her lifestyle. Other views might stress the intellectual enrichment that pursuing an intelligent career can provide, or the opportunity to draw on her personal strengths or motivation. A different perspective would point to the environment in which she worked, including the lack of support from her fellow teachers. A further perspective would point to her inner identity—that is, how she saw herself. Was she deeply committed to what she had learned in her training, and did that interfere with her further adaptation in the classroom?

As with preceding chapters, each of these viewpoints offers a different response to our chapter title, asking "Why Do You Work?" Let us examine these responses in turn, and develop a deeper appreciation of why Sarah Robinson worked, why other people work, and why you work (or seek to work). Each of the responses provides a different lens through which to view your own intelligent career.

TO LIVE OUT YOUR VOCATION

Having the desire to pursue an appealing and meaningful intelligent career may seem obvious today, but it was not always so. There was a time when young people prepared to follow their parents' line of work— peasants' children worked on farms, landowners' children managed estates, noblemen's children learned to rule. However, by the turn of the twentieth century, as young people moved to the city and an agrarian society gave way to the industrial age, the social activist Frank Parsons was one of those popularizing a new concept called vocational guidance. Over 100 years ago, Parsons wrote:

We guide our boys and girls to some extent through school, then drop them into this complex world to sink or swim as the case may be. Yet there is no part of life where the need for guidance is more emphatic than in the transition from school to work—the choice of a vocation, adequate preparation for it, and the attainment of efficiency and success. The building of a career is quite as difficult a problem as the building of a house, yet few ever sit down with pencil and paper, with expert information and counsel, to plan a working career and deal with the life problem scientifically as they would deal with the problem of building a house.[2]

Parsons's highly influential work helped lay the foundation for the widespread practice of vocational guidance in schools, colleges, and employment offices that continues to this day. In the aftermath of this work, vocational guidance was simply defined as "the process of assisting the individual to choose an occupation, prepare for it, enter upon it, and progress in it."[3] As public education became compulsory and social mobility increased, educators and governments the world over developed trade schools, professional schools, and job-training programs, as well as special programs to assist the disadvantaged. *Why* people work gradually came to be seen as an important individual choice—subject to guidance—rather than an inherited obligation.

Sarah Robinson was an easy case for vocational guidance. She had always wanted to be a teacher, and she had the ability to complete the training and do that job. Moreover, she affirmed throughout her preservice program and early teaching experiences that she was on her chosen path. She committed herself fully to the teaching profession, yet her choice still did not work out for her. Did your choice of career—or will that choice—work out for you?

TO PUT BREAD ON THE TABLE

For some people the pursuit of a vocation can seem like a luxury. In despair, Danny Hartzell and his family loaded their possessions from a no-frills apartment building into a rental truck, and set out on a ten-hour drive from Tampa, Florida, to rural Georgia. He had been laid off by a packaging plant, had found a part-time night job stacking shelves at a chain store, then had been laid off again. His daughter had bone cancer, his son would need to change schools, and Hartzell was ineligible for any further unemployment assistance. His family was moving to a new state to visit a sympathetic friend, even without the promise of new work. As he explained to the journalist George Packer in a *New Yorker* article, "If you can't climb out [of the hole his family was in], why not move?" Why not "stake a new claim" in a fresh location?[4]

The Hartzells were far from alone. At the time of their move, there were officially 9.2 percent—over 24 million—unemployed Americans. That figure excluded people who had given up looking for work, were working part-time but wishing to work full-time, or were physically or mentally unable to work. In 2010, the ten most populous nations in the world together reported over 1.1 billion unemployed. Jobs were even scarcer in war-torn or drought-ravaged nations.[5] For unemployed people, their first need is to get a job to survive. The pedagogical difficulties Sarah Robinson faced were irrelevant for Danny Hartzell, who sought only secure employment.

Dual-career couples face particular problems. Each couple needs to juggle two jobs in commuting distance from the same home, and often to stagger each worker's hours to coordinate childcare. Families headed by a single parent frequently call on help from relatives or friendly neighbors, which again restricts mobility. Evidence shows that family-friendly policies that include the opportunity to work from home can improve an employer's overall productivity by retaining highly skilled workers or allowing for longer hours of service coverage.[6]

Putting bread on the table is increasingly a focus of political life. For example, in South Africa making a living is underscored by concerns about keeping children in school, attaining greater political stability, and the effects of climate change on the water supply.[7] Putting bread (and water) on people's tables will be vital for future global prosperity. As we look toward that future, we urgently need to use intelligent careers to solve the world's current and future problems. More immediately, though, you and others like you need to make an honest living. Once you are doing that, you can turn to consider the meaning of the work that you do.

TO EAT CAKE

Rather than just bread, how about also working to put cake on the table? That is, can you find work that has greater meaning for you? This question attracted twentieth-century psychologists, who sought to tie "the scientific study of the human mind" to job outcomes.[8] In the United States, for example, the definition of "vocational guidance" was changed to helping make people aware of "their own psychological make-up, and its consequences for both self and society."[9] Popular definitions of the term, like the one in the *Collins English Dictionary*, now often assume that it is "based on *psychological tests* and interviews to find out what career or occupation may best suit a person."[10] The result has been that for more than seventy years, testing and advising people about why they work has relied heavily on a psychological approach.

The most widely used vocational tests seek to capture a person's *interests* and compare them against the interests of satisfied occupational members. A popular approach involves the "career hexagon," developed by US psychologist John Holland (Figure 3.1). This suggests that people's interests can be depicted according to six personality types, namely *realistic* (practical, hands-on), *investigative* (analytical, explorative), *artistic* (creative, independent), *social* (cooperative, helping), *enterprising* (competitive, persuasive), and *conventional* (detail-oriented, clerical). The hexagon also indicates greater similarity between adjacent types, and greater difference between opposite types. If you are interested in realistic pursuits you may also be interested in investigative ones, but less likely to be interested in social ones, and so on. Variations on similar ideas have been widely practiced around the world.[11]

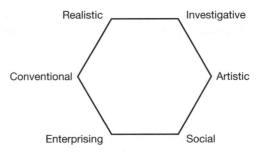

Figure 3.1   The Career Hexagon

To illustrate, the dominant personality type for a teacher is described as the social type, and the adjacent types are the artistic type and enterprising types. Looking back at the opening example of Sarah Robinson, the social and artistic types seem to fit quite well, but the enterprising type calls for competitive and persuasive interests that she may have lacked. Perhaps she could have been forewarned about the problems she encountered? Perhaps you could have been similarly forewarned? Whatever has already happened, you need to know that the approach rests on the assumption that your interests will remain stable over a time.[12] As a result, interest tests can point you in some potentially interesting career directions, but they are frequently less useful after you have developed considerable work experience.

TO BE TRUE TO TYPE

Katharine Cook Briggs and Isabel Briggs Myers were a mother-daughter team that developed the now popular Myers-Briggs Type Indicator (MBTI) during World War II. The indicator was derived from earlier work by the psychoanalyst Carl Gustav Jung, and the team's original intention was to help women entering the industrial workforce find jobs in which they would be "most comfortable and effective." The MBTI involves four dichotomies between separate pairs of contrasting psychological types:

> *Extraversion versus Introversion* (looking outward toward people and objects, versus inward toward concepts and ideas);
> *Sensing versus Intuition* (looking for tangible details and facts, rather than for wider patterns and possibilities);
> *Thinking versus Feeling* (deciding things in a detached and logical way, rather than weighing people's needs and seeking harmony);
> *Perceiving versus Judging* (where perceiving reflects a preference to "keep decisions open" and judging a preference to "have matters settled").[13]

The MBTI is a popular tool in career counseling and interpersonal communications workshops. Could Sarah Robinson have benefited from taking the MBTI? A discussion about her own personality type might have raised questions about how she was relating to her fellow workers.[14] However, you need to know that Jung's original idea was simply to highlight people's *preferences*. The point is neither to take your assigned personality type as given, nor to suggest what kind of work you are capable of performing. It is simply to raise helpful questions about where your preferences may or may not be reflected in your work.

MIT scholar Edgar Schein also takes a psychological approach in asking people to identify which of a range of eight "career anchors"—for example technical competence, dedication to a cause, security/stability, or creativity—are most important in their careers. Once you've established your own anchors through a questionnaire, you can find a partner, preferably someone outside the chain of command at work, to discuss your career history. This can help you to appreciate the relevance of career anchors and decipher your own pattern of choices.[15] Proponents of peer coaching—where you work with another person with a mutual desire to help one another—make a similar point.[16] You can learn more and adapt better if you have a good conversation with a helpful listener. To sum up, the point about exploring your psychological type or career anchor is for you—and only you—to take charge of the interpretation and application of the results.

TO FULFILL EMPLOYERS' EXPECTATIONS

However, things may not be left to you. Employers also use psychological testing to make predictions about why you work. An established favorite is the sixteen personality factor (16PF) questionnaire originally developed by the British-American psychologist Raymond Cattell. The questionnaire is claimed to have "the ability to predict a wide variety of occupational profiles" and to identify "the personality traits of successful supervisors, managers, executives, and other leaders."[17] These traits are distinguished by relatively high scores on such items as social boldness, openness-to-change, emotional stability, warmth, and group orientation, coupled with relatively low scores on anxiety and apprehension. As a result, the 16PF has been widely used in decisions about employee hiring, promotion, development, coaching, outplacement, and retirement counseling. You may well have met the 16PF, or a comparable instrument, in your own life. You may even have been denied employment because of it.

A second approach, also initiated by Cattell but subsequently developed by others, reduces the range of personality factors to a "Big Five." The Big Five are concerned with the extent of people's *openness to experience, conscientiousness, extraversion, agreeableness,* and *emotional stability.* Many scholars are confident that the Big Five provide a further platform for successful employment testing. Conscientiousness—completing work on time, paying attention to expectations, and so on—relates directly to job performance across a wide range of occupations. Extraversion and emotional stability relate to job performance for managers and salespeople, and agreeableness and emotional stability relate to job performance for customer service representatives. A composite "employee reliability" test relates elements from all five factors to job performance, on the one hand, and counterproductive work behavior, on the other hand.[18]

It has been reported that over 60% of UK employers use some form of personality testing, and that up to 70% of job applicants face such testing in the United States.[19] So the likelihood that you have been selected or rejected on the basis of such a test is relatively high. How to handle this kind of testing when you meet it? One option is to trust the employer to know what's best for you. Another option is to try to give the test administrators what they are looking for—provided you can figure out the "correct" answers.[20] In the longer term there's a third option, to claim greater control over the jobs that you seek and the way you are recruited. We will return to this option later.

TO USE YOUR PERSONAL STRENGTHS

Another way to determine why you work is to focus on your individual strengths. Former Gallup Organization consultant Marcus Buckingham and a colleague described a restaurant manager with a reputation for building and keeping successful teams. Was there any secret behind what he did? "No. . . . I think the best a manager can do is to make each person comfortable with who they are. . . . I didn't care that [my people] were all so different." Shouldn't he try to treat all his employees the same, and exercise fairness? "Of course not. . . . I think people want to be understood. . . . Treating them differently is part of helping them feel unique." Pursuing an intelligent career, for this manager, involved working to understand each of his employees. He may not have subjected his employees to psychological testing, but he was interested in individual differences.[21]

Buckingham and another colleague quickly came out with a sequel, directed toward people like the restaurant manager's employees, inviting them to "Discover Your Strengths." Globally, only 20 percent of all employees in large organizations reported their strengths were regularly in use. The remedy for the disaffected was to discover their own strengths and to find ways to exercise those strengths themselves. The book described thirty-four specific strengths—achiever, connectedness, futuristic, maximizer, self-assurance, restorative, and so on—and invited readers to lay claim to their own by completing an accompanying "Strengthsfinder." Buckingham later came back with a third book that offered a "six step discipline" for you to put your strengths to work and to "tilt the playing field" in your own favor.[22]

Buckingham's work illustrates a popular argument for intelligent career owners: the reason why you work is to make best use of your strengths, and those strengths stem from your personality and the life experiences through which you have expressed it. Some people suggest you don't need any long questionnaire to discover your strengths, you can simply sit down and complete a widely available checklist; or you can develop your own list by looking back over critical incidents in your life, or asking people who know you to make lists. Whatever your approach, the underlying point is the same. Know your strengths, know where your potential contributions lie, and make things happen. This sounds straightforward, except that it suggests your strengths remain constant.

TO BE HAPPY

Whatever your strengths, a related question concerns how you demonstrate them to others. Back in 1999, Martin Seligman, then president of the American Psychological Association, proposed that in addition to addressing mental illness psychologists needed to understand an individual's positive qualities, for example "optimism, courage, work ethic, future-mindedness, interpersonal skill, the capacity for pleasure and insight, and social responsibility."[23] Seligman, who went on to publish books called *Learned Optimism* and *Authentic Happiness*, was influential in establishing "positive psychology" as a serious discipline. The underlying credo is that happiness is to some degree a personal choice, and that you can take active steps to increase your own happiness. Thinking positive thoughts, feeling gratitude, being attentive, and becoming completely absorbed in the task at hand—what positive psychologists call "flow"—are paths to happiness.

The application of positive psychology has mushroomed in recent years. The University of Michigan *Center for Positive Organizational Scholarship* offers two self-help guides, one to "identify opportunities to make your job more engaging and fulfilling," the other to "help people identify their unique strengths and talents."[24] Other guides and self-help books are widely available.[25] There is a widespread interest—spearheaded by the UK and Australia—in adopting "positive education" across national education systems. This makes happiness the primary focus of an educational agenda, and presumes individual learning will follow. International comparisons have suggested a series of "core moral virtues," like wisdom, courage, and humanity, through which the pursuit of happiness functions. However, critics argue the approach is biased toward "a cheerful, outgoing, goal-driven, status-seeking extrovert" with proponents more driven by opportunism than scientific standards.[26] You can expect to meet positive psychology in your own life, and our best advice is that you remain open to its ideas.

You can beware of opportunism and still see connections between positive psychology and your intelligent career. There is common ground in emphasizing the dynamic interplay between your work life and personal life, your willingness to see other people in a positive light, and the link between meaningful work and job satisfaction.[27] However, pursuing an intelligent career also calls for you to more fully understand the social world in which your career is unfolding, and the relationships—positive or otherwise—through which your work is taking place.

TO FOLLOW YOUR OWN PATH

What if you don't want to spend the rest of your life exercising your established strengths, or looking happy without regard to your work situation? A professional sports player may retire early, citing the grueling lifestyle. An experienced bookkeeper may decide he'd rather try something different. A wealthy hedge fund manager may decide to open a gelato company. Boston University management scholar Douglas "Tim" Hall has long proposed the idea of what he calls "protean careers," where people thrive in responding to a changing environment.[28] What if you seek deeper engagement with your work, or fulfillment of more personal goals?

Amy Wrzesniewski of Yale University and her colleagues argue that why you work will depend on whether you see it as a "job," a "career" or a "calling." If you see your work as a job you can be expected to focus on financial rewards, and what those rewards can mean outside the workplace—food on the table, a home, a car, a social life, and so on. In contrast, if you see your work as a career you can be expected to focus on achieving greater career success over time. Finally, if you see your work as a calling you can be expected to focus on personal fulfillment—or to paraphrase Confucius, to "find a job you love and never work again in your life."[29] You may want to combine all three of these orientations, but there are trade-offs. If you were eager to find a job after leaving school you may have neglected the long-term career consequences. Or if you were too selective about your work you may have forfeited lucrative opportunities. Then there are people like zookeepers: the pay is low, the work is dirty, the chances of promotion are slim, but many still love their jobs.[30]

Intelligent careers distinguish between *objective* career success—when you succeed on society's terms—and *subjective* career success—when you do something for yourself. For example, objective career success stems from gaining greater wealth or social prestige, whereas subjective career success comes from meeting challenges you set for yourself or (like zookeepers or artists) doing something you like to do. Your objective and subjective careers influence one another, and the relationship between them is likely to change over time. Even zookeepers may need a certain level of "objective" success (that is, income) in order to live their lives. Even ambitious salespeople may sacrifice the opportunity for extraordinary income in order to enjoy more time with friends and family. A few people, like former Microsoft boss Bill Gates, gain exceptional objective success (wealth) and then seek subjective success in pledging to pass their wealth over to charity. What does success look like for you?[31]

TO WORK WITH EXTERNAL FORCES

Let us return to the idea of working to eat cake, and ask, "Where does that cake come from?" The scholar behind Sarah Robinson's story wrote two further articles about her. The first of those articles compared her with another early childhood educator, Natalie Jones, who had been similarly trained and faced comparable challenges. Jones was described to have shown greater resilience in her ability to thrive in the face of adverse, challenging, or threatening circumstances. The author went on to point out how Jones had drawn on her personal qualities of self-insight, leadership skills, risk taking, and perseverance to manage her situation more effectively. That is, she fought for her cake. The inference here, then, is that Jones supposedly had the "right stuff," but Robinson didn't. But how fair is this inference?

An alternative explanation is that the root of the problem may lie beyond individual differences. The same article went on to say that Jones had enjoyed an effective support network, a dependable mentor, and access to personal development opportunities. In contrast to Robinson, there were others helping her "bake the cake" of her early teaching experience.[32] The next article went further. A key player at Robinson's second school was her incumbent teacher's assistant, who opposed the new teaching method, persistently failed to collaborate, and refused a transfer to another class. Having consolidated her power, the assistant reportedly went on the offensive in discrediting Robinson among the parents.[33] The new teaching model also raised political problems. It had been introduced with much fanfare, the principal felt obliged to promote it, but it made severe demands on the teachers' time.[34]

Psychology can cast no light on the comparison between the obstacles that the two early childhood educators met, or how those obstacles affected personal outcomes. If circumstances had been reversed, would Jones have left the teaching profession instead? The comparison calls for other insights from, for example, economics (on funding of the schools and teachers' pay), organization theory (on the structure and authority system of the schools), sociology (on tensions among principals, teachers, and assistants and the prospects for systemic change), and social psychology (on interpersonal and intergroup issues between teachers and their assistants). Success in an intelligent career is only partly dependent on your personality. You need to be well aware of the *external* forces that are shaping your situation.

TO DEVELOP YOUR IDENTITY

Being aware of external forces is one thing, working with them is something else. Herminia Ibarra is a professor at INSEAD, headquartered in Fontainebleau, France, who has specialized in studying how we do that. Her underlying concept is one of *working identity*, meaning "our sense of self in our professional roles, what we convey about ourselves to others and, ultimately, how we live our working lives."[35] She takes us beyond the traditional psychological ideas described earlier, which see your identity as largely given. Instead, she suggests a second meaning that denotes action, and through action the further development of your identity. Her approach is useful because it acknowledges the link between your inner capacity for further development, and the importance of your employment context.

Ibarra argues that your working identity can be developed through three related sets of actions. One involves *crafting experiments*, which means trying out new work roles and activities to see if you like them. If you do, and if your experimentation encourages you to pursue those activities, the next set of actions involves *shifting connections*. This means developing contacts who can open doors for you into the world you aspire to join, and finding people against whom to measure your progress. The third set of actions involves *making sense* of your unfolding experiences, and modifying your life story as a result. The point of your modified life story is to make a link from who you were (or why you worked) to who you are becoming (or why you will work) in the future.

The connections among the three sets of actions can be illustrated in the example of Larry Pearson, a former investment banker, who was "downsized" out of his investment banking job at age 35. He had already begun to explore the nonprofit sector in search of more meaningful work, but offers of two "great jobs" in commercial banking invited him to conclude his experimentation and settle for higher standing as a banker. By contrast, his interviewers in the nonprofit sector weren't persuaded about his commitment to their world, or that his financial skills could make a difference. Yet he persisted, and found temporary work with a regional nonprofit organization developing a series of conferences. The work gave him a better feel for the nonprofit sector (more experimentation), an opportunity to meet new people (more connections) and the chance to become more coherent about how he could contribute (making greater sense).

Six months after he received his banking offers he got his first job offer in his intended sector, from a microfinancing company that eventually became his new professional home. The next step in the development of his "working identity" was over. However, if he is to maintain his enthusiasm for his new field, there will be new experiments, fresh connections, and further identity development ahead.[36] The same logic applies to you.

Developing your identity and extending your intelligent career can last a lifetime. The trick is to keep coming back to the question "Why Do You Work?" and being open to fresh answers.[37]

Let us recall the main points of this chapter. For over a century, understanding why you work has been a focus of vocational guidance, which matches your interests to a list of suggested occupations. However, it may not work for reasons that lie beyond those interests and occupations. A fundamental reason why you work is to put bread on the table, for yourself and your family. A larger reason—to eat cake, so to speak—involves meeting further psychological needs. However, all of psychological testing, finding and applying your strengths, and the pursuit of happiness fall short of identifying your uniqueness and the experiences that have shaped it. You can go further by following your own path, and pursuing your own (subjective) aspirations, rather than society's (objective) assumptions, about career success. You also need to be aware of the effect of external forces on your career, and how you can respond to these over time to develop your working identity. Expose yourself to new experiences, grow as result of those experiences, and you can expect the answer to "Why do you work?" to respond.

How Do You Work?

When you have a great and difficult task,
something perhaps almost impossible,
if you only work a little at a time, every day a little,
suddenly the work will finish itself.

—Karen Blixen

Bruce Knight never lacked the ability to learn. He enrolled in an art school in upstate New York, hoping to major in film, but disliked the large university setting. He moved back to New England and attended classes at a smaller film school, but that petered out a year later. He had a few retail sales jobs during his studies, and worked as a graphic artist for six months until the shop went out of business. Then in 1986 he saw an advertisement in the General Help section of *The Boston Globe*: "Make contact lenses; no experience necessary—will train." The job was in a small lab of three to four people grinding hard plastic lenses on specialized lathes. As Knight put it, "I was such a ****-up that's all I had open to me!"

He held the job for almost five years, during which time he also started a family. His innate curiosity led him to a deeper interest in the science behind the lens-grinding craft, which he was encouraged to learn about by the lab's director, a well-known optical researcher. When the manufacturing method shifted toward Computerized Numerical Control (CNC) machines in the early 1990s, he learned how to program the machines to design new lenses. He also learned the clinical aspects of lens fitting by working with doctors and their patients and traveling to other lens manufacturers to promote and sell his programs. The mainstream industry was moving toward flexible soft lenses, but there was still a higher-margin market for the "rigid, gas permeable" lenses that his programs produced.

With his lab director he launched a new company to market the software he had developed. Soon, though, there were disagreements with customers over licensing arrangements and an important prospect—a major eye health company—went to a competing software supplier. However, that company appreciated his programming skills, and in 2003 they employed him as a full-time consultant to support the alternative programs they had licensed. Over time, he moved toward the business end of the operation, covering pricing, regulation, technical writing, and trade show preparation and representation. When the leader of his division suddenly resigned in late 2008, the company decided it needed his skills in-house. He was offered and accepted a salaried position as Manager for Global Marketing.

The new job involved considerable travel as a principal company representative at trade shows and customer sites around the world. A change in the company's leadership also consolidated his position as a business development leader—not only visiting trade shows but also visiting hospitals and surgeries, running information sessions at medical schools, and inspiring young doctors to want to "make people see" through specialized computer-assisted lens-fitting techniques. As a natural byproduct of his work and personality, he came to know "everyone who matters" in his industry specialization. Meanwhile, his work continued to drive innovation, such as developing large-diameter specialty lenses to treat diseased corneas.

His connections were mainly in his industry, but his emergent business skills—such as communicating between specialty manufactures and their users—were transferable. He saw a potentially rewarding future in a consulting career, if for any reason his paid employment one day soured. He recognized that his early art school education went beyond graphic design to an ability to see overall patterns and abstract relevant ideas. He was also able to transfer the skills learned from dreaded "crit sessions"—where art students are asked to defend their work—to the trade show floor. There, he was successful in representing the advantages of his software to industry leaders.[1]

How does Bruce Knight work? How did he get from being a college dropout to holding a key position in global marketing? How did he succeed without more formal education, and how do other people succeed through greater commitment to formal education? How did his intelligent career develop the skills to earn the respect of leaders in his industry and to inspire young doctors—and how can you go about developing and demonstrating your skills? The sections that follow provide selected answers to the chapter title, "How Do You Work?" As you read on, please remember that ideas presented about knowledge, education, and experience will overlap. Our goal here is to help you see how they overlap, and to help you build a composite picture of how you work—or seek to work—in your own situation.

BY APPLYING AND DEVELOPING KNOWLEDGE

One way to better understand Bruce Knight's progress is to look back more than fifty years to the work of British economist Edith Penrose.[2] She argued that there are two kinds of knowledge. One she called *objective knowledge*, which can be formally taught or learned from the written word, and in turn transmitted to others. The other kind of knowledge reflected learning in the form of *personal experience.*

Objective knowledge exists independently of individuals and groups and can be, in Penrose's words, "transmissible to all on equal terms." Algebra, for example, is a clearly defined set of rules and definitions, a body of objective knowledge that can be transmitted in a classroom or through a book. You may or may not have experienced good algebra teachers in your life, but the body of objective knowledge they taught from was the same for everyone. Personal experience can also provide you with objective knowledge—for example, the knowledge an architect gains when calculating the relationship between various angles to design a building—but that experience itself cannot be transmitted to others. The architect cannot fully describe what happened over long hours at the drafting table, but those hours will have produced a change, however subtle, in the architect's knowledge.

Bruce Knight's story illustrates both forms of knowledge that Penrose describes. Although his formal, postsecondary instruction was limited, he sought out objective knowledge to become familiar with the relevant computer-programming code, and took it on himself to learn some fundamentals about marketing. However, much of his success stems from personal experience: in coding ever more sophisticated programs, networking with trade show representatives, and speaking at formal events. Recently, he left his global marketing job for a new position with a rival Japanese company, one he sees as making a stronger investment in new medical devices. The company has already employed a number of industry leaders Knight already knows. The new job will pay a little more, but he reports that the main incentive for the move is "to work on new products with people I respect."

In a changing world, you will always need to seek out new knowledge and experience. What can you learn from Knight's approach? How does the combination of working on new products with people you respect work for you?

BY USING YOUR EDUCATION

Formal education is a key factor in contributing to how people work. Nation-states frequently signal their readiness for the knowledge economy by the percentage of high school and college graduates they produce. Getting a formal education, though, is only part of the story. How can you *use* your education? Does more education always mean a better-trained mind and a more successful career? The answer may not be as obvious as it seems.

Nobel Prize–winning economist Gary Becker was one of the first to claim that formal education is a key component of our "human capital," or "the stock of competences, knowledge and personality attributes that have a direct impact on our ability to work and thus to produce economic value."[3] His writing emphasizes the benefits of formal education and advocates incentives for parents to keep their children in school, rather than expecting them to work to support the family.

Becker's argument extends to higher education, where authors Richard Settersten and Barbara Ray draw a distinction between "swimmers"—who seek out formal education, have clear career and life plans, and pursue them in a calculated way—and "treaders"—who show no interest in education and "embrace the world of adulthood too quickly."[4] The authors contend that rushing to start work limits your future career opportunities, and in turn your social and economic well-being.[5]

Is Bruce Knight a swimmer or a treader? His decision to drop out of higher education suggests that he might be a treader. Yet, his career trajectory suggests he is a swimmer, since he sought out experiences that provided the building blocks for long-term success. His career compares with those of other people—such as Virgin Group CEO Richard Branson, cosmetics pioneer Mary Kay Ash, recording magnate Simon Cowell, cookie maker Debbi Fields, the late Steve Jobs, and many others who experienced huge success without completing a college degree.[6] However, most college dropouts do not become millionaires, and in most professional careers people seek out higher education before seeking professional work. Whatever your past or future formal education, though, it can only complement—and cannot replace—your real-world experience.

BY DEVELOPING YOUR EXPERTISE

Swedish social scientist Anders Ericsson and his colleagues have developed a "10,000 hour rule," suggesting that what commonly distinguishes great from simply competent performers is 10,000 hours of additional practice. This practice involves around 20 hours a week of "struggle, sacrifice and honest, often painful self-assessment" over a ten-year period.[7] Moreover, the practice needs to be deliberate, and "focused on tasks beyond your current level of competence or comfort." Fortunately, in many fields—like piano playing—the practice sequences have already been mapped out, so that you can seek out coaches to lead you along established but increasingly challenging paths to expertise.

Popular author Malcolm Gladwell picked up Ericsson's 10,000-hour rule and, in his book *Outliers*, applied it to computer software genius Bill Joy (cofounder of Sun Microsystems, since absorbed by Oracle), composer Wolfgang Amadeus Mozart, chess grandmaster Bobby Fischer, Bill Gates (cofounder of Microsoft), and—for a change in emphasis—The Beatles. A chance meeting between a Liverpool entrepreneur and a German club owner landed The Beatles in Hamburg for a series of tours between 1960 and 1962. There, the band would play in city clubs for eight-hour shifts, often seven days a week, as customers passed in and out. The range and quality of the music the band developed by playing so many hours in Germany meant that when they came back home "they sounded like no one else." By the time they broke through in 1964, they had played an estimated twelve hundred times. Combine the marathon sessions in Hamburg with an intense practice schedule back in Liverpool, and 10,000 hours are quickly realized.[8]

What, though, if you want to develop expertise along an independent 10,000-hour path—one where the practice sequence hasn't been mapped out by other people? What kind of intelligent career work does that entail? Ericsson and his colleagues suggest you not rely too heavily or too long on any particular coach. An experienced piano coach may be accustomed to teach in a certain way, but when pursuing an individual path you need to be open to new possibilities. In this case you can develop your "inner coach," meaning that you determine your own development plans. You can pay attention to unanticipated events, how they occurred, and how they were handled. You can also ask how you might perform in a situation—say, leading a meeting—and then watch and compare yourself against someone you recognize as an expert. Regardless of your level of education, the more innovation disrupts established ways of working, the more you will need to rely on your inner coach—to practice *self-coaching*—in your own career.[9]

BY LEARNING FROM OTHERS

Having a coach or using your inner coach, however, may not fit your situation. Today's complex knowledge economy, commonly involving both teamwork and on-the-job training, means that your intelligent career often calls on your ability to learn from others. How is this done? Stanford psychology professor Albert Bandura was one of the first to articulate what he termed "social learning theory," expanding on the common-sense idea that we learn from observing one another's behavior and then imitating what we have seen. As children, for example, we learn by watching our parents, grandparents, siblings, and other family members. As adults, we learn by watching our colleagues at work and imitating them.[10]

Social learning theory also supports the basic principles of intelligent careers. It tells us that learning is a continuous process facilitated through daily interaction with others not only in the classroom but also in your professional and personal life. In this respect, how you work is influenced by the models you see among the people with whom you work. According to Bandura, this kind of learning involves four successive processes involving attention, retention, reproduction, and reinforcement. In turn, successful reinforcement can provide the motivation for future learning episodes. The stages are shown in Table 4.1, illustrated by the example of a successful episode in the training of a surgeon.

Bandura describes how our overall experience with behavior modeling leads to a sense of *self-efficacy*, which is our "judgment of [our] capability to accomplish a certain level of performance." John Krumboltz and others have applied Bandura's ideas to the process of career choice, showing that the kind of career you choose is largely determined by your observations of others.[11] Watching your parents' careers as you grow up

TABLE 4.1   BANDURA'S FOUR STAGES OF BEHAVIOR MODELING

Process	Activity (Example of a Trainee Surgeon)
Paying attention to someone's behavior	The trainee observes the surgeon performing an operation.
Retaining what you observe	The trainee seeks to retain what they observed for when they will perform the operation.
Reproducing the behavior	The trainee gets an opportunity to perform the operation under the surgeon's supervision.
Finding reinforcement	The trainee is motivated by the reinforcement received from the surgeon, peers, or their own interpretation of their performance.

may be as important an influence on your career choices as any vocational interest test. A vivid example is when growing up with a chronically unemployed parent can lead to trouble adapting to an alarm clock.[12] Community members, teachers, sports heroes, or pop stars (whom you may or may not know directly) are other likely influences over how you learn. These influences will persist in the world of work. Who are you learning from?

BY APPLYING HARD SKILLS

Drawing a distinction between "hard skills" versus "soft skills" provides another way of looking at how intelligent careers function. Psychologist and science journalist Daniel Goleman divides individual capabilities or skills into three categories: purely technical skills like accounting, cognitive abilities like analytical reasoning, and what he calls emotional intelligence (EQ)—the capability to both understand ourselves and empathize with others. Skills such as engineering, financial analysis, and numerical evaluations are best understood as hard skills, whereas emotional intelligence—including the way we write—involves the use of soft skills, to which we will return later. [13]

Hard skills are emphasized in courses on accounting principles or operations managementor, in courses with an emphasis on problem-solving or critical thinking. Yet, we also know that some skills can and often must be developed through experience. The short-order cook can only learn from experience how to multitask burger flipping on the grill. A physician who practices medicine in Haiti after having worked in the United States is likely to develop a new battery of hard skills to treat patients with tropical diseases with fewer medical resources. Bruce Knight's technical skills in the higher-margin market of gas-permeable contact lenses provided a strong platform for him to expand his experience, even though the mainstream market was moving toward soft lenses.

Revered Massachusetts Institute of Technology scholar Edgar Schein pinpoints a key principle for your intelligent career when he says that you must constantly update your hard skills because "knowledge and skill become rapidly obsolete in a dynamically changing technological world." In that world, he observes, "as technological complexity increases, the need for technical experts will increase." Schein further cautions, "as technologies in all the functions themselves change more and more rapidly, experts will become obsolete more and more rapidly." The challenge is to continually update your skills "in an organizational world that will not bear the costs in terms of money and time for this updating process."[14] In keeping with an emphasis on employability beyond any one organization, the onus to update hard skills clearly rests with the individual—that is, with you.

BY APPLYING SOFT SKILLS

Daniel Goleman asserts that soft skills are a necessary complement to hard skills.[15] A teacher's capacity to draw the shy student into class discussion is as important as their subject matter mastery. A long-haul trucker's capacity to regulate his or her sleep and endure stretches of solitude is as important as their capacity to drive. A hair stylist with a capacity to listen to clients' concerns about their appearance is as important as the ability to cut hair. Soft skills are gaining increasing attention from business schools and management consultants, because they affect what we can achieve as individuals and what we can help others to achieve.

Goleman's EQ offers a useful framework for understanding soft skills and their potential impact on intelligent careers both inside and outside of work. There are, he says, five components of EQ, as shown in Table 4.2.

As noted earlier, these five components can be divided into two groups. The first three focus your attention on self-management, whereas the last two focus on how you interact with others. Goleman and many others assert that all five skill sets are both useful in themselves, and complement the hard skills you are developing.

BY BUILDING COMPANY-SPECIFIC (OR NOT-SO-SPECIFIC) SKILLS

There is a long tradition of companies hiring graduates straight from college and putting them through carefully designed training programs. These programs add practical experience to the formal learning from a college degree—for example in accounting, nursing, social work, or teaching, and where that experience may be necessary for professional certification. For the employer, there's an opportunity to assess the employee's performance and determine whether to make a new job offer. For the intelligent career owner there's an opportunity to consider whether it would be better to take your experience elsewhere. A similar opportunity stems from management-training programs. Again, they frequently involve concentrated training in the short term, with both parties looking to reevaluate their relationship later.

How to make sense of these programs? The "brand name" of the company that trained you can be useful. The experience, for example, of cost-cutting or restructuring, may be directly applicable in a different

TABLE 4.2   GOLEMAN'S FIVE COMPONENTS OF EMOTIONAL
INTELLIGENCE

	Definition	Hallmarks
Self-Awareness	The ability to recognize and understand your moods, emotions, and drives and their effect on others.	Self-confidence Realistic self-assessment Self-deprecating sense of humor
Self-Regulation	The ability to control or redirect disruptive impulses and moods. The propensity to suspend judgment—to think before acting.	Trustworthiness and integrity Comfort with ambiguity Openness to change
Motivation	A passion to work for reasons that go beyond money or status. A propensity to pursue goals with energy and persistence.	Strong drive to achieve Optimism, even in the face of failure Organizational commitment
Empathy	The ability to understand the emotional makeup of other people. Skill in treating people according to their emotional reactions.	Expertise in building and retaining talent Cross-cultural sensitivity Service to clients and customers
Social Skill	Proficiency in managing relationships and building networks. An ability to find common ground and build rapport.	Effectiveness in leading change Persuasiveness Expertise in building and leading teams

SOURCE: Daniel Goleman, "What Makes a Leader?" *Harvard Business Review,* January 2004, 88.

company going through a similar process. More broadly, if the new work environment is similar to the old one, skills gained in the old one may be more transferable.[16] Drawing on a study of twenty General Electric alumni, Boris Groysberg and his colleagues at Harvard Business School reported that skill transferability has several dimensions, predicted to move from most to least transferable as you look down the list.[17] Other things being equal, it makes sense for intelligent career owners to invest in the skills that are most transferable.

> *General Management:* These are the most transferable skills, involving gathering, cultivating, and using financial, technical, and human resources. They include your decision-making, leadership, and functional skills, which need to constantly evolve to keep pace with greater responsibilities and new technological developments.
>
> *Strategic Human Capital:* These skills are gained through developing and implementing specific strategies such as cost-cutting measures or organizational growth, and so forth. They transfer well to different companies facing similar strategic challenges.
>
> *Industry Human Capital:* These involve skills and knowledge that are unique to a specific industry such as medicine, mining, or information technology. They are less transferable because industries operate under different management principles and bodies of knowledge.
>
> *Relationship human capital:* These skills emerge from your established relationships with colleagues and/or peers. They have more limited transferability, but if you move as part of an established team you can draw on your combined experience of working together.
>
> *Company-specific human capital:* These comprise knowledge, skills, and experience you gain in a specific organizational context, and are perhaps the least transferable form of human capital.

But what if—like most people—you aren't picked for a prolonged training program? A study in *Harvard Business Review* reports that companies think only 3–5 percent of their employees can be seen as high potential.[18]

The Economist observes, "In their rush to classify people, companies can miss potential stars." Moreover, companies that limit themselves to employees with company-specific knowledge may be creating a barrier to their own creativity.[19] Life doesn't end if you don't get tapped on the shoulder. You need to take your skills, find a job, do it well, earn respect, learn what you can, and move on when that makes sense for you. Your opportunity is to develop your own expertise—to practice self-coaching— from the start. You can seize that opportunity!

BY EXERCISING POWER

Despite widespread acceptance of value of emotional intelligence, Stanford Business School professor Jeffrey Pfeffer is skeptical. He believes that getting ahead in any organization is about seizing and keeping power. He fears you may practice self-regulation and empathize with others to the point that you "soft-pedal" instead of seizing power.[20] He emphasizes that you ought not to complain about how others play the game. Pfeffer believes you "can compete and even triumph in organizations of all types, large or small, public or private sector," if you "understand and are willing to apply the principles of power."[21] He describes eleven ways through which this can be done, shown in Box 4.1.

One of Pfeffer's examples is about Lalit Modi, child of a wealthy Indian family, who tried to establish a professional Indian cricket league featuring top foreign players. In bringing his proposal to the Board of Control for Cricket in India (BCCI) and its president, Jagmohan Dalmiya, Lalit was able to *mete out resources*, because he already had merchandising and broadcasting deals with Disney and ESPN (a Disney affiliate). When his proposal was rejected, Lalit set out to *shape behavior through rewards and punishments* by looking for support from others who might oppose the current BCCI board. In seeking to *advance on multiple fronts*, he connected with Sharad Pawar, an influential cricket-loving politician. To *make the first move*, he hired a team of lawyers to pursue charges of corruption against the BCCI's president, helped his politician friend get

Box 4.1   ELEVEN WAYS TO EXERCISE POWER

1. **Mete out resources.** *Use money, equipment, space, and information to build your power base.*
2. **Shape behavior through rewards and punishments.** *Put simply, reward those who help you and punish those who stand in your way.*
3. **Advance on multiple fronts.** *When you anticipate or meet resistance, try to work around that resistance through alternative channels.*
4. **Make the first move.** *A surprise move can catch opponents off guard and secure victory before they even know what's happening.*
5. **Co-opt antagonists.** *Make potential opponents part of your team or give them a stake in the system.*
6. **Remove rivals—nicely, if possible.** *Show people the door, preferably by finding them an attractive job somewhere else.*
7. **Don't draw unnecessary fire.** *Pick your battles carefully, and build support wherever you can.*
8. **Use the personal touch.** *Take time to be polite to and build relationships with influential people—and don't rely on e-mail!*
9. **Persist.** *Refuse to give up in the face of setbacks, and build a reputation as someone who finds a way to succeed.*
10. **Make important relationships work—no matter what.** *Some relationships will be absolutely essential to your success, so make them work whatever the cost.*
11. **Make the vision compelling.** Align what you want to do with a compelling, socially valuable objective with which others will identify.

elected, and became vice president himself. To *co-opt antagonists*, Lalit quickly procured television rights and merchandise sponsorships to show people that siding with him was in their economic interests. He soon got his cricket league approved.

Pfeffer describes power—and the political skills to acquire it—as the focus of his teaching at Stanford. He maintains that his aim is to give his students "the insights and tools that will enable them to bring about change, get things accomplished and, not incidentally, further their careers."[22] In your intelligent career, it seems fundamental that you recognize when other people are playing a power game, and in turn are better informed to respond to it. You don't want to get trampled on! However, the choice to exercise power yourself is more complicated. Was Lalit Modi's power grab good for Indian cricket, or for international cricket? Were the charges of corruption against the incumbent president in any way justified? Was he simply using his family's wealth and connections to indulge his own ego? Pfeffer's account does not raise these questions, but we submit they make a difference.[23] You need to *take charge* of how and for what purpose you apply political skills.

BY DEVELOPING YOUR WORK PORTFOLIO

The challenge to take charge applies more broadly to your own learning. What markers can you look for to ensure you are heading in the right direction? Influential management writer Charles Handy's ideas about maintaining a "work portfolio" offer a useful compass. "Going portfolio," to Handy, means exchanging the security of institutional employment for the independence of a freelance career. It means developing a work portfolio that is "a collection of different items, but a collection which has a theme to it."[24] Not all portfolio categories are developed during paid employment. In addition to wage work, fee work, and homework, the portfolio can include gift work (volunteering) and study work (learning). Years spent parenting or caring for an elderly relative demonstrate a character that is reliable, committed, and empathic. In portfolio work "people put their different bits of work into folders."[25] Architects, journalists, and photographers all bid for future work by showing examples of what they have done before. Depending on the client, different bids are likely to show different aspects of your own portfolio.[26]

Career specialists Barrie Hopson and Katie Ledger refresh and expand on Handy's ideas by reminding us that every job is now temporary, that the coin with "job security" on one side has "dependency" on the other, and that economic security no longer exists unless we create it.[27] An illustrative example is Rachel Nelken, a London area arts administrator, who works half-time as a relationship manager for the British Arts Council, works another half day for a local music program, does freelance work for a number of music funders, and offers ad hoc "action learning" programs for local arts organizations. She reports having demanding conversations while watching her kid's swimming lesson, and finishing a report on an eighteen-inch-high table at a local play center. She finds it hard to focus on deadlines when there are other demands on her time. However, she is upbeat about her portfolio career:

> I believe that each area of my work informs the other. Working with funders gives me a sense of the bigger picture, the national and regional context of my work and examples of best practice to learn from. Working on the ground gives me real-life, credible experience to draw on when talking to clients or commenting on policy issues. Running action learning sessions develops my leadership skills when I might not have the responsibility of managing a team.[28]

Your intelligent career involves building your portfolio while balancing your overall life and remaining flexible and open to new ways of work. Recognizing different categories of work also helps you to be creative: in seeing, for example, how fee work can also be study work in which you learn something new, or how initially unpaid gift work can help you learn new skills or make new contacts. Your portfolio is a growing testament to the skills and knowledge you can draw on—that is, to how you can work—in future assignments.

Finally, the energy to build a work portfolio comes from your inner motivation, values, and the way you see your professional identity. It also draws on people who, in Hopson and Ledger's words, "are so impressed by what you've done that they rave about you to others." (The same people enjoy the buzz of being recognized for knowing talented people.)[29] Portfolio work is about more than developing your skills.

To conclude, objective knowledge and personal experience are complementary kinds of knowledge. Both are necessary contributors to the question of how do you work, and the related question of how are youlearning. Formal education is often taken as a convenient measure of human capital, although it can be seen more broadly as an indicator of the kind of "swimmers" who progress to further learning through experience. For many established occupations, a "10,000-hour rule" of exceptional practice time can distinguish exceptional from merely good performers. That practice can be supervised by an experienced coach, or by an "inner coach" if the field is less well developed. Hard skills, soft skills, company-specific skills, and skills in the use of power offer further distinctions across how you perform, or can learn to perform, as you pursue your intelligent career. You can benefit from organizing and developing your skills by going portfolio, that is by describing and developing the knowledge and skills that your intelligent career has to offer.

With Whom Do You Work?

Find a group of people who challenge and inspire you,
Spend a lot of time with them,
And it will change your life

—Amy Poehler

With her signature rhinestone-studded glasses, white hair, and slight build, five feet tall and eighty-five years old, Lois Weisberg was not the kind of person you would normally think of as "the most important or powerful person in Chicago." Yet, her persistent creativity, her interest in people from all walks of life, and her reputation as "a person who seems to know everybody" gave her the kind of influence that most people can only dream about. Lois Weisberg's life is a remarkable example of an intelligent career in action. (Reader alert: You may have seen this story before in Malcolm Gladwell's writing. If you have, please bear with us. It's the best story we know to introduce the material in this chapter.)[1]

Born in 1925 on Chicago's North Side, Weisberg built an enviable career through an eclectic network of doctors, lawyers, politicians, artists, railroad enthusiasts, flea-market aficionados, singers, writers, park lovers, and actors. In the early 1950s she started a small drama troupe and, with funding from a reclusive billionaire she'd befriended at a local restaurant, hosted a festival to celebrate George Bernard Shaw's 100th birthday. The festival was a great success, not least because of the people she invited to speak about Shaw's legacy—people like dramatist William Saroyan and six-time presidential candidate Norman Thomas. This prompted her to begin a newspaper devoted to Shaw, which evolved into an underground weekly called "The Paper." The weekly opened new doors to a wider social network, this time of well-known film directors, editors, musicians, and comedians who came together to form the editorial board.

Shortly after the break-up of her first marriage, and needing money, she took a public relations job in an injury rehabilitation center. She then switched to a public-interest law firm, which fed her concerns about local issues and particularly the disrepair of Chicago's parks. The move allowed her to connect with other like-minded individuals to establish the lobbying group Friends of the Parks—a diverse collection of volunteers including nature lovers, historians, civic activists, and homemakers. Alarmed by the potential closure of a local railroad line, she set up another lobbying group—South Shore Recreation, which saved the railroad and brought her into contact with an even wider range of contacts. All of these positions capitalized on her distinctive ability to make new ties, and extended her network even further.

Her career took yet another turn when she became the executive director of the Chicago Council of Lawyers. Later, her exceptional social skills made her an ideal candidate to run Congressman Sidney Yate's reelection campaign, and in turn to work for Harold Washington, Chicago's first African American mayor. Although she enjoyed her life in politics, she was soon ready for another change. So, she quit her job in the mid-1980s, connected with the itinerant peddlers and antique dealers who ran Chicago's flea market, and set up her own second-hand jewelry business.

In 1989, fueled by her passion for the arts, she became Chicago's Commissioner of Cultural Affairs, a post she held until her resignation in 2011. In that position, she launched initiatives such as the Chicago Cultural Centre, Friends of the Park, the Taste of Chicago Festival, the Chicago Blues Festival, and the Chicago Gospel Festival. In 1990 she established the famous Gallery 37 program, in which Chicago youths created artwork under the guidance of professional artists. The original funding had been for youths from disadvantaged backgrounds, but she didn't believe that poor kids could advance "by being lumped together with other poor kids." So, backed by private funding, she extended the support to middle-income families to allow youths from *different* backgrounds to learn from one another. The program continues today and has been an outstanding success.

After a cost-cutting spat with the mayor, she resigned as Commissioner for Cultural Affairs in early 2011. Asked about her plans for the future, she said her children wanted her to slow down, but she had other ideas. "I am writing a book." she added, "A lot has happened to me since I entered the world of big city politics, but I had a pretty big life before getting here."[2]

Lois Weisberg's "pretty big life" involved working with many other people, across different walks of life. How about you? With whom do you work? What kind of ties do you have, either in your existing workplace, or in other workplaces, or with family and friends? How can those ties help you, or how can you help others? What networks or teams are you associated with, and what can you get from or give to them? What about volunteer groups or online social networks? Finally, where have you built or can you build trust, and again with what value for your intelligent career? As with previous chapters, let us speak to the opening title with a series of alternative responses.

WITH WEAK TIES AND STRONG TIES

Lois Weisberg is an outstanding example of someone who makes the most of what sociologist Mark Granovetter calls "the strength of weak ties." According to Granovetter, the strength of a tie is based on a combination of the time spent, emotional intensity, mutual confiding, and reciprocity between individuals. In your own career, you are likely to have strong ties with family members and close friends or colleagues, and weak ties with people you feel less emotionally close to. In his research, Granovetter found that weak ties are especially valuable in a job search because they "are more likely to move in circles" different from your own and to have access to different information that you would otherwise receive.[3] In other words, weak ties can open new doors for you.

Weak and strong ties play an important role in encouraging greater cohesion in professional and social groups. If you have strong ties with people in one group and weak ties with people in other groups, you can provide your strong ties with what Granovetter calls "bridging," facilitating the flow of ideas, influence, and information can travel. Bridging explains why Lois Weisberg's Gallery 37 program was able to connect professional artists with Chicago youth. Bridging also explains the popularity of networking sites such as LinkedIn or Facebook, where some people claim thousands of "friends." The value of having the right balance of strong and weak ties is that it allows you to benefit from close relationships at the same time as you maintain connections to a wider world. Your overall combination of strong and weak ties amounts to your *social capital*—your advantage created by your location in a structure of relationships.[4]

Influential University of Chicago scholar Ronald Burt has extended our understanding of social capital by emphasizing a third situation, where neither strong ties nor weak ties exist. In this situation, if you map all your existing relationships you will simply see a "structural hole." You could build a bridge across that structural hole. Why might you want to do that? Because your bridge can help you see what others can't see.

Suppose, for example, Robert and Jessica meet at an industry trade show. They are in different occupational groups—say, marketing and production—and making a connection allows each a window into the other's world. From this beginning they can go further, with perhaps one inviting the other to fill a small part in a project team. Over time, they develop a high-trust relationship where each admires the other's work and trusts him or her to do what needs to be done to complete the next project (Figure 5.1).[5]

At the next stage, Robert and Jessica realize that the high-trust relationship between them can anchor a project team. Robert places greater

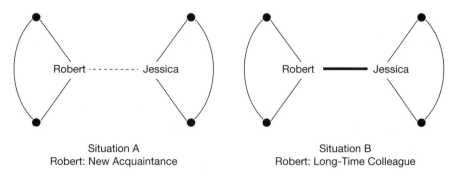

Situation A
Robert: New Acquaintance

Situation B
Robert: Long-Time Colleague

Figure 5.1   Robert and Jessica Build a New Bridge

trust in Jessica's contacts, and vice versa. That leads to an advantage for them in choosing between alternative approaches and "framing a proposal to be attractive to needed supporters."[6] Together they are more likely to broker deals that please a greater number of stakeholders. This situation is commonly found in advertising projects, for example, where two key "creatives" are the copywriter, who provides the script, and the artistic director, who provides the visual art. Having once succeeded as a team, the same two creatives often stick together—even through changes in their employment. As they do, they rely on each other to recruit complementary photographers, graphic designers, and TV and Web advertising and other experts they may need for the successive projects they take on.[7]

WITH SOCIAL NETWORKS

Beginning in relatively recent times, strong and weak ties have been supported by the Web. In earlier days there were always social networks, but they were maintained by regular physical contact between participants—supported by letters, telegrams, telephones, fax machines, and more recently e-mail. The Web has changed all that, so that now most of us assume social networks refer to digital networks such as Facebook, Twitter, LinkedIn, and Tumblr and their equivalents around the world. Participation in these contemporary social networks is widely prescribed for the benefits it can provide across both your personal and professional lives. Why so? Career consultant Pam Lassiter puts it this way in her book *The New Job Security*:

> They can dramatically improve your sources of information and your career management results. If you're not using them and your competition is (and, I promise you, they are), you're at a disadvantage. Using them is fun, too. You can find people that you haven't seen in years, from high school friends to former employers and neighbors, as well as meet new people with similar interests. You will discover ways that you can help each other that you never would have known about before.[8]

Yet, despite their much-vaunted advantages, and their apparent usefulness in bridging structural holes, social-networking sites need to be used with caution. Lassiter suggests that you think through four major areas of concern, about what she calls being found by others, making or breaking reputation, promiscuous networking, and valuing what others share.

Being found by others: A principal concern here is—what can companies find out? Even if you're a passive job candidate (someone's interested in you, but you don't know it) your public information is likely to be vetted without your knowledge. The simple response is to keep your information up-to-date. Let people find you, and determine they want to know more about you.

Making or breaking reputation: The Web is the custodian of your reputation, and the "brand" that you have created around the work you can do. Take care to protect and build that reputation. Most of all beware "digital dirt"—that potential collection of Web hits you would prefer other people not to find!

Promiscuous networking: When is it appropriate to reach across to others, for example to "friend" on Facebook or "connect" on LinkedIn? Lassiter suggests two filters in determining whether to approach someone. Do you know the person reasonably well, and would you be willing to write them a reference?

Valuing what others share: There's a new etiquette around social networking. Most of all, it involves being sure to thank people for small favors, like providing that introduction or "retweeting" that message. This valuing in turn can help build trust between distant collaborators.[9]

In sum, social-networking sites can be immensely useful—as long as you take charge of the way you use them. It can help you find other people and be found yourself in a way that wasn't previously possible. It can also complement more focused approaches to relationship building, like those we discuss below.

WITH MENTORS AND PROTÉGÉS

Ties to other people are often a starting point for individual learning. Mentoring—a process that provides for one person to learn from another person's experience—is usually seen as passing from a senior person to a junior one. Typically, a mentor wants to teach, a protégé wants to learn, and the two parties come together. Commonly no money is exchanged, but the protégé reciprocates by taking the mentor seriously and trying to be a good student. Conversely, the mentor benefits through the respect he or she is shown and the opportunity to teach. In your intelligent career, you will need to play both mentor and protégé roles, reflecting both your past experience and your future learning interests.

For example, Yong Bing Ngen left school in Malaysia at age sixteen and started his first job clearing tables and washing dishes in a small "zi char" (cook and fry) restaurant. Upon watching the cutting skills on show around him he "was so impressed that [he] decided [he] was going to become a chef." From these humble beginnings, Yong, the son of a duck farmer, learned the art of cuisine by working alongside his "Shi Fu"

(Master) Leong Mun Soon at the Kuching Hilton's Chinese restaurant. In Yong's case he was given a wider lesson that "before a chef can cook good food, he needs to build good relationships with everyone in the team." Leong also showed his protégé how to befriend and learn from other hotel employees—for example housekeepers, purchasers, and engineers— about how their methods could also be applied to kitchen activities such as cleaning, inventory control, and equipment maintenance.[10]

Mentoring expert Kathy Kram and others emphasize that mentors can support protégés through two basic functions: *career* and *psychosocial* mentoring.[11] On the one hand, career mentoring can help you learn new skills relevant for a present or future job, or to anticipate a transition to a new line of work. On the other hand, psychosocial mentoring can give you emotional support—helping you to improve your confidence and self-esteem, or to cope with difficult personal challenges. The mentor is frequently, but not always, the older party. To return to the aforementioned example, when Yong took a position in the famous Raffles Hotel in Singapore in 2003, he struggled with a menu he had never cooked before. "But the cooks under me were patient enough to explain things to me. And as much as they taught me, I tried to share with them my Chinese cooking skills too."[12] Mentor and protégé roles are best shaped by what you can each offer one another.

WITH DEVELOPMENTAL NETWORKS

It used to be common to talk about finding a single mentor who could "show you the ropes and open the right doors." However, in the knowledge economy, a single relationship, or even a series of relationships, may not meet all your needs. As Kathy Kram and her colleague Monica Higgins ask, "How can one teacher know enough to help you keep up with rapidly changing technology, as well as navigate the challenges of globalization, a multicultural work force and team-based decision making? People who have served as mentors may need as much or even more help than their protégés in staying abreast of all these changes." So rather than think about one or even several mentor-protégé relationships, you can do better thinking systemically about your "developmental network" and what you would like to both take from and give to the people in that network. Building your own developmental networks involve five key steps.[13]

1. ***Know yourself:*** Be prepared before you ask for help. Know your goals, strengths, and weaknesses and reflect on the feedback you've received. Think about where you would like to go and how you would like to get there. What skill and knowledge gaps would you like to fill? Who are the people, inside and outside your present employer, who can help you? Who knows you well enough to help you? How comfortable are you in approaching these people, and where would you like to make a start—for instance with a supportive partner, or a long-term friend?

2. ***Know your Context:*** Knowing yourself is only half the story; the other half is knowing your context. What are you trying to achieve, in terms of promotion, learning, entering a new field, work-family balance, or whatever? Do you know enough about the employment system, information sources, industry background, or family support systems you may want to use? Where do you need fresh contacts, and how can you go about making them? What can you offer in return for the help you are seeking?

3. ***Enlist developers:*** Next, go out and enlist your network members. You may need help in, say, negotiating company policy, understanding new markets, or researching a new technology. Here, outsiders such as fellow alums, family contacts, or professional association members can be helpful. Think about the diversity of your network and the value of receiving different viewpoints. Think about what you can offer people, beginning with your commitment, your gratitude, and being a good student.

4. ***Reassess regularly:*** What you need from your developmental network is going to change. This does not mean you need to throw off old friends, but it does mean that your behavior needs to be intentional. You can bring new people in without discarding

trusted allies, and be selective about whom you seek advice from in any particular situation. Keep asking which members of your network can help you meet your goals, how you can get sufficient access to them, and—not least—what you can provide in return.

5. *Develop others:* Remember that high-quality relationships are mutually beneficial and that your developmental network needs to reflect this. As a relatively junior party you can be a dependable worker, an able presenter, a willing team player, an open-minded listener, and an enthusiastic learner. As a relatively senior party you can be a leader, a role model, and a source of wisdom. In either position, you can reinforce your commitment to the underlying developmental approach and its mutual benefits.

Finally, remember that members of your network are also developing themselves. They, too, will be learning new skills, making new contacts, and changing employers from time to time. So it's important to keep up with people, and to stay on top of how their development can further support your own, and vice versa.

WITH FELLOW ALUMS

As people grow older, attachments from much earlier in their lives can exert a powerful force. When he was just seven years old, David Thomson was a student at Upper Canada College riding his bike with a young classmate. The classmate turned to him and said, "My mother is so happy that we are friends because you are going to be able to do so much for me later in life." At the time Thomson didn't understand what his young friend meant. However, since Thomson came to head up Canada's largest family fortune and be appointed chair of Thomson Reuters, the picture becomes clearer. The boy's mother was apparently thinking about the potential power of "old school ties." Moreover, it's not just about meeting people in class. As the school's director of alumni relations notes,

"A lot of people send their kids to school so that they can build those networks not only while they're here, but also after they graduate."[14]

While institutions such as Upper Canada College have formal and long-established alumni programs, alumni communities can also be driven by their individual members. Lois Weisberg's Gallery 37 program provided an opportunity for youth from disadvantaged backgrounds to connect with middle-income youth. Both groups could learn from and build bonds with each other as well as enjoy their shared experience and interest in art. Whether institutionally or individually driven, maintaining connections with people from one's past can provide opportunities for future relationship building.

Alumni communities can involve graduates from the same high school or higher education establishment, former members of the armed services, people who worked for the same company or government department, contributors to the same political campaigns, players on the same sports teams, participants in the same weekend retreat, and so on. Other career-relevant communities can involve sharing a common religious, ideological, or political affiliation. In each case, members identify with one another and are likely to provide career support to one another when they can.[15] Today, with the availability of the Web, they have a far greater opportunity to stay connected and in turn develop deeper attachments.

WITH VOLUNTEERS

At the beginning of this chapter we saw how Lois Weisberg's work experiences included being a volunteer, often working alongside other volunteers, as when she joined the Friends of the Parks. We also saw how those experiences led her to new work opportunities and interests, both paid and unpaid. Whereas much focus has been given to paid work, voluntary work is an increasingly common part of people's work experiences. Studies in the UK have reported that just under half of all adults take part in formal voluntary work and around two-thirds take part in "informal" or unstructured voluntary work.[16] Why so? According to the late John Raynolds, former president of "Outward Bound," volunteering is an excellent way to develop and enhance both paid work opportunities and professional networks.[17]

Clare, a graduate of Oxford University in the UK, provides a useful insight into the value of volunteer work. After graduation, she went on to get an MSc in development from the School of Oriental and African Studies in London. However, she soon realized that her formal qualification wasn't enough to fulfill her dream of working in the field of human rights. Rather, it was common knowledge among her peers that to get paid work she first had to get some volunteer experience. This led her to the North End Community and Refugee Project in inner-city London, where she found a regular volunteer position. The position was demanding, requiring almost daily attendance, and Clare even gave up her paid job to spend more time at the Project. However, in her eyes it was worth the effort: It allowed her to gain hands-on experience, and increased her chances of meeting people in her field and finding full-time work.[18]

The benefits of volunteering extend beyond professional opportunities to better health, improved self-knowledge, and extended life experiences.[19] However, perhaps the biggest opportunity in volunteering is to try something new—rather like an informal apprenticeship—where you can meet with and learn from people already active in your field of interest. Volunteering has also gone global over the Web, for example when people "crowdsource" to provide bird-watching data that ornithologists had never previously imagined they could collect.[20]

WITH REFERENCE GROUPS

Maria from Barcelona, Spain, was discussing her career future. "As far back as I can remember," she said, "I would always hear about the kind of work that generations of my family members have done. My grandfather was a dentist. Two uncles were dentists. My father is a dentist." And what are her career plans? "I'm going to be a dentist."

Harrison was graduating from an MBA program with a choice between a two-year "fast track" rotational leadership position and a position with an investment banking firm. After listening to his MBA program peers and his family he concluded, "My gut wants the leadership program, but my head says I'd be crazy to turn down this great I-bank offer." So he took the investment banking offer.[21]

Both of the above examples are about reference groups, people we respect and want to please, and their influence on the kind of career opportunities we pursue. Family members are one important reference group. Peers—in the classroom, the hobby room, or the workplace—are another. People who don't know you but who are visible to you—rock stars, war heroes, activists, politicians, and CEOs can also be part of your reference group. "They," as you are likely to call your reference group, are the people whose approval you would like to have about your own intelligent career contributions. What may be surprising is that people's reference groups can differ substantially, even if they are in the same organization and have similar employment histories.[22]

One particular reference group involves people you see as part of the same *occupational community*. These may or may not be colleagues working for the same employer. They are people with whom you identify because of the education and training you've received and the shared understanding you have of how your occupation contributes to the world outside. Engineers, lawyers, nurses, teachers, and many other kinds of professionals are likely to affiliate with others in the same occupation, and may associate with one another rather than with other people working for the same employer. In classical terms, they present themselves as "cosmopolitans," rather than as "locals."[23] Recent evidence suggests identification with a profession rather than a particular employer is increasingly likely. In your intelligent career that makes a lot of sense, and doesn't prevent you from caring deeply about your employer as well.[24]

Many professionals now exchange knowledge over the Web with other professionals, or with occupational communities. For example, the Advanced Practice Nurses Listserv provides an online forum for nurses, educators, administrators, physicians, and other critical care professionals to collaborate by sharing knowledge and experiences. The site is particularly useful for people who live in geographically remote places or don't have colleagues at their workplace to draw on. As one nurse describes it, "I'm the only critical care nurse specialist in my hospital, in the whole town as a matter of fact. . . . [It] helps me to be in contact with other nurses from all across the country online on a regular basis. It allows me to ask questions . . . helps me to validate my practice and get knowledge that I need quickly."[25] Schoolteachers, relatively isolated from one another in physical space—across schools, education boards, and states—make it a point to share classroom designs and curricula in virtual space.[26]

Occupational communities can also enrich the range of people you work with by creating a more diverse network of connections. This might make your relationship with your employer a little more complicated, but it can be a good thing for both parties. It allows you to better appreciate how your occupational community adds value to your intelligent career. In turn, that allows you to better appreciate how your career adds value to your employer.

WITH TEAMS

A particular opportunity to develop ties and build social capital involves working in teams. Harvard Business School professor Amy Edmondson recalls that we used to think teams typically had relatively stable memberships, were physically located in the same place, and—like sports teams or musical groups—learned and performed together in pursuit of common goals. But what happens, asks Edmondson, if you are working in an emergency services facility where the staffing changes every shift? What if you are in a temporary project team formed to solve a complex problem? What if you are called on to reconcile both individual and shared responsibilities? How can you contribute to more effective performance in those situations?[27]

The answer, suggests Edmondson, is in contributing to *teaming*. This involves coordination and collaboration without the benefit of stable team structures, and where individual memberships frequently change. In this kind of temporary team, you need to develop and use new capabilities for sharing crucial knowledge quickly. You need to build on what she calls "four pillars" of teaming success:

Speaking up: Contributing to honest, direct communication by asking relevant questions, seeking feedback, and discussing errors.

Collaborating: Assuming a collaborative mindset to drive the process, both within and beyond the team's direct membership.

Experimenting: Taking a tentative, one-step-at-a-time approach that recognizes the uncertainty of the situation the team faces.

Reflecting: Consistently looking at specific questions and processes the team faces, and addressing them in regular meetings.

Edmondson describes how the application of these pillars contributed to the success of the Motorola RAZR mobile phone, which combined a groundbreaking "clamshell" design with technological advancements to achieve a breakthrough ultrathin phone. Meetings were held daily, and despite missing their first deadline the team persevered, enabling Motorola to sell 110 million RAZR phones over a period of four years.[28] Of course, long before those four years were up the team was disbanded, its members moving on, we trust, to apply the same four pillars across the range of different teams they subsequently joined. And if they were practicing intelligent careers, they were still in touch with one another.

WITH PEOPLE YOU DON'T YET KNOW

The idea of dynamic teaming leads on to our final topic. Earlier in the chapter, we introduced the idea of structural holes—gaps in a network structure. Here, we introduce the related ideas of *brokerage* and *closure*. If you are a member of a group, brokerage involves connecting with someone you don't yet know in another group, thereby creating an external contact with that group. In contrast, closure involves staying inside your own group and deepening relationships with other members of your group. Traditional ideas about employment often suggested that closure was enough; you ought to concentrate on your relations with fellow employees. However, a wide range of recent evidence suggests that in the knowledge economy—for example across total quality management, mental healthcare, student project, senior management, screenwriter, and semiconductor research groups—effective brokerage is essential to a group's overall success.[29]

You can help yourself and the world by looking beyond high-closure situations. Figure 5.2 illustrates four kinds of groups with which you might be affiliated, representing alternative combinations of low and high brokerage, and low and high closure. The high-performing groups described above are in Box A. In contrast, the low performing groups are in Box C. Now think about a group in which you participate—a work group, professional group, church group, student group, hobby group, or whatever. Does it sustain both high brokerage and high closure (as in Box A)? Or, in contrast, does it persist with both low brokerage and low closure (as in Box C)?

Consider your group again. Does it appear to have too much brokerage for its own good (Box D)? Or does it appear to have too much closure for

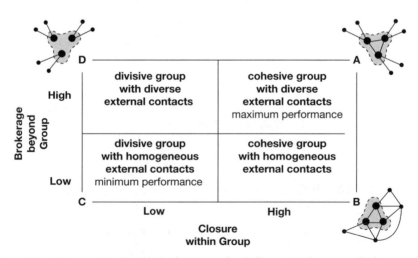

Figure 5.2   Comparative Group Performance for Different *Brokerage and Closure* Combinations.

its own good (Box B)? Look across all four boxes and notice the differences between the illustrated internal and external connections. Now ask yourself: What can I do to better serve my group?

Your temperament or life circumstances may have led you to favor either brokerage or closure in your career at this time. However, Figure 5.2 presents you with a larger question. It asks not only what behavior do you favor, but what behavior do you encourage from others? Can you do more to stand up for brokerage *and* closure in your group activities? If your answer is yes, you can anticipate contributing to higher performance, both as an individual *and* a group participant in the knowledge economy.

To summarize, the people with whom you work or are relevant to your work reflect two forms of social capital: weak ties, involving relatively low emotional attachment, and strong ties, involving relatively high emotional attachment. In addition, structural holes—gaps in the prevailing social structure—provide opportunities to extend your social capital. Learning through social relationships involves taking on contrasting mentor and protégé roles and sustaining developmental networks through which you can pursue your own learning agenda. Pursuing volunteer opportunities, seeking out reference groups (including occupational communities), and contributing to effective teamwork are other ways in which to build social capital. In collaborative work it is important to encourage the complementary contributions of both brokerage (going outside your group) and closure (staying inside your group) to overall group effectiveness. Paying attention to those with whom you work is a vital part of your development.

When Do You Change?

The past,—well, it's just like our Great-Aunt Laura,
Who cannot or will not perceive
That though she is welcome, and though we adore her,
Yet now it is time to leave.

—Piet Hein

Thirty years ago, Jean-Luc Brès took an entry-level advertising position in Polydor Records (now part of Universal Music Group) in Paris, France. Since then, he has watched music sales shift from vinyl, to tape, CD, videodisc, Web downloads, and Cloud storage. Meanwhile, he has progressed through roles as advertising representative, advertising manager, marketer, marketing director, and more recently "development manager," all within the same company.[1]

He describes his present job as "developing new business forms around the music." That means not only selling the music but also tying in related activities such as the sale of T-shirts, promotion of concerts, and licensing arrangements. One recent project involved working with mobile phone providers on personalized music opportunities for their customers. This opened up both new markets for the music and new ties to show business.

Another project involved partnering with retail banks to develop a "music card" to merchandise credit cards to a new generation of cardholders.

He likes to make ideas work, and laughs when he also says he likes making money. He likes to convince people about new projects by sharing his ideas. He argues that you have to tell your bosses what you're thinking without too many details, so that they see you as the only person for the job. Then you need to make your project succeed by using your relationships, and your marketing and product knowledge. You cannot simply transfer all your knowledge to other workers, since you need to have the creativity to face unforeseen situations. That creativity, he insists, belongs to people, not to companies.

He believes that innovation is essential. However, innovation is more than simply hatching a new idea. The difficult part is to make an idea work and to think about and act on all the elements involved. He likes change, and likes to promote it in his company. Neither he nor his company can afford to stand still. He says making a mistake is only a problem if you don't react to it. It's like cycling. If you stop cycling, you fall. If you keep cycling, and looking for a new direction—whether it's in a good or bad direction is another question—at least you continue.

His choice of projects has been driven by a mix of the money he can earn, his interest in the work, and the people he can work with. The money enables him to live and to enjoy a comfortable lifestyle. The work feeds his appetite for new learning, about changes in recording and distribution and incorporating them into the company. That means collaborating with newspaper publishers, media outlets, telecommunications companies, retail banks, and performing artists. His relationships with performing artists are "human, rather than economic." He values working with a good team. "You get money once a month, but you have to work with people every day."

Despite his thirty years at the same company, his advice to others is to have no set career plan. He acknowledges that some companies, like Procter and Gamble, have proposed a company career model. However, he asks, "How many people are there in Procter and Gamble who have had 20 years in the same group? Maybe the system did work out for some of them, but I suspect for many it did not. You need to set yourself a target to take on a new position every three years, and you always need to be mobile. You can use your three years' experience with Procter and Gamble to ask for a better position in another company."

Since the interview for his story was conducted, Jean-Luc Brès has taken on another position, this time as CEO of Universal Music and Brands, France, which represents contracted artists to partnering corporate brands. He has persistently changed what he does as his industry has changed. How about you? When will you change? Once more, let us explore our opening question through a series of alternative responses, this time covering your experiences with employment contracts, learning, losing a job, starting a project, finishing a project, taking your time, managing risk, breaking free, or diagnosing your current situation.

WHEN YOUR EMPLOYMENT CONTRACT CHANGES

Nearly all jobs, long or short term, involve an employment contract where employee and employer agree to certain legal terms, usually meant to protect both parties. But what exactly are you doing when you add your signature to the dotted line? Are the terms set in stone, or can they be revised?

Management professor Denise Rousseau of Carnegie Mellon University has described how in a range of traditional societies employment contracts were based largely on worker obligations. In feudal times the peasant farmer was obliged to be loyal to an overseer lord. In contrast, today's employment contracts, and the democracies behind them, are based on individual freedom of choice:

Contracts are a product of free societies. Choice underlies the existence and meaning of contracts. Freedom gives new meaning to promises and gives contracts a special significance. Motivationally, having a choice can engender a great personal commitment to carry out a promise. As the trend toward democratization continues worldwide, more countries will wrestle with what it means to make and keep a contract.[2]

Rousseau went on to say that countries' and employers' ability to compete called for a fresh approach to employment contracts. These would need to respond to both changing technology and the developing marketplace. For people, the "psychological contract"—the set of beliefs an individual holds about the terms of their employment—would need to change.

Rousseau saw that both parties to the employment contract could benefit from more flexible arrangements, and has followed up by describing the kind of "idiosyncratic deals" employees can bargain for themselves.[3] These evolve from the informal ways that employees and employers, like Jean Luc Brès and World Music, have sustained work arrangements flexible enough to meet each other's needs. He rejects the idea of a company career, insists that creativity stems from individuals, and seeks a new position every three years. Yet, his track record suggests he has served his employer well.

Both Rousseau's writing and the Brès example also point to the importance of *context*—national context, economic context, industry context, company context, and the more immediate employment context in which people work.[4] He survived in a rapidly changing music industry, but workers adhering to more traditional psychological contracts may have been less fortunate. Both parties to the employment contract need to adapt to a changing world.

WHEN YOU LEARN

What is it like *not* to learn? Your responses to questions about how you work remain constant. You continue to do the same things, use the same skills and knowledge, and draw on the same advice from others. You may help the same patients or settle the same accounts in the same way, or apply the same methods in situations you have met before. Your initial enthusiasm for your work has given way to a sense of routine, boredom, or even alienation. You still find meaning in providing for your family, or serving a worthy cause in your spare time, but you are missing out on the opportunity to learn from work.

In contrast, doing what you know—that is, *knowing*—and developing what you know—that is, *learning*—can be a potent combination. If you get the knowing-learning combination right, you can deliver value today while expanding your knowledge for tomorrow. What's more, given the pace of the information age in which you now live, the range of new discoveries being made, and the way in which work is constantly being reassessed, you need to ask an important question: Can you afford *not* to learn?

Let us return to the Jean-Luc Brès story. It is a story about getting the knowing-learning combination right over a thirty-year time period. However, he still needs to work for another ten years, whether at Universal Music or elsewhere. He insists he does not make plans but prefers to be open to opportunities. Perhaps he'll spot a job with greater autonomy, or a creative advertising challenge, or a chance to open a new subdivision? If he does, he'll think about what it offers, including the learning it will open up, and make his choice about whether to pursue it.

As University of London researchers Tom Schuller and his colleagues have put it, learning "gives people a sense of horizon, agency and purpose in their lives."[5] In this regard, Brès has been fortunate, as new opportunities have kept things interesting. What, though, if the story were different? What if he was caught in a job that allowed little discretion over his use of time? What if he got stressed out or didn't fit in? What if he lost his job? What if any of those things happen (or have happened) to you?

WHEN YOU DON'T HAVE A JOB

Statistics from around the globe tell us people have problems in finding jobs. At one end of the spectrum, young people are having a hard time finding a job after finishing their education. There is clearly a structural problem.[6] At the other end of the spectrum, older workers who have lost their jobs struggle to find new ones. Again, there is a structural problem.[7] If you are reading this book and don't have a job, you can take heart that you are not alone. However, one thing you can do is choose not to rely on the established system. Statistics tell us that most people don't find work through orthodox means—that is, waiting for a job to be advertised and responding to it. You can show more initiative than that.

Consider the case of Titan Gilroy. After growing up with an abusive father, prolonged bullying, and a series of school expulsions, he tried his luck as a boxer in Las Vegas. One of his trainers thought he could make it as a professional, but he got into a brawl at a nightclub and spent the next three years in prison. After that, he returned to boxing but then got into a fight with a neighbor. Handcuffed, but never charged, he realized how easily he could lose his freedom—and the wife and son with whom he'd recently reunited.

He quit boxing the next day, moved back to his native California, and found an entry-level job at a small machine shop. He took evening classes in computer numerical control (CNC) and was rapidly promoted to head programmer and shop foreman. Later, financed by a business partner who invested $110,000 by remortgaging his home, and by a company owner who extended full credit of $300,000 on four CNC machines, he founded his own machine shop. Both of his backers had seen him work and had complete faith they would be paid back. He took in over $1 million in revenue in his first year of operation, survived a subsequent recession, and now employs a stable workforce of around 20 people. He said it was "a matter of persevering, going forward and just never giving up."[8]

Chantell Quill was an aboriginal member of the Cree Nation struggling to raise two daughters and earn her Canadian high school diploma. She applied for a Bank of Montreal scholarship offering financial support and summer employment. The people in her office befriended her and asked her to return for a second summer. They then encouraged her to go on to complete an undergraduate degree and become a loan officer. Like Titan Gilroy, she never gave up and found friends to support her.[9]

Some people end up losing their jobs through changes in their personal circumstances such as personal injury or illness, losing someone they are close to, or through some form of discrimination. Whatever the cause, you need to find a way to move on. Job loss can be "a blessing in disguise" if you see it providing an opportunity for reflection and consideration of previously unexplored possibilities.[10] That involves some combination of doing your homework, getting help from others, keeping yourself motivated, and demonstrating that you have the right skills to achieve your goals. What combination can work for you?

WHEN YOU START A NEW PROJECT

If "innovation is essential," as Jean-Luc Brès suggests, how can you contribute to it? Science writer Steven Johnson has borrowed biologist Stuart Kauffman's idea of the "adjacent possible" to help us understand and make the most of the opportunities available to us. An example is the video-sharing website YouTube, launched with immediate success in 2005. YouTube relied on users having the necessary graphical and video-sharing software and a high-speed Internet connection. The founders of YouTube recognized that their idea had become possible, and the number of potential users could rapidly grow.[11] In Johnson's words, the adjacent possible is "a kind of shadow future, hovering on the edges of the present state of things, a map of all the ways in which the present can reinvent itself."[12] YouTube's founders got their timing right, and their innovation caught on.

Johnson invites you to imagine yourself in a room with four doors, the one you came in and three more. If you have become familiar with the room, you are ready to look beyond it, so you go through one of the other three doors. Then after you become familiar with the next room, you have the choice of a different set of doors. The change you undergo in each room influences which room you choose next. Johnson is writing about innovation, but he could just as well be writing about Brès's career. If a room represents one of his three-year projects, then he has gone in and out of ten or more rooms. As he completed each project he saw a new door to further opportunity—a key to why he worked. In the new room he would both apply his expertise and seek new learning—keys to how he worked. He would also draw on existing relationships and build new ones—a key to with whom he worked. Figure 6.1 suggests a "virtuous cycle" of personal experience, and of the way why, how, and with whom you work can contribute to one another as projects unfold.[13]

Projects are everywhere. All employers—including public sector employers—need to innovate to remain relevant. Brès's projects in developing new products have their parallels in a wide range of industries—automobiles, biotechnology, consumer goods, financial services, healthcare, information technology, pharmaceuticals, and many more. Many industries have an explicit project-based approach to organizing—such as accounting (audits), construction (roads and buildings), filmmaking (movies), law (cases), software (programs), and so on. Even where those projects are led by large established firms, the underlying employment arrangements rely on a continual flow of new projects. Where are your projects?

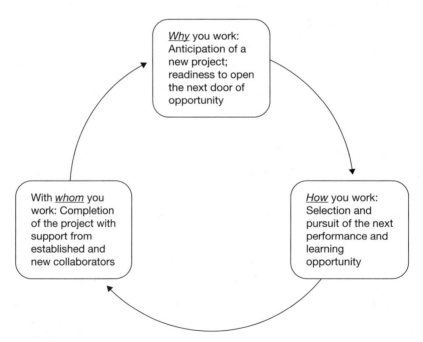

Figure 6.1   Links Between Why, How, and with Whom You Work as Projects Unfold

WHEN YOU FINISH A PROJECT

Let us look more closely at filmmaking. Typically, a new production company is established for each new film. Then the producer, director, screenwriter, financial backers, and lead actors are secured. The process goes on through the rest of the cast, camera operators, set designers, wardrobe specialists, special effects people, stand-ins, grips, personal assistants, accountants, and—not least—runners, whose lowly positions often provide privileged learning opportunities at the heart of the action. You get invited to join a new project based on the commitment you've shown before, the skills you've demonstrated, and the people you've come to know. Each project requires change.[14]

For each of the film crew's participants, their objectives are twofold: First, play your part and do what you can to help the project succeed; second, learn something new, both for its own sake (it keeps work interesting) and to better position yourself for future projects. Regarding the first objective, the film industry is already organized to celebrate the separate contributions people can make. A movie can fail to win critical acclaim and still earn "Oscars" or similar awards for its actors, screenwriters, cinematographers, and so on. The range of awards means that reputation is built largely in the specialization for which each person was invited to join up. Regarding the second objective, filmmaking may offer a relatively privileged environment. There is regular "down time" between shoots in which people can get to know each other better, gain a wider perspective, and trade experiences. Learning happens on the set as well, when actors, crew, and directors hone their complementary talents.

Not everyone in filmmaking gets the same opportunity for down time, and not everyone takes the same advantage of it. However, people in filmmaking have it better than people in many other kinds of projects. Mainstream guidelines about project management focus on using people efficiently and completing the project both on time and under budget. Project managers' performance is typically measured on these criteria, and the notion of projects providing fresh learning opportunities for their participants is largely absent. The guidelines may suggest that you reflect back on the project after its completion, but that advice comes too little, too late, for the intelligent career owner's purpose.

The solution is to seek out fresh experiences for yourself and on your own terms. You can bring parallel objectives to (1) make a contribution to the project and (2) learn as you go. You can see the two objectives as synergistic with one another, since demonstrable commitment to project success is more likely to earn learning opportunities from others. To paraphrase Denise Rousseau's message from earlier in the chapter, the end of a project means a return to free society and the opportunity to take on something new. The renewed motivation, enhanced skills, and additional contacts you have made are yours to bring with you.

WHEN IT'S TIME TO CHANGE

Some projects call for greater commitment than others. Being a producer or principal actor on the *Harry Potter* film series or a director or special effects provider on *The Lord of the Rings* trilogy takes a longer time commitment than making just one movie. Even longer time commitments may be made by scientists working on the particle accelerators at CERN, the European Organization for Nuclear Research in Switzerland, whose fundamental questions of physical science may take decades to solve. In other fields, musical and mathematical prodigies, athletes, and dancers are known to peak relatively early. In contrast, where professions require a long training period and accumulated experience—for example, medicine, law, academics—a person usually takes longer to reach professional maturity. You need to figure out what time means to you.

We used to think that time unfolded as we moved through predictable life stages: childhood, adolescence, early adulthood (when we begin our careers), midlife (after we have made progress in our careers), and so on. If you follow the old formula, you would retire at a "ripe old age" with a comfortable pension. However, today's pace of change, and new appreciation of people's capacity to adapt, have changed those ideas. Carl Jung's distinction between the "morning" and "afternoon" stages of life—the first in which we look ahead, the second in which we become more reflective—still seems attractive. Many women, though, have made a dramatic shift from devoting the "morning" of their adult lives to raising children. Many couples are sharing family caregiving responsibilities. People who have retired from conventional jobs find the energy to embark on a new chapter in their careers or take up new hobbies. Moreover, since intelligent careers are tailored to individual preferences, a typical timeline is difficult to define.

Malcolm Gladwell has highlighted that the time it takes to learn something is a function of both the skills you start out with and the further skills you need to realize your vision. Consider two major 20th-century painters. Pablo Picasso had a distinctive skill set, but approached each painting with a clear idea of what he was going to do. He seemed not to use his painting time for any kind of experimentation. In contrast, Paul Cezanne was a "late bloomer." His focus was on experimentation and what it might mean to the vision he held for his work. Some of his early paintings were relative failures in the public eye, but by the later stages of his life he had a clearer idea of where he was going. His paintings were also more widely appreciated.[15] This comparison suggests that you can have your own schedule, even compared with others in a similar field.

WHEN YOU MANAGE RISK

Career consultant Pam Lassiter emphasizes in her book *The New Job Security* that to effectively manage risk you need to "track the trends" as they relate to your individual work situation. Moreover, this kind of tracking calls for personal attention, as Lassiter remarks:

> Good career management means that you are making your own conclusions about how the trends affect you. Your company is not tuning in to what works best for you as an individual. You can't afford to wait for them to take action. You have to know what's going on in your field to protect yourself.[16]

TABLE 6.1   TRACKING AND UNDERSTANDING KEY TRENDS

Domain	Where to Look	Questions to Ask
Skills	At the next job you would like to have	What are the key skills involved? How (and from whom) can you learn those skills?
Competition	At the other candidates who might be going after the same job	What might they offer, and with what limitations? How can you stand out in relation to them?
The Global Scene	At the global business environment	In what ways is that environment changing? How can you prepare for the changes that you see?
The Local Scene	In your area	What's happening with local companies, business trends, or recent career moves? What does this information mean for you?
Thought Leaders	At the "big thinkers" in your field	What are they contributing? How can you join the conversation?

Lassiter lists a series of questions, which we have adapted in Table 6.1, on what you need to track about relevant skills, competition, global trends, local trends, and major thought leaders if you are to do this well. The good news is that staying well informed is much easier these days than it used to be. Search engines like Google make information much easier to find. However, they also make it easier for others to find that information, too, so you're missing out if you're not searching.

Even if you are up to date in your tracking, you still need to think through how you will use the information you have gained. *Wall Street Journal* writer Andrea Levit suggests there are five main things you can do:

- *Think long term.* It doesn't much help to think about your present situation, or even your next move. Where do you want to be in five years, and what actions will you have to take to make sure you get there? What are the challenges and the opportunities? More specifically, what is the "upside" if the risk goes well?

- *Consider the downside.* In contrast to the upside, what is the worst-case scenario, and what effect can it have on your career? Is that scenario something that can be overcome? Can you maintain a back-up plan?
- *Keep looking for clues.* Keep on assessing if the risk is getting worse. What clues are out there to help you? Do your research, and seek counsel from experienced people.
- *Believe in yourself.* Self-doubt and negativity can only harm your chances, so part of managing risk is to project confidence in your chosen path.
- *Learn from the experience.* Deal with disappointment. Take stock of what went right and wrong. Make notes to do things differently next time. Be better informed, but don't be deterred.[17]

This list connects to related ideas about crafting *experiments* that take you closer to the work you might want to be doing in the future, without letting go of the work you are doing now. Setting up a series of experiments can divide what might seem like one daunting risk into several more manageable stages. Each stage can serve as a stepping stone, helping you to move further ahead without necessarily cutting off the past—at least until you are clear that the next step is within your reach.[18]

WHEN YOU LEAVE YOUR "CAVE"

Sometimes, you may want to consider a more radical approach to risk. In Plato's *Republic*, he invites readers to consider the allegory of the cave. Imagine a group of prisoners chained and held immobile since childhood. Their arms, legs, and heads are held still, so that the prisoners must gaze at a wall in front of them. A fire burns behind the prisoners, and between the fire and the prisoners is a raised walkway. The prisoners see the shapes cast by travelers, not knowing they are shadows. They also hear muffled sounds off the wall, not knowing they are echoes.

Imagine a prisoner is freed, and turns to witness the walkway and the fire. Imagine the prisoner going outside and seeing the day, the night, the seasons, and the changes in animal and vegetable life that accompany them. Imagine the prisoner coming to appreciate the power of the sun on all that took place beneath it. Now imagine that same person returns to the group still chained inside the cave. On the one hand, knowing that the world is different makes it harder for the returning person to relate to former colleagues and to join in their conversations. On the other hand, it is hard to introduce them to new ideas. Trying to describe what lies outside the cave is beyond the others' imagination. What should the free person do?

Plato's *Allegory of the Cave* argues that everyone has his or her own cave. You can interpret the "cave" to be the specific family and social background in which you grew up, and from where you drew specific assumptions about the world and your place within it. The cave you grew up in—socioeconomic, geographical, ethnic, religious—helped define how you saw yourself, what education you got, and what roles you took on either within or beyond the places in which you grew up. Over time, as you met other people who came from dissimilar backgrounds and held dissimilar assumptions from your own, you had a series of choices to stay with what's familiar, or to venture "into the light" and try to understand what's unfamiliar.

Moving on from what's familiar can be painful, and the journey can be lonely. In Plato's *Allegory*, when the prisoner first ventured from the cave, his eyes hurt from exposure to the bright light. The longer he stayed outside the cave, the more his eyes adjusted. In today's global economy, where technology allows us to Skype a colleague in Mumbai while sitting in Geneva, to stay within the confines of our upbringing is to be like Plato's prisoners—chained in a cave where shadows are mistaken for reality. Think of an intelligent career as something you pursue once you are out of the cave. It can involve thriving from interactions with cultures and mindsets different from our own. It can also be rewarding, especially if other people care enough to help you on your way. And it can be rewarding when you have made sufficient progress, in turn, to help others. Commonly, you get help from more experienced people and later give back to less experienced people. You help the world go round, one learning opportunity at a time.[19]

Over the past 150 years, society has witnessed major advances in film-making, broadcasting, telecommunications, the World Wide Web, and smartphones. These have greatly enhanced your ability to connect with other groups, cultures, and peoples. Yet, the world is still a dangerous place, and at least some of the world's leaders seem more concerned to keep their citizens inside separate caves for the foreseeable future. Can you perhaps contribute to a safer world, by reaching out to others and building wider understanding?

WHEN *WHY, HOW,* OR WITH *WHOM* YOU WORK CHANGES

At the start of this chapter, we reported that Jean-Luc Brès said he used three criteria—the money, the work, and the people—in his assessment of new opportunities. Later in the chapter, we described the way that why, how, and with whom he worked formed a virtuous cycle as he progressed through the projects he has undertaken. The money, and the lifestyle that it provided, responded to the question about *why* he worked and provided a link to how he worked. The efforts he made to develop new business opportunities and seek new learning answered the question about *how* he worked and provided a link to with whom he worked. The cultivation of relationships with his bosses, clients, and colleagues reflected with *whom* he worked and provided a link to *why* he worked. That virtuous cycle is represented in Figure 6.1.

However, to present Brès's or any other intelligent career owner's life as either succeeding or failing to provide a one-way, virtuous cycle would be to miss out on what else is possible. To stay with Brès's example, *why* he works can also influence with *whom* he works, through the positive or negative attitude he adopts when he interacts with fellow employees and customers. With *whom* he works can in turn provide or deny the resources for fresh learning that can influence how he works. In turn, *how* he works in witnessing the implementation of his ideas can reinforce or call into question why he works. Figure 6.2 illustrates the wider set of links among why, how, and with whom you work can occur.

Following on from the above, Figure 6.2 invites you to take a wider view of your situation. If your response to the question about *why* you work exhibits a positive attitude, that is likely to have a positive influence on how you work and also on the people with whom you work. However, if you bring a negative attitude, perhaps provoked by a bad experience, why you work can have a negative influence on both how and with whom you work. If your response to the question about *how* you work is to perform it well, that is likely to reinforce your motivation about why you work and encourage you to deepen or extend your relationships with whom you work. If your relationships with others *with whom* you work are positive,

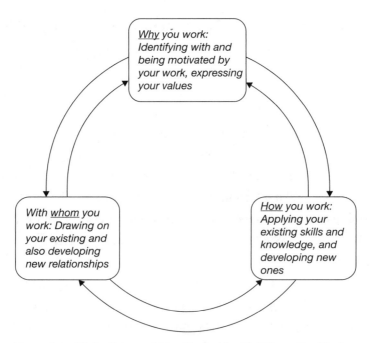

Figure 6.2   Links Between Why, How and with Whom You Work

they can reinforce why you work and whether you pursue new initiatives in how you work. If, though, you are dissatisfied about how you work, or discouraged by those with whom you work, the further influences are likely to be negative.

We therefore invite you to think about Figure 6.2 as a diagnostic tool. How do the links between the three ways of knowing line up for you? Can you appreciate the positive links, but also question the unsatisfactory connections? For example, is the reason why you work simply to put bread on the table? If so, what effect might that be having on how and with whom you work? Or, are you blocked in how you work by a boss who doesn't want to show you anything new, and how is that influencing why and with whom you work? Or, is it hard to find good advice from the people with whom you work, and how is that affecting why and how you work? If you take a long hard look at the figure, what can you see about why, how, and with whom *you* work and the links between them? And what can you *do* to change what you see?[20]

To sum up, freedom of choice about the employment contracts you take on is fundamental to a democratic society. Knowing—applying what you know—and learning—extending what you know—are complementary approaches to how you work. Losing a job is often a trigger to deeper personal change, inviting you to reflect more fully on, search more widely for, and get help in pursuing other work you are willing to do. In starting a new project you can think about the "adjacent possible," that is, the kind of project you are now qualified to take on, as members of a filmmaking crew do as they move from one film to another. The time to change who you are and what you do will vary; some occupations call for lifetime commitment, while others offer steppingstones to greater opportunities. Changing jobs can be risky, but you can manage that risk by taking incremental steps to help show the way forward. In contrast, not changing jobs and staying with the same reference group can leave you blind to other possibilities. Seeing your situation as a series of interdependent links among why, how, and with whom you work can provide a helpful diagnostic tool, both in both seeing where you stand and changing what you see.

Taking Action

I n this second part of the book we support you in taking *action* in your future intelligent career. That is, we help you change focus from where you are to where you want to go. The six chapter titles use action verbs that lead you toward a deeper appreciation of the topics "Making Sense," Embracing Technology," "Investing in Communities," Working with Employers," "Sharing Your Story," and "Building Your World." Here, we are referring to your own social world, in which your intelligent career interacts with other people's careers, and where together you make a sustained contribution to the world of employment.

In the introduction to Part I, we made reference to various debates about the future of work, and the importance of being aware of them. Here, we invite you to see yourself as both a subject of those debates and a contributor to their outcomes. You are making sense of your own place within the world of work, and doing things that respond to and reshape the technology, communities, and institutions with which you interact. A major factor here is the pace of change, including your own contribution to that pace. Owning an intelligent career doesn't mean holding on to a job. It means being involved in the way job changes get introduced.

In a healthy, knowledge-driven economy, new ways of working will continually replace old ways. As this book goes to press, an Oxford University study has concluded that 47 percent of US jobs are at risk.[1] A survey of CEOs by PriceWaterhouseCoopers Global shows 81 percent looking for broader skills in their new hires.[2] *The Economist* has asserted that freelance workers "will reshape the nature of companies and the structure of careers."[3] The world of work will keep changing, and you must focus on how you can join in, on your own terms.

Making Sense

Nothing can ever happen twice.
In consequence, the sorry fact is
that we arrive here improvised
and leave without the chance to practice.

—Wisława Szymborska

Barbara Harris, a thirty-year employee of the International House of Pancakes (IHOP) and mother of three boys, didn't know what she was getting into. In 1990, after the boys had left home she began to wonder if she could have a daughter. However, this time she concluded, "the only way was if I went and became a foster parent and asked for one."[1] She and her surgical technician husband, Smitty, filled out the necessary forms, took the required training, and submitted to a background check. The mixed-race couple—she was white, he was African American—asked for a newborn child and waited. Soon, a California social worker called and asked would the couple consider a girl eight months old? They said they would, and drove to the foster home. There, they were shown a beautiful baby, but a social worker told them she had been born addicted to PCP (angel dust), crack cocaine, and heroin. Barbara and Smitty were undaunted and they took the baby home.

Four months later there was another call. The same birth mother had just had another baby, this time a boy. Would Harris and her husband like to keep the two children together, and take him straight away? They said yes, but this time there were more problems, as the baby exhibited withdrawal symptoms and wasn't able to take his formula for several months. A year later, there was another call, and a second girl from the same birth mother was offered. A year after that, another boy was offered. They took him too, upgraded their car to a van, moved into a bigger home, and set about raising all four of the extra children they had taken on.

Later, Harris reflected on what she had seen. Why was the same birth mother able to repeatedly visit the hospital, deliver a drug-addicted baby, and simply walk away? She tried to get a "child endangerment" law passed to address the problem, but her attempts failed. At that point, she concluded, "I had to come up with something else. I had to be creative."[2] In 1994, she came up with the idea of paying the addicted mothers to commit to long-term birth control. The payment would be $200 (it's now $300), and the addicts would be offered an intrauterine contraceptive device (IUD) or an implant, or a third choice of sterilization if they had already had a child. She announced her initiative on her front lawn, got some early publicity on daytime television talk shows, and had soon collected $150,000 from a diverse group of supporters. Now she was involved with another birth—this time of what was to become the registered charity Project Prevention.

By March 2013, Project Prevention was reporting it had provided long-term birth control to over four thousand drug-addicted women, as well as vasectomies to around 75 drug-addicted men. The charity now operates out of North Carolina, where Harris and her husband moved to be closer to Harris's siblings. Outside the United States, an anonymous person gave $20,000 to launch a spin-off program in the UK. An alert Kenyan student saw an opportunity to address a wider problem of children being born with and frequently dying from AIDS, and launched a program there. There was talk of getting similar initiatives underway in Hawaii, Ireland, and South Africa. Harris is no longer just making a difference in her neighborhood, but also around her country and the globe.

Barbara Harris's story raises a range of issues relevant to this chapter. Most fundamentally, they are about you *making sense* of your career situation. We use the term alongside its compound form *sensemaking*, popularized by University of Michigan management professor and social psychologist Karl Weick.[3] This can be simply defined as the process by which you give meaning to experience.[4] It involves "choice, irrevocability, and visibility," leading you from the past to the present, and from the present toward the future, in taking and maintaining ownership of your career.[5] One approach to sensemaking is to identify the underlying *themes* that guide you in your present situation. Related approaches are to picture or unravel different aspects of your life that presently concern you. Various other approaches involve making fresh sense of a change in your work situation, reflecting for example on job loss, a missed promotion, leadership challenges, and economic crises.

In the rest of this chapter we take you through a series of illustrations of how other people have made sense of their own situations, with a range of different outcomes. Our overall purpose is to leave you with a better appreciation of how to use your intelligence to work in a fundamental way, that is to make greater and, we hope, more productive sense of your present work and life situation.

IDENTIFYING YOUR THEMES

A useful first step in making sense is to identify the overall *themes* through which your career is developing. This involves adopting a broad lens on your life and career, as advocated by MIT management scholar John Van Maanen. Your themes provide a framework for understanding your present situation and for locating that situation in a wider stream of work and life events. They cover more than your interests, or your self-described strengths, although these can contribute to a wider understanding. They also cover more than the skills or knowledge you possess, or the support or reputation you enjoy with others. In part, your themes will reflect why, how, and with whom you work. However, they will also tie why, how, and with whom you work together. They will reflect your present identity and your life and work situations. They will draw on your past experience and look ahead to future action.[6]

Let us take Barbara Harris's case as an illustration. From what has been written about her, we can suggest the themes that drove her when she first set out to explore foster parenting included the following:

New energy: As her own children began to leave the nest, she found herself having new energy to take on fresh challenges.

Stuck at work: Her job at IHOP had become predictable and routine. She didn't see that as a source of further stimulation.

A good team: Harris and her husband had worked together to raise their own children, and were ready to reapply their parenting skills to benefit other children.

Distinctive experience: As a participant in a mixed-race marriage, she and her husband envisioned she might be particularly helpful in certain foster-parenting situations.

Stability of location: She had an established home and children still around that home, so staying in the same geographic location was important.

An affordable commitment: Foster parenting operates through government programs that provide limited compensation for the services provided.

We can expect that these themes were active when Harris and her husband first set out to explore the foster-parenting option. That quickly led to receiving and accepting an offer to take the first foster child they were offered. The first offer in turn led to three subsequent offers. When they accepted each of those children, the same themes appear to have still been active, perhaps supplemented by a further theme that valued keeping orphan siblings together. Your life and work will reflect your own unique themes, in all likelihood quite different from Barbara Harris's and most other people's themes.

PICTURING YOUR SITUATION

A complementary approach to making sense of your career is to draw a "visual timeline." Like the identification of themes, this approach is also grounded in present time, reflecting on the past and preparing for the future. It also insists on a broad view of your situation that takes both personal and environmental factors into account, as well as the relationships between them. Moreover, drawing a picture can provide a way for you to surface sensitive or complex issues that may be difficult to express verbally. Discussing your visual timeline with a friend or coach can also help you to look more deeply into your personal situation.[7]

The procedure goes something like this: Allow an hour of your time. Take a relatively large, clean sheet of paper and a set of colored markers. Begin on the left with when you first started thinking about your adult life and career, and conclude on the right with how you see the future. Find a way to indicate the principal life and career events that have brought you to the present and led you to see the future the way that you do. Use symbols, such as happy and sad faces, stick figures, and images to show the key people, groups, employers, and institutions with which you have interacted. Allow your picture to communicate with you as you proceed, so that one image leads to another and the picture becomes a richer source of information. If your picture becomes too messy, or you run out of space, you can redraw it later. The main purpose, for this hour, is to capture what comes to your mind.

The next step—and this is where you may most benefit from a trusted friend or advisor—is to talk about your picture and either make notes or have someone else make notes about what you have drawn. Talking about your picture can help you bring out and organize what's most important in your life and career right now.

An example picture is shown in Figure 7.1. It was drawn by an immigrant from what was war-torn Serbia adjusting to living in western Europe. He explained his picture as showing a zigzag sequence of events, reflecting early investments in education, marriage, and starting a family,

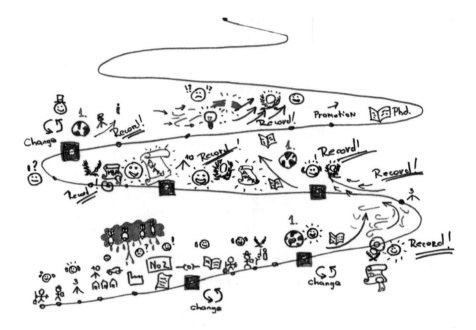

Figure 7.1   An Example Visual Timeline

and subsequent successes—"records," in his terminology—in two different marketing jobs. Successes in each job involved, first, carving out a
new business opportunity in one European country, then, second, repli-
cating that success across a wider range of countries. The final part of his
picture anticipates continuing success through a further promotion and
the future completion of a PhD program in which he recently enrolled.
At present, he sees the uncharted future reflecting a stable and supportive
family life and even greater success in his adopted business field. Good
luck to him—but how would your picture look?

UNRAVELING LIFE STRANDS

A different approach to making sense can be helpful if you feel you are
struggling to find a place for an intelligent career among other life and
family obligations. Mary-Dean Lee of McGill University and her colleagues suggest you can picture your life history from past to present as a

set of "entangled strands" representing personal, work, family, and community strands. (Community here refers to the act of *communion*, that is, of building relationships with other people.) With this picture, you can be less concerned with any chronology of events than with how your different life strands came together, or got entangled, as your life progressed.[8]

To try this approach, think about three things: First, what *events* happened at particular points in time—getting a job, being laid off, being transferred, arrival of children, family illness, losing a loved one, or whatever? Second, what particular *actions* have you taken? These can reflect choices you made in responding to related events, such as accepting or declining a job offer or taking time off to support your family. Or, they can be actions taken on your own initiative, for example to seek out new opportunities or make new connections. Third, what gradual *developments* occurred over time that influenced how your strands worked together? In asking these questions you can create a picture comparable to the one shown in Figure 7.2. Gaining a deeper understanding of how your own life strands became entangled in the past can leave you better positioned to untangle them in the future.

To illustrate how entangled life strands can become, consider an executive vice president that Lee and her colleagues found. He was in a challenging leadership role when his superiors broadened the scope of his

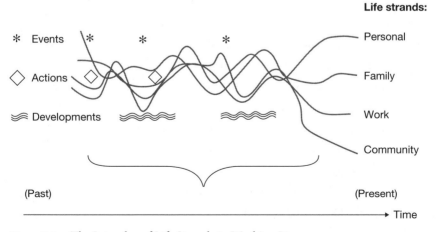

Figure 7.2   The Interplay of Life Strands in Working Lives

job, raised his performance targets, and cut back on resources. Then a merger that his company had been working on failed, the chairman quit, his boss jumped ship, and he received a severance package. He took another job, but that quickly fell apart as the new company ran out of funds. Soon after, his father died, and he had to close the family home and find his mother somewhere to live. He quickly came up with another job, but found himself trying to implement a new program when his mother fell ill. After she died, he realized he was in a state of physical collapse, a colleague sent him home, and his doctor ordered him to take a six-month medical leave. While he was on leave, his company decided to repackage and outsource his job, and he received another severance package. It arrived in the mail on the same day that his fifteen-year-old son blew up at him and moved out.[9]

We do not wish on any reader the problems this particular vice president faced. However, we do hope, whatever your life situation, that you can work on understanding it better and begin to take steps to improve it.

SEEING THINGS YOUR WAY

Marge Lahtinen was a journalist at a Finnish newspaper that needed to downsize. She wasn't directly laid off, but felt she was forced out because too many journalists were fighting over a smaller amount of available work. Feeling insecure, she chose to leave and take the opportunity to join her husband, who was working overseas. When she returned a year later, she struggled to find a new job and started to resent the lack of appreciation her old employer had shown for her loyalty. Moreover, as a woman over forty she saw her future employment prospects as gloomy. As a result, and despite a lack of support from her husband, she chose to set up on her own as a freelance journalist.[10]

Using a combination of the previous contacts she had made and the writing skills she had demonstrated, she was soon able to find short-term contract work that suited her talents. Moreover, word quickly got around that she was an able and dependable writer who could turn her hand to a variety of short-term projects.

> "So although in a way I'm a sort of substitute and temporary worker it's in my own hands much more. I'm this kind of media entrepreneur and because I offer my services I don't have to change who I am because of who I work for. This is exactly the stability I was looking for, where you don't constantly have to change who and what you are."[11]

Lahtinen has found that a series of contracts has produced a stream of work, and in turn this stream of work addresses her need for security. However, she now sees the stream being generated by her own efforts, rather than from dependence on any one employer. Although at first she felt pushed into entrepreneurship, she has become relatively optimistic about her future as an independent contractor, where she feels there is room in the market for freelancers to work on short-term contracts. Because of this sensemaking, she now describes herself as a "media entrepreneur," rather than as someone simply earning wages from part-time jobs.

MANAGING CAREER DOWNFALLS

One instructive way to better understand sensemaking and its consequences is to notice how people respond to career downfalls. Management researcher Roxanna Barbulescu and her coauthors investigated how workers in Wall Street's financial district dealt with career downfalls related to the 2008 stock market crash. They found three kinds of response, reflecting what they called downward spirals, unfinished searches, and virtue discovery.[12]

> ***Downward spiral:*** In a downward spiral, an initially negative assessment of a situation becomes more negative. That in turn

emphasizes your feelings of helplessness, failure, and despair. For example, one individual reported, "The destruction of the economy has destroyed the future of the country. The country is not interested in correcting any of the problems necessary to build a new and solid economy. Therefore, I no longer have a career."

Unfinished search: In this, an initial negative valuation remains unresolved. However, you hope for a positive future. For example, one individual described a three-part plan to (1) investigate an alternative career in consulting, (2) determine whether consulting with "increasing sales targets and slaving to make partner" really made sense, and (3) establish "what I really want to do when I grow up."

Virtue discovery: Here, there is a progressive sequence where an initial negative assessment becomes positive, and you achieve closure. For example, one individual had to lay off staff for the first time, and reported that the burden of doing so was hard to bear. However, an initially distressing experience was soon seen as an exercise in personal survival and an investment in the future health of the employing firm.

The virtues that can be discovered through a career downfall fall into a variety of categories. One reflects *justice* (for example, joining a smaller firm but gaining a more considerate boss). Another reflects *prudence* (for example, downsizing one's home and lifestyle to be better prepared for an uncertain future). A third reflects *magnificence* (for example, claiming to have survived better than most and projecting oneself as a future leader)— be careful with this one! Various other virtues include amassing *wisdom* or demonstrating *courage*. The underlying message is that you need to be able to see some virtue stemming from your downfall, if you are going to progress to a more positive interpretation of your experience.[13]

MAKING SENSE FOR OTHERS

Sensemaking frequently has a social dimension, involving you helping other people make sense of their situations, and vice versa. One way to explore how you can help other people make sense is through a comparison between the orchestra and jazz forms of music. In the orchestra form, the composer tries to be clear about what he or she wants, leaving explicit notes in the manuscript from which the music will be played. The conductor in turn mediates between the composer and the musicians, keeping everyone in line to produce the desired effect. The job of the musician is essentially to "play along," that is to perform as requested. In contrast, jazz music is commonly organized into 12-bar or 16-bar sections, which provide musicians with a series of different entry and exit points into and out of the performance.[14] Some jazz leaders simply buy the "orchestra" approach, clearly prescribing what their musicians will do. However, others leave room for something different.[15]

For example, here's what bass player Darren Taylor had to say about the composer and bandleader Duke Ellington:

> "[Ellington] just wrote a lot of triggers so that musicians at the time could express who they were. In a way, that is a mark of genius because you allow the personalities to express themselves and then just glue all of those things together, so he got the best performance from everybody by having a very informal structure that actually bound people together."[16]

In a similar vein, here's how music writer Bill Evans described Miles Davis's approach to recording his landmark album *Kind of Blue*:

> "As the painter needs his framework of parchment, the improvising musical group needs its framework in time. Miles Davis presents here frameworks which are exquisite in their simplicity and yet contain all that is necessary to stimulate performance with a sure reference to the primary conception. . . . The group had never played these pieces prior to the recordings and I think without exception the first complete performance of each was a 'take.' "[17]

The comparison may be a little unfair to orchestral music, but it does help make a point. How much space can you leave for other people to improvise—that is to make sense of what they can do with the opportunity provided? In a wide range of situations from theater direction to product development to information technology to project management, how much flexibility can you provide for other people to take responsibility for their own contribution after the "trigger" you provide them? And how might their sensemaking further contribute to your own sensemaking, as an innovator, people developer, or team leader?

LEGITIMIZING YOUR ROLE

The idea of legitimizing your role relates to the two previous sections. You can see it as combining the virtue-discovery element of managing career downfalls with the underlying process of making sense for others. To put it simply, legitimizing your role ultimately involves making what you do look good to others. However, the process behind legitimizing your role has predictable underlying stages. Here's an example.

Piers Gilbert, a CEO in an asset management company, uncovered fraudulent behavior by a dealer that threatened to bring down the whole company. He determined the issue needed to be reported to the regulators, and as a result a number of people reporting to him would be disciplined. His solution was to offer his own resignation, so the regulators "got the head of the business." In turn, he felt other people below him would not be unjustly punished and the company would not be jeopardized. He also saw he would be expressing his "core values" rather than "being chameleon-like in your principles." His resignation was not accepted, but the act of offering it added to his reputation and legitimized his continuation as company leader.[18]

Gilbert's approach to legitimizing himself toward others can be seen as *defying the odds* and consisting of three parts. First, he cast himself as being in an especially difficult situation. This involved the reality of the fraudulent behavior and its potentially disastrous consequences. Next, he projected himself as having the fortitude to deal with the situation. His offering to resign demonstrated that fortitude and showed he was putting the company's interests ahead of his own. Third, he projected himself as a future hero for steering his company out of trouble. If he were to succeed, he would be cast in a more favorable light once the present crisis was overcome.

Other approaches through which business leaders seek legitimization can be described as *staying the course* (remaining the "captain of the ship" and being resolute), *succeeding through talent* (using exceptional skills and winning out on merit), and *giving back to society* (eschewing material success and acting with compassion). In each case, the sensemaking occurs in present time, but the sensemaker has an eye toward the future and toward moving on from any downfall that has occurred.

FACING THE OPPOSITION

Let us return to the Barbara Harris story, and consider how other people might react to what she was trying to do. To what extent would they support or oppose her, and how would she react?[19] One group of critics accused her of spreading "dangerous propaganda" for suggesting that addicts are unsuited to having children.[20] Others claimed that her program involves "racial profiling" and labeled her work as "eugenics," reminiscent of the white supremacist policies of Adolf Hitler's regime.[21] Regarding her international initiatives, the UK British Medical Association took the sterilization option off the table, but did not object to the rest of the program. The director of an Irish addiction treatment center called the approach "absolutely horrendous."[22] The Kenya program has been criticized for detracting from more comprehensive AIDS treatment efforts. Meanwhile, the South African health department said it would bring the project before the Human Rights Commission if it began operations in that country.[23]

For her part, Harris has become better at responding to such criticism. She has changed her charity's name to Project Prevention from the more confrontational name, CRACK (Children Requiring a Caring Kommunity), that she started out with. She also interviews each of the mothers that the charity serves, and uses their own words of appreciation to support its mission. She fends off the racial-profiling allegations with statistics about the diversity of addicts treated, and with words, arguing, "I'm the only white face in my family." While she regrets a remark she made while being interviewed on a talk show about "women literally having litters of children," she also points out that it has been taken out of context. Moreover, she holds firm to what she is trying to achieve: "I guess it depends on where your heart is. Some people are so into the women and their rights to get pregnant that they seem to forget about the rights of the kids. They act like these children don't matter." She also has an invitation for her critics:

> "If they feel so strongly about it then they need to start an organization that does what they are telling me to do. I am concentrating on women who are addicted to drugs who are getting pregnant over and over again. That is really my focus."[24]

The simple point here is that her work has met resistance. Moreover, much of the resistance seems to have come as a surprise, or what MIT professor John Van Maanen has called "at least a momentary unhinging" of the person from [their] accepted everyday reality.[25] Surprise that the same drug-addicted woman was having more children; surprise, perhaps, at the support she found once her program was publicized; surprise at the opposition she faced for what she believed to be a useful service for both the addicts she served and the society in which they lived. Harris's is an unusual case, but your own life circumstances are also subject to change depending on how you make sense of what is happening to you. As your experience grows and the world continues to change, you will undoubtedly face further surprises. The question is, what will you make of them?[26]

DEVELOPING YOUR THEMES

Making sense of surprises connects back to the idea of career themes covered earlier. At the time Barbara Harris volunteered for foster parenting we identified several prominent themes: She had new energy once her sons were older, she felt stuck in her waitressing role, she and her husband made a good team, they had distinctive experience as a mixed-race couple, she needed stability in her present geographic area, and there was at least some financial compensation. However, by the end of the story she has moved on from her restaurant job and the geographic location to which she once felt committed. She has maintained her energy, but it is no longer directed toward foster parenting. The "good team" and "distinctive experience" themes with her husband still prevail, but are directed toward running a charity rather than foster parenting, where she's more of a spokesperson and he's more of a dependable supporter.

There are also some new themes:

Representing the cause: Her work is now dedicated to assisting drug-addicted women to find access to long-term birth control if they so desire.

Public speaking and influence: She learned she needed to sharpen her public speaking skills, and be more tactful in representing her cause.

Facing the opposition: As noted previously, her work has been criticized, and she has worked on responding to that criticism.

The new themes suggest that she has extended her self-belief in response to her changing situation. This is interesting, since self-belief is often promoted as a goal of effective leadership training programs, for example for nurses, police workers, or organizational managers.[27] In Harris's situation, her self-belief has grown in response to her deep commitment to the work she does and her readiness to face new challenges.

You may or may not identify with the cause that Barbara Harris has taken on, but either way you can still appreciate how she has built on and extended her career themes. You can also expect to build on and extend your own career themes in a similar way—testing how well they work, revising old themes, and introducing new ones as your experience grows.

In this way, you can manage your own self-belief rather than wait for any training program to help you along.

SIMPLIFYING WHAT'S COMPLEX

The title of this chapter is "Making Sense." It is presented as part of a wider agenda concerned with you pursuing a more effective intelligent career in a rapidly changing world. At first sight, it puts you in the horns of a dilemma. On the one hand, here are all these ways to make better sense of your situation, to see it this way or that way and to celebrate novelty. On the other hand, today's world calls for a bias toward action. To keep reflecting on the past, and in a sense living in the past, limits your ability to adapt to the future. How can you come to terms with this dilemma?[28]

Back in the nineteenth century, celebrated social scientist and novelist William James offered an interesting analogy between a bird's "perchings" and its "flights." When it is perched, a bird can be considered to be making sense, reflecting on what's gone before and considering what to do next. However, when it is in flight, that bird is taking action.[29] The analogy suggests that, like the bird, we need to regularly alternate between sensemaking and action. Does this mean that as the bird gains experience its perchings become more complicated? In a sense yes, but in another sense, no. In its perchings the bird internalizes where sources of food are likely to be found, or where cats or other predators are likely to roam. Once this sensemaking is made, the bird can move to other challenges like finding a mate, choosing a site, and building a nest. So it goes with your intelligent career. At the outset, the next round of sensemaking makes work and life seem more complicated. However, as you occupy your perch, you can see how old sensemaking challenges have receded and new ones have come to the fore.

Seen in the above light, you can find consistency across all of the sections in this chapter. Each of them says, "Now try seeing things this way," and contributes to a repertoire of sensemaking approaches. However, the common purpose is to help you move toward a new level of simplicity in your life. Nowhere is this better illustrated in the two snapshots of Barbara Harris presented at the start and near the end of this chapter. Her themes have changed considerably, yet those changes seem understandable, given the way her own intelligent career has developed. You are not Barbara Harris, but you too are likely to be living through fresh experiences. You too will need to rest on a perch and make fresh sense of your life, take flight, and rest again. That is the nature of you, your career, and the world in which you live.

In this chapter, we have introduced sensemaking as a fundamental approach to interpreting your past and taking ownership of your future intelligent career. One way to do so is to develop a list of themes that help you describe your present career situation. Other ways to make sense of different aspects of your career involve visual approaches such as making a drawing of your career situation or life strands. You can also reinterpret a changing situation from your own vantage point, recognize and face your opposition, and manage career downfalls in a way that helps you to move forward from a troubling situation. You can also work with other people or groups in helping them make sense of their situations and in legitimizing the role you play for them. You can revisit and update your career themes as they change over time, and you can keep abreast of a challenging agenda by regularly "perching" to appreciate your situation, confirm what's most important, and take flight once more on your own intelligent career journey.

Embracing Technology

He picks up scraps of information
He's adept at adaptation
Because for strangers and arrangers
Constant change is here to stay

—Rush, Digital Man

Doug Gould is a 50-year-old advertising veteran and an associate creative director at the Allen & Gerritsen agency in Boston, Massachusetts. His résumé includes more than a dozen industry awards, and two memorable Super Bowl advertisements—fresh, closely watched, and typically highly expensive productions airing at the most expensive time during American football's big game. However, he understands that he can't rest on his laurels. When he started out, the tools of the advertising trade were a drafting table, a haberule (a kind of plastic ruler designed to measure how much type could fit into a given space), a set of "letraset" transfers (to select a typeface and rub selected characters into the space) and an impressive collection of colored markers. Not long ago he "thought [he] knew everything." However, he later reported to the *Wall Street Journal* columnist Sue Shellenbarger, "There is new technology out there I don't know the first thing about, [which] could easily turn me into a dinosaur if I don't continue to adapt."[1]

And he has tried hard to adapt. He took to Facebook fairly quickly, but had a harder time with Twitter, wondering how useful it was to restrict communications to just 140 characters. He got over that, and in recent years has enrolled in a wide range of information technology courses. Moreover, instead of leaving the detailed work to junior workers, as many other account managers do, he insists on doing it himself. As a result, he can be regularly found on his computer working with new design and animation programs, trying out new social networking applications, or using the advanced software he has learned to generate Web-ready html code. He explains, "If I become a manager and nobody wants a manager, how am I going to thrive in my later years? The lifeboat for me is to be able to still do the work."

One thing that drives him is his recollection of an earlier wave of technology in computer graphics programs that occurred when he was in his late twenties. He witnessed older colleagues who "didn't want to learn, or were afraid to learn" and determined he would avoid the same fate. Witnessing the upheaval that digital technology and social media have brought to his industry has made him more determined to survive. The ghost in the mirror is "that person who fails to keep up." Younger colleagues call him "Uncle Doug" or "Coach," which he acknowledges gracefully as terms of endearment. However, he says you can still read between the lines and hear "old guy." He has taken other steps to stay relevant, moving to his present firm from the larger Hill Holiday organization to seize the opportunity to help a midsize agency grow. Both formally and informally, he is an active participant in his agency's "reverse mentoring policy," trading his experience in client relations and presentations for technological savvy from his younger colleagues.[2]

You may be facing some of the same technological challenges in your work. Or you may already be competent in the technologies he has worked to learn. Whatever your present competencies, though, both you and he will need to continue to face up to the persistent pace of technological change. How can you adapt? How can you work with technology? How can it bring you and other intelligent career owners together? Or, as our chapter title suggests, how can you *embrace* technology as part of your everyday life? Let us explore these questions in the subsequent sections.

LOOKING BACK

Spanish sociologist Manuel Castells is perhaps the most insightful voice on the changing nature of the Internet. In a new preface to the 2010 second edition of his book *The Rise of the Network Society*, he emphasized the importance of coming to terms with "the crises and conflicts that characterized the first decade of the twenty-first century." Among them—and visible wherever people lived—were a global financial crisis, parallel disruption in business and labor markets, disturbing trends in the growth of the criminal economy, and "the backlash of the disaffected" in terms of religious fundamentalism, intolerance, and violence.[3] Moreover, it was apparent that the widespread upheaval "was brewed in the cauldrons of the new economy, an economy defined by a substantial surge in productivity as the result of technological innovation, networking, and higher education levels in the work force."[4] Yet, that substantial surge brought unanticipated consequences. What next?

In your intelligent career you are living in two worlds. One is the virtual world, functioning over the Web, through which knowledge flows and the knowledge economy functions. As a participant in this world you want the Web to be effectively maintained, something you can rely on so you can produce and deliver your work to collaborators and customers. The other world is the physical world, the region and country in which you keep a home and participate in society. Not too long ago it was popular to think of these as worlds apart. Each had little effect on the other, and that was the way it would stay. By the end of the first decade of the twenty-first century, however, a new order was emerging where the Web was increasingly used as a tool for government or the pursuit of social change. You are a participant in both of these worlds. How can you contribute as a knowledge worker? And how can you simultaneously contribute to society?

In this chapter, we focus principally on the first question above. That is, we help you better appreciate your working relationship with technology. However, we also help you consider the arguments of technology's critics, people who say it is becoming too powerful and too harmful to simply be left to power further innovation. In turn, we invite you to "embrace" technology, as suggested in our chapter title—to appreciate its assets and be aware of its liabilities—in a way that helps you to also stay connected with your physical world, wherever you live and whatever form of society you are experiencing.

HEARING THE NAYSAYERS

Let us hear directly from the naysayers, those who say the Web is a negative force in our everyday lives. Nicholas Carr's book *The Shallows*—a finalist for the prestigious Pulitzer Prize—was also published in 2010, and provides a convenient contrast with Castells's writing. Carr celebrates that the Web, or the Net, as he calls it, has "been a godsend" to himself as a writer, as well as a timesaver in online banking, shopping, bill-paying, travel arrangements, sending greetings cards, and handling social invitations. Yet, he laments:

> What the Net seems to be doing is chipping away at my capacity for concentration and contemplation. Whether I'm online or not, my mind now expects to take in information the way the Net distributes it: in a swiftly moving stream of particles. Once I was a scuba diver on the sea of words. Now I zip the surface like a guy on a Jet Ski.

Carr goes on to ask, "What if I do all my reading on the web not so much because the way I read has changed . . . but because the way I *think* has changed?"[5]

The subsequent material offers a series of arguments about how the Web may be changing the way you think, rather than serving your larger interests. One disturbing argument is that the recently discovered plasticity of the brain makes you a likely victim of the Web's temptations. You have the capacity to leave behind, in the relative blinking of an eye, mental abilities that have been useful for centuries. Bad habits can replace good ones, as technological power drives you forward. One particular ability at risk is your capacity for "deep reading," that is, for paying the kind of sustained attention required to read a demanding book.[6] Another concern is memorization: If that is now delegated even partly to the Web, what happens to your brain's capacity to call on your memory later?[7]

A further argument is that you lose your sense of context. This applies particularly to your use of search engines, and their capacity to zoom right in on the phrases that you submit. As a result, when you search the Web you "don't see the forest," you "don't even see the trees," you only see "twigs and leaves." A related problem is that the Web disrupts your concentration. Indeed, that's what many of its developers are trying to achieve, to attract your attention, to draw you in, to make you a customer. You are exposed to a "cacaphony of stimuli" that takes you away from the original purpose of your search.[8]

There are responses to these kinds of charges, notably in contrasting evidence that the Web can be good for your mind and good for your social life as well.[9] There can be little question, though, that familiarity with an established technology has, once again, come into conflict with a new technology. This has happened before—for example with the introduction of the printing press, the factory, and the automobile—where, despite people's resistance, new technology has changed the course of human experience. The Web has arrived, and you are both a witness and a contributor to its consequences.

ACCOMMODATING MOORE'S LAW

Moore's Law is the assertion that over the history of computing hardware, the number of transistors on integrated circuits—that is, on computer chips—doubles approximately every two years. The chip is at the heart of home and office computers and the servers through which computers are connected, so we can expect the power of these to double every two years as well. The assertion has held true for over 50 years, since Gordon Moore, a cofounder of chip manufacturer Intel, first published it in 1965. The progression of the law over its central years is depicted in Figure 8.1. One of Moore's former colleagues at Intel has even

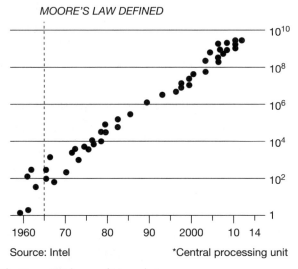

A persevering prediction
Number of transistors in CPU*
Log scale

MOORE'S LAW DEFINED

Source: Intel   *Central processing unit

Figure 8.1   Fifty Years Evidence of Moore's Law

proposed that processing power doubles every year and a half, when the combination of both more and faster transistors is taken into account. Most people predict that Moore's Law will continue to hold for the fore-seeable future, further lowering the cost of computing and extending the range of applications. In your intelligent career, you must expect to see the world of computer technology continually changing, and to adapt to that change as you work.[10]

The challenge of adapting to Moore's Law is compounded by two related phenomena. One concerns the underlying technology and its application. The manufacturing science of photolithography—transferring geometric shapes to the surface of a silicon wafer—has not only consistently lowered the cost of chips and increased their reliability but also brought about related gains in the cost of hard disk storage, computer network capacity, pixel density in photography, the cost of online library storage, and in turn the proclamation that we are living in an "Information Age."[11] The breadth of these gains is so wide that pioneering computer scientist Jaron

Lanier muses about whether his six-year-old daughter will ever learn to drive a car, rather than simply use self-driven ones. Whatever the exact timing, the rite of passage of learning to drive a car will soon be on its way out, just as learning to drive a horse and buggy was on its way out a hundred years before.[12]

The second phenomenon in the adoption of Moore's Law is that it has become something of an industry standard. Across all of research and development, strategic planning, marketing, and engineering departments it has become the primary reference point in pursuing new business. Predict a lower rate of chip development and you're not taken seriously; predict a higher rate and you've got to work hard to make your case. The very fact that Moore's Law has survived for fifty years makes it harder to dislodge. Moreover, the standard is adopted wherever computer chips are prominent, for example in the digital camera and watch industries, and—as mentioned above—the digitally controlled car.

Writing about Moore's Law's 50th birthday, Computer History Museum's David Laws has described it as "the most important graph in human history." Moore himself has predicted the Law is good for at least another ten years. However, *The Economist* cautions that while transistors can still be shrunk further, the cost of doing so may lead to the Law's demise.[13] That may be so, but right now you'll do better to join the anticipation of further technological advances than to resist their coming.

GOING WITH TECHNOLOGY'S MOMENTUM

Information technology professor and writer Tim Wu proposes the following thought experiment: Take an educated time traveler from 100 years ago. Introduce her to a friend of yours hidden behind a curtain. Then ask her to use what questions she pleases to assess your friend's intelligence. With little delay, your friend can recite passages from Shakespeare, perform challenging calculations, speak foreign languages, describe almost any part of the earth in extraordinary detail, and give thoughtful answers to relatively complex questions. The time traveler might reasonably conclude that our species had evolved to a new level of "superintelligence" unheard of a century earlier.

Draw back the curtain and your friend is just a regular person, very much like the time traveler of 100 years ago but equipped with a smartphone. However, your friend has the advantage of a massive body of research that led to the emergence of the Web. One pivotal research project funded by the US Defense Department sought "a new and systematic approach to improving the intellectual effectiveness of the individual human being." The ideas were taken up by Xerox Parc research center in Silicon Valley, where a "graphic user interface"—combining a screen, a keyboard, and a mouse—was developed. That interface was adopted by Apple Computers, soon leading to the Web and the smartphones we know today. What seemed like superintelligence to the time traveler was just an act of deception.[14]

Or was it? One thing that the thought experiment highlights is that technology's developers have moved in different directions. As the above account implies, these include the establishment of online libraries, mathematical tools, language translation programs, global mapping services, encyclopedias, and other forms of knowledge assimilation and utilization. Other prominent directions include generation of online music, videos, games, communications systems, control systems (in a crisis, an Airbus jet is likely to take over the controls, because it can make critical calculations far faster than any pilot), chat rooms, virtual reality environments, and so on. Technology's developers not only open up new paths but also clear the ground for others to go further. The forthcoming driverless car is just one of many fields where we can witness momentum not brought about by technology alone, or by the assumption of Moore's law, but by diverse groups of developers recombining to produce the eventual product.[15]

In thinking about the combination of technology and its developers, you can become aware of what technology *wants*, as Kevin Kelly, former editor of *Wired* magazine, would have it.[16] To put it simply, technology wants what its developers can do with it. Keep an eye on those developers, and you can get a good idea of where things may be going.

MAKING FRIENDS—WITH ROBOTS

A particular example concerns robots, which Kelly projects will become commonplace as we move through this century. He illustrates his argument by reference to Baxter, a prototypical robot designed to work alongside humans. Unlike previous robots, Baxter can "see" in the straightforward sense that it has eyes that can detect the presence of nearby people. Baxter can work beside you but still keep out of your way. Baxter is also easy to train. You take its arms and demonstrate what you'd like it to do. It's capable of repeating the motion, for example to remove and restack a pile of timber from a truck, without expensive programming. Baxter is also relatively inexpensive, at around the price of a midsize car. Baxter and his descendants seem set to rewrite the book on both how and where traditional manufacturing will be performed. And that's not just Kelly's opinion; a subsequent special feature of *The Economist* has affirmed Kelly's projections.[17]

Robots will become more active in the services sector, too. Amazon.com already has plans to use them for package delivery. And as people build trust in what robots can do, the applications will multiply. How can you keep track of and benefit from these developments? Kelly's writing suggests a simple four-quadrant framework (Figure 8.2). Start in quadrant 1. What parts of your present job will in future be performed by technology—that is, by the likes of Baxter? Move to quadrant 2. To what extent does your job already rely on the likes of Baxter? Move to quadrant 3. What new contributions can you make in your job that can't yet be done by technology? Move to quadrant 4. Some things lie beyond your imagination right now. That's OK, as long as your imagination keeps working![18]

BRINGING BACK DISCOURSE

Once upon a time, not too many generations ago, pen, paper, and ink were hard to come by, and there was a strong oral tradition in the way people lived. That tradition was idealized by the ancient Greeks in their

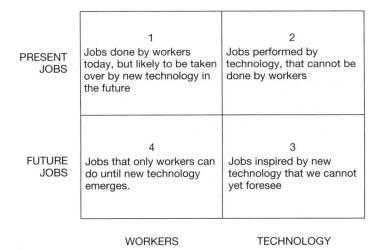

	1	2
PRESENT JOBS	Jobs done by workers today, but likely to be taken over by new technology in the future	Jobs performed by technology, that cannot be done by workers
	4	3
FUTURE JOBS	Jobs that only workers can do until new technology emerges.	Jobs inspired by new technology that we cannot yet foresee
	WORKERS	TECHNOLOGY

Figure 8.2   The Shifting Relationships among Jobs, Workers and Technology over Time

"Socratic method" of social discourse, and reaffirmed at the beginning of the European Reformation in the early fifteenth century. At that time, artists' portrayals of people going about their everyday business challenged a prevailing orthodoxy: one where the ruling classes governed by their monopoly of the written word.[19] Then along came the printing press, industrialization, the spread of literacy—the capability to both read and write—and bureaucracy. Bureaucracy and people's ability to read became codependent on one another, so that for most of the twentieth century, society's expectations for people to write were relatively minimal. Filling out forms was usually enough to get by, and the term "illiterate" was commonly taken to refer to lack of reading rather than writing capability.

The typewriter slowly began to change things, expanding the ability to generate the printed word to a wider group of people. The personal computer changed things even more, providing every user with the opportunity to generate and modify printed materials. The Web changed that again, extending people's reach to a wider group of readers, and social networking software has changed the situation yet again. We e-mail, text, tweet, blog, and post, so that writing is a much bigger part of the picture than it was until relatively recently. In 2013, science writer Clive Thompson tried to come to terms with how much writing was taking place: in the United States, on Facebook alone, 16 billion words per day; in China, on the microblogging site Sina Weibo alone, 100 million updates per day; by text messaging, globally, 12 billion words per day. Thompson's overall projections amounted to the equivalent of 36 million books being posted every day, compared with the total holdings of the US Library of Congress of just 35 million books.[20]

For you, and for other intelligent career owners like you, reading and writing are back together again. However, Thompson also emphasizes how much better the average writer has become. Working with typewriters was a start, but the literal constraints of the "cut and paste" approach ended with the arrival of the personal computer. The computer also meant you could try different ideas, look things up, check your grammar, and develop your material in a way that wasn't previously possible. But what really changed things, says Thompson, was when people began writing for an audience. The very act of writing pushes you to clarify what you mean to say. Having an audience, even a small one, encourages you to write more clearly, getting feedback on your writing nudges you even further forward. You have evolved to the kind of discourse celebrated by the ancient Greeks and reintroduced at the start of the Reformation, but this time using both the spoken and the written word.[21]

GOING BEYOND LITERACY

Literacy refers to your "knowledge of letters"—that is, knowledge of one or more alphabets and all that springs from them.[22] However, there's more going on. Let's begin with the usual package of computer programs found in Microsoft Office or its various competitors—word processing, spreadsheet, and slide-presentation programs. These call on you and your collaborators to exhibit a new set of capabilities, concerned with numeracy as well as literacy, and with presentational skills that involve the visual display of summary arguments and related images. Familiarity with all three types of programs is a commonplace expectation of intelligent career owners. Moreover, as those programs become better, other people's expectations of your capabilities will change. A simple example involves tracking changes in shared documents. A more substantial one is the advancements in data visualization, where the representation of comparative data goes well beyond traditional "PowerPoint" capabilities. An example is show in Figure 8.3.

Beyond extensions of traditional "Office" programs, digital technology is also changing the possibilities in the application of photography and film. These may have first become prominent in your social life

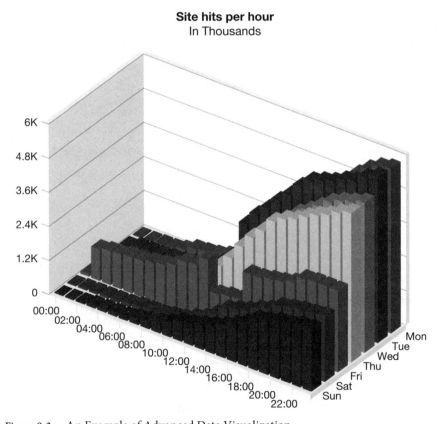

Figure 8.3   An Example of Advanced Data Visualization

rather than your professional one. However, they are rapidly becoming integrated into professional lives, too. The web service Instagram was originally developed as a way to help you apply "digital filters" to your pictures and movies before sharing them with your friends. However, it was quickly adopted for business applications—for example to show off products, processes, or premises, or provide tours to visit selected customers.[23]

LIVING THE NEW MOBILITY

Technology has also brought about a new meaning of worker mobility, where that mobility no longer refers to a change of employer. It refers instead to mobility in the location from which you connect to the Web. Let us turn to the African continent for two examples.

The first example concerns Ushahidi (the Swahili word for "testimony"), the website that emerged to track instances of apparent government violence after questionable elections in Kenya in 2007. A group of four friends realized they could use cell phones in conjunction with maps from Google Earth to witness where violence was being perpetrated. Not only could the violence be recorded but also help could be rapidly directed to its victims. The friends' website soon attracted funds from interested donors as well as growing interest in using their software for other purposes. As a result, Ushahidi was successfully used on the Haitian earthquake of 2010 to locate rescue sites and direct first responders to where their help was urgently needed. It has since been used to provide relief across other disaster sites, for example in Australia, Chile, Japan, New Zealand, and Russia.[24]

Ushahidi is an example of *crowdsourcing*, whereby you invite previously unknown volunteers to help you provide a new or improve an existing service. Popular commercial examples include Goldcorp, a mining company that found eight million ounces of new gold by simply posting all its geological data online and asking for help; Proctor and Gamble, which realized its R&D department couldn't cover most customers' needs and now does most R&D through "open innovation"; and GlaxoSmithKline, which in 2012 released all of its clinical trials online and welcomed new drug-development assistance from outside firms and scientists.[25] If you work in the not-for-profit or public sectors the same argument applies.[26] Noncommercial and nongovernmental examples of crowdsourcing include getting volunteers to help search the solar system to find new stars, or to help decode fragments of ancient papyrus.[27]

Another example of the new mobility stems from a recent study of employment patterns among information technology specialists. A worldwide survey of technology-savvy workers identified a new group of so-called #GenMobile workers, who habitually worked from home, did so during irregular hours, and were more focused on finding flexible work arrangements rather than higher pay. As a result, the workers were requesting that their employers provided reliable high-speed "WiFi" connections as well as the software systems and underlying trust to accommodate the flexible hours the workers preferred. In a nutshell, the request was for employers to reorganize the work around the mobile devices that the workers carried with them.

South African workers appeared to prefer the new mobility as much as anyone: 72 percent reported that their mobile devices help them to manage their lives, 64 percent would prefer to work from home two to three days a week, 53 percent of them said they believed they worked more efficiently before 9 am or after 6 pm, 42 percent thought WiFi was better than other connections (like the slower "4G," "3G" or "wired" connections). The poor state of repair of many South African roads further added to the workers' preference to stay out of the employer's office.[28]

In these and many other examples, we see a widespread reversal of the logic of you having to go to the office to accommodate the technology. Instead, you carry the technology wherever you go, and the office has to accommodate you.

ADVOCATING OPENNESS

Canadian writers Donald Tapscott and Anthony Williams have been persistently upbeat about technological change and its consequences. In their 2007 book *Wikinomics*, they argued that the Web had opened up new possibilities for people to be active in the global economy.[29] In 2010, they wrote *Macrowikinomics*, arguing that people could apply Web-based tools to make the world more "prosperous, just and sustainable."[30] In 2013, their book *Radical Openness* described technology as inspiring an "unstoppable march" toward greater transparency, and through it "a global economy in which everyone can participate."[31] Tapscott and Williams focus on the world of business, but they insist that you, the intelligent career owner, are both the driver and the beneficiary of the change that they see. Are they right? Is the Web leading you toward a new, sustainable economic order in which everyone can participate?

Or, are Manuel Castells's forebodings about religious fundamentalism, intolerance, and violence, and their reflection in politics and government, closer to the mark? At this time of writing, does Russia's annexation of Crimea signal a hardening of national differences that will be difficult to reverse? Does the US government's intolerance over leaks about national security signal tougher times for transparency advocates? The authors of *Radical Openness* see their ideas applying to both businesses and governments. They also see transparency—being free from pretense and deceit and characterized by visibility and accessibility of information—as a fundamental principle. The kind of message control assumed to be acceptable in the early twenty-first century is no longer seen as tenable.[32] One example is General Motors, where eleven years of secrecy about potentially dangerous ignition switches suddenly became costly and brought about an apologetic shift toward a transparent approach in 2014.[33]

The radical openness argument connects back to the virtual and physical worlds mentioned in the discussion of Doug Gould at the start of the chapter. It also connects to the roles you play as both an intelligent career owner and a member of society. If you work for a newly chastened organization like General Motors, join the commitment to change! Help make sure that your company doesn't fall back into its old ways! Similarly, if you work for companies like Proctor and Gamble or GlaxoSmithKlein— recently committed to open innovation—get on board! If you work in the not-for-profit or public sectors, the same argument applies. Wherever you work, how can you join others in seeking to promote a more transparent company culture? Or if you don't like what you see, how can you change the company you work for in order to have a clearer voice within its culture? What about beyond the workplace, as a member of society, and hopefully as a contributor to a democratic process? What can you do there?

These ideas relate to others about teaching digital *citizenship*, commonly defined as reflecting both how you use information technology (your skills) and why you use it (your values). Digital citizenship is increasingly seen as a vital part of educational curricula in schools and colleges.[34] You may have caught something of that education, or it may have arrived too late for you. In either case, your present and future challenge is to effectively contribute to the virtual world through your career. Advocating openness offers a way for you to embrace technology and to insist it serves you well, and serves others well at the same time.

In summary, new technology, and in particular the World Wide Web, has transformed the world of work. Changes across technological innovation, networking, and higher education that began in the late twentieth century became more visible in the first decade of the current century. What were once seen as independent physical and virtual worlds are now clearly interdependent. You need to recognize what's happening at the same time as you incorporate technology in your intelligent career. The Moore's Law prediction about the pace of technological change will hold true for the foreseeable future. Contemporary workers armed with smartphones or tablets appear far more intelligent and productive than their counterparts from the recent past. As robots become more familiar in the workplace, you are being encouraged to become more literate in your communications. The emergence of the Web means that the new mobility refers to technological access over the Web, rather than to physical mobility, and that transparency of organizations and governments is a more viable goal than ever before. Technology offers a shifting invitation for you to embrace it on your own terms.

Investing in Communities

Pull up a chair.
Take a taste.
Come join us.
Life is so endlessly delicious.

—RUTH REICHL

n the early 1990s Sarah Horowitz landed a job at a New York law firm
and was told she would not be receiving the customary benefits—
health insurance, pension plan, or paid vacation—employees usually
received. The snub proved to be temporary, but the message struck home.
She had a degree in labor relations, her father was a labor lawyer, and her
grandfather was a trade union activist. She realized an increasing number
of the work force were in the same predicament as her, and in 1995 created the nonprofit organization Working Today. The idea was to represent independent workers' needs and develop collective power in both
employment markets and politics.

Working Today attracted attention from both grant providers and independent workers, and by 1997 had generated a network of 35,000 freelancers. The members were later described by *New York Times* reporter
Steven Greenhouse as including "lawyers, software developers, graphic
artists, accountants, consultants, nannies, writers, editors, Web site

designers or sellers on [the handmade goods website] Etsy."[1] Horowitz and her advisors began to develop a policy agenda for those freelancers—almost all intelligent career owners—focusing on inequities they faced around healthcare, taxation, and unemployment protection. Further experimentation with the idea of establishing portable benefits for New York freelancers led to the official launch of the Freelancers' Union in 2003. Over subsequent years, the union helped gain national recognition of the particular problems that freelancers faced, developed health insurance and pension plans, and embarked on political lobbying. The membership reached 100,000 people in 2009, and by 2016 had grown to over 300,000.[2]

After listening closely to her members, Horowitz realized they had a major problem with healthcare insurance. This is commonly denied to freelance workers in the United States and expensive to purchase on your own. The Freelancers' Union moved quickly to fill the gap, attracting $17 million in start-up grants and low-interest loans from sympathetic foundations, developing its own cooperative health insurance policy, and opening its own clinic in Brooklyn, New York. The US federal government was impressed, and awarded the Union $340 million in low-interest loans to establish additional healthcare cooperatives in New York, New Jersey, and Oregon. These would cover not only freelancers but other uninsured workers as well.

A further benefit that Freelancers' Union members receive is Horowitz's own lobbying efforts. She has worked closely with politicians in both New York State and Washington, DC, to reverse the inequities freelancers face. For example, she helped get New York City to reverse a punitive "unincorporated business tax" on freelancers, and the federal government to recognize the unique challenges faced by 42 million workers. She sees the Freelancers' Union as a response to an established system of secure employment, and accompanying health and pension benefits that's breaking down—and not only in America. She has written a wide-ranging *Freelancer's Bible* to help people become and succeed as independent workers.[3] She describes her union as wanting people to have "meaningful independence" by "freeing them of [their] insecurity to give them the ability to take risks because somebody has your back."[4]

The story of the Freelancers' Union raises a range of issues for your intelligent career. What opportunities do you have to connect with other career owners, and to stand by one another, in your work? In what circumstances can you and others develop a sense of community around your work? How can communities support your working identity and help you develop new skills? Where do occupations fit in, how can your geographic place of work affect what you do, and how much can so-called virtual communities dislodge or complement communities traditionally grounded in physical space? What can you or other people do to get new communities started, and how can you draw on community attachments in your overall working life?

NEITHER BOWLING NOR ALONE

At the same time as Sarah Horowitz was taking the first steps that led to the Freelancers' Union, Harvard University sociologist Robert Putnam was publishing his highly influential essay "Bowling Alone." In the essay, Putnam argued that the behavior of US bowling league participants was symptomatic of a wider decline in the "social capital" of American life. People were still bowling, but were opting out of "the social interaction and even occasionally civic conversations over beer and pizza" that occurred around the leagues.[5] As it went for the bowling leagues, argued Putnam, so it went for society in general. Overall, he saw strong evidence that "the vibrancy of American civil society ha[d] notably declined over the past several decades." The point did not apply only to the United States; evidence from a recent World Values Survey suggested it applied to other countries, too.[6]

The larger question, as Putnam acknowledged, was whether traditional forms of civic organization had been offset by countertrends of "vibrant new organizations." At the time, Putnam argued forcefully that wasn't the case. At one extreme, large institutions, like chain stores, were laying claim to member "communities" although the level of social connectedness among the members was low. At the other extreme, there was a rapid expansion in so-called support groups, in which 40 percent of US citizens were taking part. However, he was dismissive of these groups' larger possibilities:

> The social contract binding members together asserts only the weakest of obligations. Come if you have time. Talk if you feel like it. Respect everyone's opinion. Never criticize. Leave quietly if you become dissatisfied. . . . We can imagine that [these small groups] really substitute for families, neighborhoods, and broader community attachments that may demand lifelong commitments, when, in fact, they do not.[7]

Other things were going on. More women were working, and their participation in civic life was declining. There was a growing number of one-parent families. There was more relocation between jobs and in turn less residential stability. And there was what Putnam presciently called "the technological transformation of leisure," referring to the influence of television, videocassette recorders (remember those?), and virtual reality helmets in displacing more socially directed activities.[8] It would have been hard to predict what technology would bring over the next twenty years, but the question Putnam posed remains valid today. Was—and is—technology driving a wedge between people's individual interests and their collective interests? What about your individual and collective interests?

The US-Canadian scholarly team of Lee Rainie and Barry Wellman suggests two responses to the above question, favored by "doomsters" and "enthusiasts" respectively.[9] The first group regrets what we have lost, while the second group celebrates the gains we have made. In particular, the second group argues that technology has enhanced community-building opportunities. Most significantly, it has given rise to widespread patterns of social networking that were previously unimaginable. This social networking can supplement the physical interactions of traditional social groups, or it can provide for the greater interaction of more dispersed groups (like professional societies and the specializations within them). As we discuss later, technology has also given rise to "virtual communities," where social interaction occurs in virtual space rather than physical space.[10] Most intelligent career owners don't participate in bowling leagues, but whether they participate more or less in communities is a complicated question.

STEPPING UP

What is a community? Let us defer that question for a moment, and talk about how groups of people can come together. There will have been moments in your life—in social or professional circles—where you have felt strongly about something and asked others to support your interests. In some cases, you prevailed and your point of view was adopted or included in a wider agenda. In other cases, someone else's view prevailed, or people went their separate ways, or you were directed to a related initiative that was already underway. In all of those cases, you were part of a process that could lead to the development of an informal group centered on its members' shared interests. In some of those cases, the group could have developed the staying power to become a permanent part of the landscape.[11] Let us return to the story of Sara Horowitz and the Freelancers' Union to consider how this process occurs and how it relates to your own situation.

Suppose you are a freelancer living in New York at the same time as Horowitz is beginning her pioneering work. You become aware of that work, and—to use the metaphor of the dining table from our opening quote—are invited to "pull up a chair" and "take a taste" of what is going on. If you like what you taste, then the follow-up invitation to "come join us" makes good sense. You become a member of the Freelancers' Union because of the overlap between your individual interests and the union's collective interests. So you join up, and others join up, because the union's invitation appeals to you. There is also a further opportunity to convert your overlapping interests into an agenda for action. Perhaps, then, life can become "delicious."

If you joined the Freelancers' Union would that make you a member of a community? That is at least partly up to you. The meaning of a "sense of community," has been described by scholar/consultant Philip Mirvis as "the emotive experience of feeling close to others, being connected to them by reciprocity or empathy, and even of living at least some of your life with and through them."[12] Put simply, if you get close to other people and take action together, you are part of a community. Does that mean you live in the same neighborhood, or meet face-to-face? Not necessarily. Does that mean you can also be a member of other communities? Of course you can. One of the appealing things about community attachments is that you can make new ones, or sustain or deepen existing ones, according to what you are trying to do with your life. Let us explore further where and how community attachments can be developed.

EXPRESSING YOUR IDENTITY

Ten years after the publication of Putnam's "Bowling Alone" essay, labor economists Michael Piore and Sean Safford offered a different interpretation of events. People had not given up on collective interests, but had found new mechanisms to express those interests. The shift had gone from the collective expression of identities concerned with social class, industry, and occupation (frequently through trade unionism or professional associations) to the expression of identities concerned with gender, race, ethnicity, age, disability, and sexual orientation. Moreover, these groups were loosely organized under an umbrella precept of diversity—so that, for example, the telecommunications powerhouse AT&T had more than fifty "diversity initiatives" including groups representing Asian, African American, Jewish, disabled, Christian, former military, women, "over 40" workers and other minorities.[13] According to the simple definition introduced in the previous section, these groups can all be experienced as communities.

Similar communities have evolved at both local and national levels, and become engaged in politics at each level. Similar communities again can now be found *within* trade unions and professional associations pressing a case for their separate agendas. In sum, the initiation and development of communities has become more individualized and has shifted from a one "big tent" approach to a larger number of "little tents" that more precisely reflect the identities of their members. This pattern makes sense with the rise of the knowledge-driven economy. If you are looking out for your own career in this economy, why shouldn't you look for support among your own kind of people? And why shouldn't you affiliate with more than one "little tent"—perhaps as a member of church, alumni, professional, and hobby communities—if you feel you belong in each?

One example of a relatively little tent involves being a newcomer, taking your first job in your adopted field, and trying to make sense of your experience. Take teaching, for example, where new appointees face a sudden shift from theory to practice when they first set foot in the classroom. A common response is to form newcomer communities in either physical or virtual space, where members can reflect on their early experiences. In physical space, teachers in the same geographic area create "peer mentoring communities" to find mutual support and learn from one another. In virtual space, communities form online, where members seek support and learning from writing blogs and developing discussion boards.[14] Newcomer communities are likely to have a limited life span, at least for the purpose for which they were first formed. However, their influence can endure through the long-term friendships that they promote.

DEVELOPING OCCUPATIONAL BONDS

Management scholars John Van Maanen and Stephen Barley have argued that a central opportunity for workers to engage with one another is through the shared interests and mutual regard they develop through occupational communities. A simple indicator of an occupational community is whether conversation about work spills over from work time into leisure time. More formally, an occupational community can be defined as:

A group of people who consider themselves to be engaged in the same sort of work; who identify (more or less positively) with their work; who share with one another a set of values, norms, and perspectives that apply to, but extend beyond, work related matters; and whose social relationships meld the realms of work and leisure.[15]

The description builds on the common ground architects, engineers, nurses, and many other groups of intelligent career owners find with one another. As a reader of this book, you either already are or have the potential to become a member of such a community.

A similar idea comes from other research on "communities of practice," where these communities develop a shared sense of meaning from the work that they do, and from the reinforcement they experience from the products or services they deliver. More specifically communities of practice—among teachers, nurses, engineers, or whatever—reflect the interplay of three dimensions. These three dimensions reflect the sense of joint enterprise that the members experience, the shared repertoire that they practice, and the mutual engagement through which they interact, as shown in Box 9.1.[16]

The three dimensions relate closely to the underlying questions of why, how, and with whom you are pursuing your career. They provide a way for you to relate your own intelligent career investments to the wider value of occupational community membership. This membership can be a source of support in your present job, and provide greater continuity when your employment arrangements change. It can also suggest a clearer community-centered learning agenda for your future career.

LEVERAGING WHERE YOU LIVE

The idea of occupational communities offers a fresh insight to the way we think about industry clusters. Take the archetypal example of California's

---

Box 9.1   THREE DIMENSIONS OF COMMUNITY ATTACHMENTS

Joint enterprise is principally concerned with the way members are accountable to one another, adapt to the ebb and flow—or "rhythms"—of their work, and deliver a joint response to the customers or clients for their work.

Shared repertoire involves the concepts, tools, and skills members bring to and share in the workplace, the related actions taken, and the way the repertoire is maintained through stories and developed through fresh experiences.

Mutual engagement reflects the way members do things together, maintain the social relations that underlie the community's work, and develop the necessary coherence to underlie the quality of the work members perform.

Silicon Valley, where—despite the growth of large firms like Apple, Google, and Oracle—freelancers, or contractors, are still prevalent. As scholars Stephen Barley and Gideon Kunda report, those contractors enjoy distancing themselves from the "politics, incompetence, inequities of organizational life" and are largely successful in developing their individual skill sets and finding new work.[17] Barley and Kunda also describe regular contractor community-building. It was "usually spontaneous and informal, and driven less by conscious design than by contractors' efforts to solve immediate problems," which could involve both technical and nontechnical support. In addition, the contractors were shifting toward more "virtual" communication in seeking technical support and market information.[18]

Various studies of other industry clusters in other parts of the world have confirmed the relevance of occupational networking and occupational communities to those clusters' success. A comparison between a German biotechnology cluster with low employment turnover and a UK cluster with relatively high turnover demonstrated that underlying interfirm networks were similar in each case. That is, the German employees maintained external links with outside occupational members even though the likelihood of them changing employers was lower.[19] An examination of Minalogic, a high-technology cluster around Grenoble, France, suggested that workers participating in interfirm projects developed dual loyalties—to the employer that assigned them to the projects and to fellow workers in the cluster as a whole.[20]

More than half of the global population is urban, and the trend toward greater urbanization continues. Cities are also major engines of innovation. As Edward Glaeser writes in his book *Triumph of the City,* "The streets of Florence gave us the renaissance, and the streets of Birmingham gave us the industrial revolution. The great prosperity of contemporary London and Bangalore and Tokyo comes from their ability to produce new thinking."[21] Intelligent careers need cities, and cities need intelligent careers. Yet, there is a paradox, since proximity seems to have become more valuable even as the costs of connecting or communicating around the globe have fallen. Cities are "proximity, denseness, closeness. They enable us to work and play together and their success depends on the demand for physical connection."[22]

One example of people working and playing together is advertising "creatives"—people who develop the images and storylines in an advertising campaign—located in and around Soho, London. Creatives begin as peripheral members of their own community, and progress toward greater inclusion through a process of "learning through immersion." This brings them into contact with other advertising professionals and provides an opportunity to build reputation. The learning process leads through successive challenges that can result in greater inclusion in the creatives' community and prospective leadership of a creative team.[23]

BUILDING YOUR OWN COMMUNITY

Entrepreneurship is commonly viewed as the work of lone heroes— of people who dare to go where others don't, and take risks that others won't in order to start a new business. Yet, as Martin Ruef, professor of entrepreneurship at Duke University, reminds us, entrepreneurship is more typically a group activity. In launching a new venture, you look for people you trust who like your idea and want to support you. Those people, in turn, may invite others to the entrepreneurial table. Some may bring particular skills or knowledge, others may bring money, so that together your group accumulates the resources to help your business succeed.

Ruef tells the story of Bob Moog, founder of University Games. He began with the idea for a murder mystery game, and recruited a business partner, Cris Lehman, to join in. He then reached out to two child psychologists, Patricia Stewart and Edna Maples, who had been writing and selling mystery games from their own homes. Moog and Lehman also drew inspiration from others, including the two founders of a weekend adventure getaway company. The group of advisors and company employees spread, but with each addition there was a genuine attempt to describe what University Games was trying to achieve and to invite the newcomer to both identify with and contribute to the business's success.[24] The process is illustrated in Figure 9.1. University Games subsequently grew to become the fifth-largest game company in the United States.

We can make sense of Ruef's example by applying the three dimensions of communities of practice described earlier: Ruef and his collaborators were able to build a joint enterprise, reflecting the members' commitment

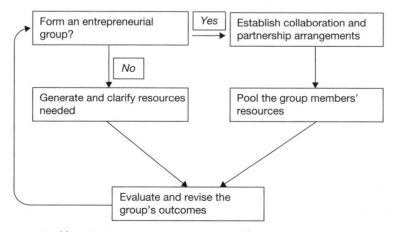

Figure 9.1   Building Resources in an Entrepreneurial Group

to helping the business succeed. They also developed a shared repertoire, not so much in the direct overlap of people's skills, but in the complementarity of those skills to meet the business's needs. Finally, they promoted mutual engagement, as the founders and their collaborators worked together to provide entertainment for their customers.

You don't need to be starting a for-profit corporation for the idea to make sense. You can think about founding your own nonprofit or charitable organization, or a local chapter of an institution that's been adopted in other places. Or you can simply form a group of friends who share the same ideas and hobbies as you do, meet a few times, and see what happens. In each case, you will be taking the initiative, seeking out other interested parties, getting a group started, and seeing where your initiative leads.[25] You may not always end up with a successful business, or any enduring sense of community, but you will have taken an opportunity to express your own interests and build your network.

JOINING VIRTUAL COMMUNITIES

Until the development of the World Wide Web, communities developed largely in physical space. Workers in industry clusters or cities were relatively privileged in the range of community attachments they could make, but people in rural areas had fewer choices. The Web brought fresh possibilities, and one of the first groups of intelligent career owners to take advantage of these possibilities was the Linux community. It grew from a simple request by a young student in Finland, Linus Torvalds, for help with a new computer operating system he'd written over the summer. A young student? Finland? One summer? Any of these questions might suggest the requester had little to contribute to the development of global computer operating systems. Yet, a key collaborator from Australia quickly signed up, and other early collaborators added to an impressive mix of global talent. The mix of talent added to the Linux community's momentum, so that twenty-five years later it still thrives, widely supported by the major software companies once seen as its competition.[26]

Linux also showed others what was possible for virtual communities, and writer Howard Rheingold quickly took up the cause:

> The technology that makes virtual communities possible has the potential to bring enormous leverage to ordinary citizens at relatively little cost—intellectual leverage, social leverage, commercial leverage, and most important, political leverage. But the technology will not in itself fulfill that potential; this latent technical power must be used intelligently and deliberately by an informed population. More people must learn about that leverage and learn to use it, while we still have the freedom to do so, if it is to live up to its potential.[27]

Some people objected to what they saw as hyperbole in Rheingold's language, claiming that communities ought to be seen as more local and more enduring than anything Rheingold observed. However, Harvard Law School professor Yochai Benkler has argued that virtual communities will "come to represent a new form of human communal existence, providing new scope for building a shared experience of human interaction."[28] European sociologists Marie-Laurie Djelic and Sigrid Quack have argued forcefully that *transnational* technologically enabled communities are becoming an increasing feature of the social landscape.[29] Social networking sites like Facebook, first launched to help people express themselves, now provide a straightforward system for the building of virtual communities.

JOINING THE CROWD

Technology writer Jeff Howe, who coined the term "crowdsourcing" with fellow *Wired* editor Mark Robinson, introduces his book on the subject with a story about the T-shirt company Threadless. Its founders invited people to submit designs for new T-shirts, asked users to vote on which design they liked best, and selected the winning designs for production. At first, designers just got store credit for their efforts, although the company raised the remuneration later. Nevertheless, as Howe saw it, the principal motivation for the designers wasn't money. Rather:

> It's about cred, or to give that a more theoretical cast, it's about the emerging reputation economy, where people work late into the night on one creative endeavor or another in the hope that their community—be it fellow designers, scientists, or computer hackers—acknowledge their contribution in the form of kudos and, just maybe, some measure of fame.[30]

What can crowdsourcing mean, though, for your intelligent career?

Crowdsourcing has subsequently been defined as an "online, distributed problem-solving and production model."[31] And community-building over the Web—among fellow designers, buyers, innovators, hobbyists, data gatherers, problem solvers, and other shared identities—is a common part of the experience. Moreover, you don't need to form a company or have the money to start one in order to make crowdsourcing work for you. In a variation called crowdfunding, websites like Kickstarter offer to bring your ideas directly to potential funders. You simply describe your project, choose a deadline, and post a minimum funding goal. If you don't meet your minimum goal, the monies pledged go uncollected. But if you do meet your goal, you are pretty much free to invest the money raised without further restriction.[32]

A twist on crowdsourcing occurs when community-building in virtual space leads to improved community living in physical space. One example involves citizen water-testers in rural India. They use a simple water-testing device and send the results over a cell phone to a central data processing facility. In turn, that facility aggregates results and highlights local problems for immediate action.[33] Another example is that of citizen crime-fighters in Malaysia. They watch what's happening in their neighborhood and submit crime-watching observations to law enforcement authorities over the Web. Then those authorities prioritize the observations received to make better use of available resources. [34] Both examples point to how crowdsourcing can provide an efficient solution to historically insurmountable challenges. What can crowdsourcing do for you?

BECOMING MORE CONNECTED

In many circles, it has become customary to think of the world in institutional terms. In these terms, you count for little except the overall goals of the institution. You are part of a classification scheme—a type of customer, a citizen, a voter, an employee, or a "resource"—that defines the institution's interest. How you see yourself, what you stand for, your essential identity as a human being, are of little concern beyond the institutional purpose you serve. Yet, there's a different approach. It begins with your identity, and extends to the people with whom you seek to relate. In turn, you reach out to other individuals and groups with whom you have something in common. You engage in collective behavior. You help form or build or sustain communities, driven by your own and your collaborators' direct interests and enthusiasms.

There are people who seek to preserve the term "community" for attachments that, as Robert Putnam once put it, "may demand lifelong commitments."[35] There are others who seek to preserve the term "collective" for institutional use, as in "collective bargaining." If you listen to them too closely, you may risk devaluing what you have found. If a group, real or virtual, feels like a community to you, why not go ahead and call it a community? When you do, you can see the world from both an individual and a collective perspective. Figure 9.2 is derived from the work of Stanford professor Jure Leskovec and his colleagues, and illustrates prospective overlapping attachments for a group of Facebook users. Leskovec was once skeptical of the term "community," suggesting the world could be equally understood by simply looking at interpersonal networks. However, he has since changed his view. Communities, and the common ground they represent, make sense. Moreover, the figure highlights how particular communities can overlap with other communities, including transnational communities. Yet, the significance of the individual—of yourself—is never lost.[36]

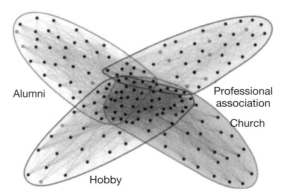

Figure 9.2   Illustrative Overlapping Communities in the Knowledge Economy

Networks occur within and beyond communities; they can help you see how your communities are connected to other communities, and how you might successfully "bridge" between one community and another. You may not know everyone in your own community, but if you have graduated from the same school, experienced the same campaign, or taken on the same cause, you can reasonably introduce yourself. Moreover, recent evidence suggests it's good to build bridges across communities and that it's your own circle of connections (rather than any friend's connections) that is most valuable.[37] Make a map of your own communities, express yourself, invest in them, reach out to other people across both physical and virtual space. You owe that to yourself and to your fellow members.

To summarize, changing times invite you to invest in changing patterns of community formation and attachment, such as those exhibited in the founding and growth of the Freelancers' Union. As a result, your community attachments are less likely to revolve around any bowling league or other straightforward leisure activity. In contrast, they are more likely to express your underlying identity as a person or occupational specialist and to look for support from others. The physical space around where you live provides a natural opportunity for community-building, including finding people to support an entrepreneurial idea. However, virtual communities are becoming an increasing part of the intelligent career owner's landscape. They allow you to both pursue an initiative of your own and support someone else's initiative using virtual approaches such as crowdsourcing. Finally, the pursuit and maintenance of *multiple* community attachments can provide you with the resources and support you may need to pursue your own intelligent career.

Working with Employers

I was once afraid of people saying,
"Who does she think she is?"
Now I have the courage to stand and say,
"This is who I am."

—Oprah Winfrey

Pierre Albert finished engineering schooling in France, completed a year of military service, and looked around for his first job. He had a good degree, but had not been a "straight A" student. However, he was comfortable in social situations and willing to travel. He was the kind of engineering graduate sought by electronics companies to go into technical sales, to talk with customers rather than work on the engineering bench. Such an opportunity was ideal for him. He wanted to get around and meet people, and find out how the industry worked. That getting around would soon take him outside his home country.[1]

He joined the Paris office of a major American computer chip manufacturer, Lonestar Instruments, as a sales associate. He was attracted by the early training the company offered, not only in sales but also in quality management and interpersonal relations. He also liked what he called the "Texan culture," where "people have to perform [and] the way you present yourself is very important." He was charged with selling computer chips to the French auto industry and developing long-term plans, quality plans, pricing contracts, and mutually beneficial higher sales numbers with key customers. He had never seen a customer when he was first assigned, but he quickly learned "the customer trains you." Customers knew that his company regularly brought in young people, and liked it because young people were eager to please.

However, entry-level jobs at Lonestar didn't last forever. Two and a half years later, he could have stayed at Lonestar with modest increases in money and responsibility, but chose to take a position with a competitor, Telerola, as a key account manager. The work would be similar, but it paid more, carried a higher title, and exposed him to the related field of telecommunications in another American company. Two years after joining Telerola, he was invited to join an MBA program at the company's expense. It was a multicultural program, coordinated by Purdue University in the United States in collaboration with partner schools in Rouen and Budapest. The only cost was to sign a letter saying he would stay with Telerola for three years after the MBA. He studied with "people from everywhere," and got the feeling that he could "do what [he] wanted to do" working in the international arena.

After he finished the MBA, Albert was promoted to a manager position responsible for a team of six coordinating the sales of key customers in overseas markets. In this role, he frequently traveled to customers' "centers of competency" to collaborate over new business opportunities. Two years later he was expatriated to Germany, and put in charge of a sales and marketing group responsible for the auto industry across both Europe and the Asia-Pacific region. However, one year later Telerola decided to take the sales and marketing work back to the Unites States. In Albert's view, the decision was political, based on a claim that US automakers Chrysler, Ford, and GM were leaders not only in sales volume but also in technology. Telerola had a global sales director position waiting for him back in France, but he determined it was time to take his experience elsewhere. He stayed in Belgium and built an international marketing organization for a start-up focused on the assembly and testing of computer chips.

Pierre Albert's career experiences raise a range of questions for this chapter. What happens on each side of the employment contract in a rapidly changing world? What are an employer's and an employee's obligations to one another? What can you do to better serve (1) your employer and (2) yourself as you perform your work? What boundaries will you cross, or attachments will you develop, through your work? Speaking of the employment contract, what does being a *contractor* mean for you—either literally or figuratively? And what about having an *agent*, either directly or indirectly through the reputation you build? Who owns the knowledge you have generated through your work, and how can you stand up for your rights to that knowledge? Let us look at these and other issues in the sections that follow.

THEIR SCRIPT, YOUR STORY

Pierre Albert's first job with Lonestar Instruments made sense to the employer and employee for fundamentally different reasons. For Lonestar Instruments, he was just one of a number of new recruits who would be given a chance to get their feet wet in entry-level sales positions. There was a standard "script" for these positions, designed to provide recruits with early career experience and create a pool of applicants for later promotions. For Albert, it was an opportunity to begin his first job after his university training, and it fulfilled his desire to meet customers and gain industry knowledge. It would provide the first chapter in the "story" of his individual career. There was a separate, short-term logic that made sense for each party.

After two years in an entry-level position, from both the employer's and employee's perspectives it was time to move on. Lonestar Instruments came up with a new script to encourage Albert to stay with them. However, the Telerola script meant the next chapter in his story would provide him with combined knowledge of the electronics and telecommunications industries. Third, fourth, and fifth chapters in his story lined up nicely with successive Telerola scripts when he was offered the MBA opportunity, the international sales management position, and the leadership of the Europe and Asia-Pacific auto industry sales and marketing group.

However, Telerola abruptly changed the script in deciding to move responsibility for his work to Detroit. He disagreed with the logic of the
decision, and took steps to continue the story of his career elsewhere.

Pierre Albert's experience can be generalized in Figure 10.1. Employers
and their employees are active in the global knowledge economy.
Employers need to pursue their separate missions and develop related employment scripts, which result in the job descriptions typically assigned
to individual workers. Employees need to develop their individual stories,
the next chapters in their careers, through the jobs that they perform.[2] It's
hard for either party to look very far into the future, and each needs to look
after their own interests. You can develop your story by varying your job,
but you are still expected to fulfill your obligation to the employer's script.
So far Albert's intelligent career has involved both him choosing to change
employer to develop his story, and having an employer take his job script
away from him. What about your career story so far? What has happened
in your employment relationships? And what do you see in your future?

The essential lesson is to see both sides. The better you can understand
both your company's and your own interests, the stronger position you
are in to negotiate. The same applies to seeking out a new employer. The

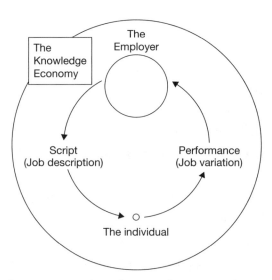

Figure 10.1   Employer Scripts and Employee Performance in the Knowledge Economy

better you can understand its interests, the better you can show how you can deliver value. Let us look next at something you can offer to each side: to your employer, fitting in with the established culture, and to yourself, "crafting" the way you do your job.

SURVIVING AN ORGANIZATION'S CULTURE

The interaction between the script your organization wants you to perform and the story you seek to develop takes place through your organization's established *culture*. Edgar Schein describes this in *The Corporate Culture Survival Guide* as "a pattern of shared tacit assumptions" that has "worked well enough to be considered valid," and is routinely taught as the "correct way" to address the organization's problems. Culture is the medium through which your script is made available, and through which you are expected to respond. However, much of an organization's culture is likely to remain invisible unless you make a particular effort to uncover it.

Schein invites you to uncover that culture at three distinct levels—artifacts, espoused values, and shared assumptions—moving from the largely visible to the largely invisible, as follows:

Artifacts are the most visible aspects of organizational culture, covering relatively obvious things like dress codes, office layout, jargon, and levels of formality, as well as behaviors that take a little more working out, like how conflict is handled, how decisions are made, and how you learn things.

Espoused values: An organization often publishes its proclaimed mission and related values, or they can be found in its published codes of ethics or employee guidelines. Some deeply held values, though, may not be written down.

Shared assumptions: These are deeply established but largely invisible beliefs that frequently reflect the founders' influence, and draw on national, ethnic, religious, and other forces, as well as assumptions about human nature or the state of the world.[3]

Next, Schein offers an exercise in "deciphering your organization's culture," and suggests it be used by a group charged with managing organizational change. However, the skill to decipher an employer's culture seems an essential part of the intelligent career owner's tool kit, so we adapt the exercise for your individual use in Box 10.1.[4]

Ideally, you might expect an organization's culture to adapt to both a changing world and its changing membership over time. However, this is all too rarely the case. University of Waterloo economist Larry Smith has written persuasively about the effects of "worker-bee" cultures that provide little room for fresh insights and cultivate "an epidemic of lowered expectations."[5] You need to work with an organization's culture, contribute through it, build reputation and maybe even contribute to a broader "culture change" initiative. However, your antennae need to be tuned to a culture's potentially deadening outcomes.

CRAFTING YOUR JOB

Your response to the script takes place through the job that you perform. However, that job also allows room for you to influence your developing story. In job *crafting* you change the way you do your job, rather than waiting for someone else to suggest changes for you. It involves seizing opportunities to enhance what you do and add to any or all of the gratification you receive, the skills you develop, and the relationships you build. You can exercise job crafting through three different approaches:[6]

> ***Expand or reduce the tasks you perform:*** Focus on the range of tasks that you do and the skills that you add or develop in doing them. For example, Emma Stanton, a recent college graduate, worked the telephones and corresponded with prospective clients and sponsors of a not-for-profit organization. She started to help other associates with particular writing challenges and soon became the "go-to" writer in her group. This has also helped her with her own writing,

Box 10.1   SIX STEPS TO DECIPHER YOUR
ORGANIZATION'S CULTURE

1. **Select the business problem:** For you, that's surviving and contributing in the established culture.

2. **Identify and list your organization's artifacts:** Step through the examples given on the previous page, notice patterns in your own and other people's behavior, and ask newcomers what it's like to work in your organization.

3. **Identify your organization's espoused values:** Check out what's written down on the organization's website, or in its employment policies, and notice and gather information on "the way we do things here."

4. **Compare your lists of artifacts and values:** Highlight differences, for example claims to having an "open door" policy versus bosses habitually being "too busy" to talk, or between promises versus practice in interdepartment relations.

5. **Assess the shared assumptions you have found:** These will stem directly from the comparison you've just made, but you are likely to still have unanswered questions. Why do we *really* do this, and not do that, or whatever?

6. **Decide the next steps:** Adapt your behavior to what you have learned, and keep revisiting steps 2 through 6 to gather more information.

adding to the value she brings to her job and positioning her for future leadership opportunities in her field.

Change the relationships around your job: Focus on altering the range and extent of your interactions with other people. For example, Paula DeCampo had gradually risen to a relatively senior position as a policy analyst and responded to a request to speak about her work at a local university. She prepared well, enjoyed the experience, and decided she would like to do more public speaking on her company's behalf. In the process she has become a more valuable spokesperson for that company, or for other companies she may choose to work for in the future.

Change how you see the job: See your job in a way that helps you identify with and feel a greater sense of purpose in what you are doing. For example, Gary Anderson had been an outgoing rock musician who subsequently became a schoolteacher. He soon realized that he could put on his "stage face" and take command of his students the same way he had taken command of his musical audience. Moreover, in making the class more interesting and more fun he was putting his students in a better position to learn new material.[7]

What kind of job crafting can you apply in your present job? What wider view of your work can you take to feel more involved, see greater purpose, apply or expand your skills, and develop relationships or build reputation? The proponents of job crafting focus directly on the job a person performs and how that particular job can be changed. However, you can take a broader view, expanding on and seeing connections among the approaches described, and deepening your intelligent career investments as you go.

CROSSING BOUNDARIES

Boundary-crossing in your work is a relatively simple idea. You do something that takes you beyond a recognizable boundary to communicate with someone else. Straightforward examples include speaking to someone in another department in your company, or to someone in another company (for example, as a salesperson or designer), or to members of your occupation, or to participants in your industry who work at other companies (for example, at trade shows). Frequently, boundary-crossing involves taking up particular projects to solve organizational problems or build interorganizational relationships. It can also take place within projects, where the project brings together people from different occupations such as new product developers, marketing specialists, lead customers, information technology experts, and so on.

Management writers have commonly seen boundary-crossing as a feature of one organization communicating with another organization. As a result, there are various sets of advice about what to expect: in engaging with a different organizational culture, communicating between different occupations, or bridging across national or linguistic boundaries. However, these sets of advice commonly subordinate you to the organization and are not necessarily helpful to your career. In contrast, scholars Nicholas Kinnie and Juani Swart see this subordination as problematic and describe three kinds of "commitment tensions" between the organization, its client and your profession.

> *Your organization and your client:* These kinds of tensions can occur, for example, when you are being called back to meetings or team-building exercises in your own organization instead of supporting the work being done at the client's location. Or, you are being asked by your organization to apply the letter of your original contract rather than absorbing subsequent client changes.
>
> *Your organization and your profession:* One particular tension that can occur is when you feel a sense of ownership over what you know and want to be selective about when and how you share that information. Another problem can involve you seeking to develop your professional knowledge, while your organization is most concerned to see you finish the task at hand.
>
> *Your profession and your client:* Tensions can occur, for example, between creative marketing consultants who seek to be more innovative than their clients' conservatism demands. Or, there can be tension between the client's claim on your time and the opportunity for you to attend what you see as important professional development courses.[8]

From the individual intelligent career owner's perspective, there is no ideal response to the tensions portrayed. However, you can work on what's best for you by asking, with which of the three kinds of commitment do you identify most? If it's your organization, it suggests you are most committed to supporting its mission (at some sacrifice, perhaps, in gaining fresh work experiences). If it's your client, it suggests you are committed to the effective application of your work. If it's your profession, it suggests you are committed to how your profession is developing. There is, of course, an opportunity to show commitment to all three parties, but if you want to do that you need to understand the trade-offs.

Recent writing on boundary-crossing extends the range of conversation. What about prospective employee spin-offs and whether they will involve new or old technologies? What about boundary-crossing as a means to innovation, rather than assuming innovation occurs within the employing organization? What about discontinuities in teams, especially virtual teams, whose members may be pursuing different agendas? What about being a knowledge broker? What about being a contributor to new knowledge generation?[9] All of these questions are relevant to your own boundary-crossing, what you seek from it, the work you are willing to put in, and the kind of relationships you would like to build.

GOING UPSTREAM—OF THE HUMAN RESOURCES DEPARTMENT

The section before sees you as a contributor to, rather than simply an employee within, the knowledge economy. It sees you having the opportunity to assert yourself, clarify what you bring to the table, and make the most of your situation. It also sees you claiming a larger role for yourself than your organization's human resources (HR) department might imagine. Let us turn to that department here.

Despite your best efforts, you may feel that the best opportunities for learning in your present organization are already behind you. Or, more urgently, you may have already parted ways with your organization and are looking for a new job. The most straightforward approach is to see who's hiring and put in an application. Or is it? University of Pennsylvania HR scholar Peter Cappelli has examined the hiring process and found it wanting. His focus is on hiring in the United States, but there are lessons to be learned wherever you may live. One problem lies with overspecification, for example when a company sought all of marketing, publishing, project management, accounting, and finance expertise, yet claimed it was merely "holding out for the right fit" when the job went unfilled. Another problem is that it's hard to reach a real person. Instead, recruiting often relies on software, and your résumé gets scanned to see if it matches the hirer's job requirements.[10]

The software, too, can be overspecified. One company had an ideal person already doing the work advertised, but wouldn't hire her because of some questionable personality assessment built into the software. According to a *Business Roundtable* report, almost 40 percent of job postings look for additional background information—education, prior experience, and so on—that is irrelevant to the job being posted. The software can also seem silly, as when a program specified experience with a particular quality-testing tool when the applicant had already designed a similar tool for a competitor. In addition, the software reflects government regulation, which can call for all manner of checks on ethnicity, gender, nationality, citizenship, drug use, and more. All of this goes beyond the fundamental need to find someone able to do the job. There's also a reluctance to make exceptions to the software, for fear those exceptions may transcend company policy or the law.[11]

The above problems can also occur if you are looking for a new position *within* your present employer, and where company policy may seek to apply similar recruitment standards to both external and internal hires. What to do? The answer for both internal and external candidates is to leverage or extend your boundary-crossing behavior. Go *upstream* of the HR department. Find out about the need for the kind of help you can offer before any job gets posted. Get yourself in the decision maker's mind as a strong or ideal candidate. If possible, preempt the hiring process. If you can't do that, try to get the job description written with you in mind. Another way to go upstream is to sign on as a contract worker, and in doing so avoid much of the red tape associated with direct hiring arrangements. We say more about this below.

DECODING TALENT MANAGEMENT

The term "talent management" has been around for a while. You may well have already been exposed to it. Look behind the term and you will find it is synonymous with "strategic HR management," which perhaps sends a clearer signal about what's going on. The term "talent management" was reportedly coined by the management consulting firm McKinsey in the late 1990s.[12] In raw form, it was about directly shaping the talented employee's career in the employer's prescribed direction. To be recruited to a talent-management program was flattering, but it was only about you to the extent that you could deliver what your employer wanted. At least the ground rules were clear.

More recently, it has been claimed that talent management can be "customized" through computerization, so that "the organization you work for today is designed to fit you, rather than demanding that you fit it." The pitch to the organization's leaders—this time from the consulting firm Accenture rather than McKinsey—goes like this:

> Think of this approach to customization as similar to the concept behind the McDonald's Happy Meal® product; just as you can choose from a predefined list of which types of food (an apple or yoghurt? a hamburger or chicken nuggets?) and prizes (a clown or a dinosaur?) to include in your child's McDonald's Happy Meal®, this approach lets employees or their managers select from a list of predefined, limited choices based on what suits their needs and preferences best.[13]

You may be wondering: Is being compared to a kid getting a Happy Meal a good enough reason to buy into a talent-management approach? Let us pursue this by returning to our opening story of Pierre Albert.

Before he left Telerola, Albert had gained valuable experience in global sales forecasting—a complex, database-driven approach tying sales forecasting to competitor analysis and regional pricing. The job with the start-up, mentioned earlier, and a later job with a Singaporean semiconductor company both extended his sales forecasting experience, but each only lasted around eighteen months. Wiser for his experiences, Albert next found a global sales and marketing opportunity with a key division of a Belgian computer-imaging company. He enjoys being responsible for 120 people worldwide, and values the close face-to-face relationship he has with the division president. He better appreciates the politics and uncertainties of global technology-driven marketing, yet after three years he is ready for another promotion. He firmly adds "If it doesn't come within the next two years, I will be out."

We do not know where Albert would have been if he had stayed with Lonestar or Telerola. We do know that in directing his own career he has become a valued contributor in the field of global business, and in particular in the highly challenging field of global marketing. He did not build the experience he has gained by allowing himself to be treated like a kid getting a Happy Meal. On the contrary, he has persistently moved to situations where he can develop his own talent on his own terms. He seems determined to keep doing so, but with greater wisdom about what kind of situation he will take on. How's that as an example of managing your own talent? And how does it apply to you?

DEVELOPING CONNECTIONS—AND REPUTATION

If you are to build your own talent, developing connections and building reputation are critical. Take Mary LaFleur, who went to law school in Boston, Massachusetts, where there is a prominent financial services industry. Just before her graduation, she was contacted by Joe, whom she had met at a law firm where she had interned. Joe was now working for Sweeper Investments, and offered her a job negotiating contracts between derivative traders and their counterparts. She accepted the job, but soon after got drawn into the investigation of an employee who had engaged in rogue trading. She quickly became the go-to person around trading desk compliance, earned further promotions, watched her company merge with a major European bank, moved into the related field of risk management, and got promoted again.

About eighteen months after the merger Lafleur got a call from Bob, the chief compliance officer (CCO) at the investment bank Weaver Steers, asking if she would interview for a position reporting to him. Bob had got her name from her former boss Kathie, and Lafleur accepted a position as Vice President, Head of Trading Practices. She managed a Code of Ethics team, worked with the trading desks, and led teams involved in two examinations called for by the Securities and Exchange Commission. A few years later she received a call from Pam, a former colleague now at the portfolio management company Bearcub Capital.[14] Lafleur interviewed with the CCO and accepted a position as Managing Director, Head of Trading Practices. She has been at Bearcub for the last several years, is now a CCO in her own right, and continues to be exposed to new opportunities and challenges.[15]

There is a pattern to Mary Lafleur's career. She has never been anxious to leave a job, and never searched for a new one. All three of the companies she has worked for after law school found her through the reputation she had previously built. We can expect her to continue to build and benefit from her reputation in the future. Her career also demonstrates that your reputation can travel through *other people's* mobility. As your contacts move from one position to another, they can see fresh opportunities for your talents. Your job search can take place without you knowing anything about it![16]

BEING (OR ACTING LIKE) A CONTRACTOR

Contract work—working on short-term contracts without long-term security and frequently without the further benefits often associated with permanent jobs—is controversial. On the one hand, the major agencies in the temporary help industry—companies like Manpower—have culti-vated a growing market for their services. On the other hand, they have obliged prospective regular employees to become contract workers in-stead. In many people's eyes, the agencies have replaced "good jobs"—permanent jobs with related benefits and future prospects—with "good temps"—contract workers who'll take what they're offered and perform the required work with minimum supervision.[17] However, an alternative view is that the fundamental nature of work has changed.[18]

The growth in knowledge workers adds to the pace of innovation, and in turn to the pace of change. However, as management scholars Karl Weick and Lisa Berlinger argued over twenty-five years ago, there is a direct trade-off. Innovation drives both new learning *and* changing em-ployment arrangements. The best jobs for new learning are likely to be the most insecure jobs.[19] Looking at it another way, most innovation takes place through projects, and new projects call for new teams while com-pleted projects don't need the same teams any more. Life moves on, and intelligent careers move on too. Whether you are in so-called permanent employment or temporary employment you are in essence a contract worker, moving between positions that can help you learn and in turn prepare for later positions.

Seeing yourself as a contract worker also means someone performs the role of agent. Either you find your next job, or you leave it to some-one else to find it for you. Your agent can be any or all of yourself, your boss, your employer, a headhunter, members of your network, or a com-pany set up for the specific purpose of connecting contractors with work opportunities—that is, a formal employment agency. Opinions about these agencies vary, from seeing them as directly responsible for disman-tling an established system of enduring jobs to seeing them as pioneers of a new market for employment opportunities. Whatever their history, if you use an employment agency you want to derive value from it.

How do you know if you're getting value? Scholars Stephen Barley and Gideon Kunda have described the "good" agency as being involved in two conversations. One is with prospective employers, regularly meeting with hiring managers, finding out what their businesses are up to and what staffing needs they might have. The other is with prospective contractors like you, checking out your skills, collecting references, and getting clear about your own priorities—for more money, new learning, a different location, the chance to work with other people, or other factors. Whatever your work situation, the roles of contractor and agent need to be played, and played for your benefit.[20]

PROTECTING YOUR (INTELLECTUAL) PROPERTY

Acting like a contractor involves being free to exercise your skills and knowledge without interference. However, many employees are already signatories to *noncompete clauses* that compromise their freedom. Wikipedia describes a noncompete clause as a legal provision where an employee agrees not to enter into or start a similar profession or trade in competition against the employer.[21] The terms vary, but traditionally they have required the employer to show a "reasonable" hardship and have been constrained in both time (often a two-year period) and space (in earlier times, around 20 miles). In many cases, though, the constraints placed on what you may view as your own skills and knowledge—your intellectual property—are more severe, and large organizations use their "deep pockets" to discourage protest. However, that may be changing.

The state of California has long held out against the widespread pattern of noncompete agreements, or "noncompetes" as they are commonly called. Moreover, the emergent evidence is that the state's resistance to those agreements stimulates a higher rate of innovation than in other states. As University of San Diego professor Orly Lobel puts it in her book *Talent Wants To Be Free*:

California is in the minority among states in its belief in talent mobility. Other states assert that noncompetes are essential and without them their state would grind to a halt, and yet California, which doesn't allow noncompetes, still moves. Not only does California continue to move, it thrives. It is home to some of the world's most successful industries. Despite not having the ability to require non-competes from their employees, companies in California compete vigorously and successfully on a global scale.[22]

The Californian example points to a global problem, and the message may at last be getting out. Several recent studies have supported the claim that regions and cities with relatively lenient enforcement of noncompete agreements promote higher levels of innovation. These studies reflect a growing movement across national and cultural borders to challenge non-compete clauses and to place greater faith in intelligent career owners like you to make good choices.[23] The evidence suggests your choices will lead to richer "innovation networks" and greater prosperity in your corner of the world. There may already be people in your region working on your behalf, and a quick computer search can bring them up. Your intellectual property, and the effect of noncompete clauses on that property, are your business.

To sum up, the ideal employment arrangement has changed. Specifically, you are in charge of your own employability and through it your career. It's your employer's script but your story, and it's to your advantage to understand both. Deciphering your organization's culture and crafting your job can add to the advantage you hold for your career. Crossing boundaries in going outside of the organization to engage with fellow professionals or clients, or upstream of the HR department to look for unannounced jobs, can also serve you well. Unless you are content to be treated as a standard component of a Happy Meal, you need to take control of your *own* talent management. This can help you build reputation (and have jobs come to you) and see yourself as a contractor taking successive jobs on your own terms. Finally, the shift in employment arrangements calls for an equivalent shift in intellectual property arrangements. So beware of noncompete clauses!

Sharing Your Story

To improve the golden moment of opportunity,
and catch the good that is within our reach,
is the great art of life.

—Samuel Johnson

An aspiring actress in New York City, Mary Lakis needed a job that would allow her to fulfill a busy schedule of lessons, try-outs, and performances. She found what she wanted in a local call center of the package delivery company Fedex. She was a dependable employee, and her boss felt he got good value from the irregular hours she was prepared to work. One day while she was recovering from a serious car accident, and questioning her long-term commitment to acting, a temporary position opened up. Her boss had noticed her excellent communications skills, and recommended Lakis to cover for the district manager's secretary about to go on maternity leave. She was able to help the district manager by converting his rapid-fire conversation into digestible English, while learning more about Fedex's business.[1]

She knew the secretarial job would be temporary, so she looked out for other Fedex opportunities. She saw there was a vacancy for a position as a district coordinator of hazardous materials. She had no experience in that line of work, but had learned something about both the district and hazardous materials through her secretarial activities. She was invited for an interview with the hazardous materials manager and his two lieutenants, and set out to "nail it!"

She walked in wearing a lab coat and a pair of false glasses. She introduced herself saying, "You don't just need a coordinator, you need a scientist," and that she would bring "a little biology, a little chemistry and a little physics to the role." She brought out a petri dish, saying "Let's start with biology, how can we grow?" and went on to argue Fedex's highly profitable hazardous materials business could be fertilized by the company's established reputation. She then brought out a glass vial filled with a blue energy drink, added, "Let's turn to chemistry," and spoke about making sure materials were safe to travel by air. Next, she showed a ball to shift to physics, adding, "What goes up must come down—and get delivered" and addressed challenges in getting goods landed, through customs, and on to the customer. She peered at her props one last time, then handed over a magnifying glass and said, "Can't you just see it?" She got the job.

Later, still at Fedex, she wanted to prove herself in a fresh environment, without the support of the managers she already knew. She interviewed as the only "unknown," the single out-of-district person in a pool of eight applying for an operations manager position. The city in which she was interviewing had a long tradition of professional baseball, so she donned the appropriate cap and compared the company's thirty-, sixty-, and ninety-day quarterly reporting system to being on first base, then second base, then third base. She described what needed most attention as she moved sequentially around the three bases, ending by pulling a ball out of her bag, throwing it to the district manager and asking "Put me in, coach!" He did.

The relevance of Lakis's example is not that you need to be a trained actor to succeed in an interview. And before we get to her interview performance, we can note that her example raises a range of questions relevant to this chapter. One key question asks, what overall narrative—and what episodes within that narrative—are you developing through your intelligent career? A related question concerns how you select from that narrative—or tell a good story—in situations such as a job interview. Also, how do you present your abilities, or your "product," in the best light? What kind of homework can you do, and how can you prepare for the unexpected? How, too, can you make the most of the limited attention your résumé will receive, or that you will receive in a chance encounter? Another important question concerns how to cope with disappointment if things don't go your way. Two final topics, about personal branding and career resilience, affirm the importance of telling your story in a constructive way.

DEVELOPING YOUR NARRATIVE

As suggested, the stories Mary Lakis told in her interviews, and the way she told them, were part of something larger—the developing *narrative* of her life and career. The *Oxford English Dictionary* defines the everyday usage of the term "narrative" as "an account of a series of events, facts, etc., given in order and with the establishing of connections between them."[2] More specifically, the focus here is on the account you are developing about *yourself*. It is an account that is grounded in your past, gets reported in the present, and projects onto the kind of person you want to be in the future.[3] What events, facts, and so forth, have you experienced up to this point in your life, and how do you see them piecing together? In particular, what *episodes*—coherent sections within your narrative—do you see? Narrative episodes reflect social interactions that vary "in their visibility, the stakes involved, and the relationships between the parties."[4] Yet, you may only recognize these episodes with hindsight.[5]

At the time Lakis was involved with the interviews just described, each story she told would seem like a fresh episode in her developing narrative. However, when she looks back at those interviews she may see them as elements of a larger episode, such as for example her "Fedex years." What may seem like a relatively small experience at the time, such as going on a job interview, can take on much greater significance later on. Perhaps you are offered a job that leads to a whole new series of experiences. Perhaps you get laid off, which precipitates experiences you hadn't anticipated. Perhaps you find or lose a soulmate. Perhaps your personal circumstances influence the jobs you take, or don't take, and how you perform in those jobs. Whatever your situation, you will be able to recognize episodes, and links between episodes, that have contributed to your developing narrative. You can also expect your narrative to develop through new episodes in the future, as it has in the past.

Your narrative centers on you, but it is not all about you. On the contrary, your narrative keeps bumping into other people's narratives—people who are applying for the same job, seeking the same customer, and doing a job on which your job depends or vice versa. Other people's narratives can create groups and invite you in, or form cliques and keep you out. In the global knowledge economy, personal narratives often evolve and interact across national borders. Some of what's going on may seem fair to you, some may seem unfair. You cannot change the past, but you can influence the present and the future.

Whatever your personal situation, it comes down to how you respond to a series of important questions: What is the underlying narrative of your life to this point, what would you like to do next, and how can you draw on your narrative—that is, share your story—in a way that helps you move forward? In the rest of this chapter, we cover different approaches to getting your story out there.

KNOWING YOUR PART

Let us look closer at the Mary Lakis example. Perhaps her acting skills helped her. Let's leave her skills aside, though, and consider the way she applied her underlying theatrical knowledge to her interviews. In doing so, we can see that her approach illustrates what scholar-consultant team Herminia Ibarra and Kent Lineback call the "key elements of a classic story." Those elements trace back to Aristotle more than 2,300 years ago, and unfold as follows:

*A **protagonist:*** The protagonist is you, the interviewee. Your immediate task is to make your audience relate to you. Lakis's approach was to take on novel "roles" (the scientist, the baseball player) at the start of the interview to capture her audience's attention.

*A **catalyst:*** In the standard three-act play, much of the first act is concerned with establishing a catalyst that has driven the protagonist to action. In a job interview, the catalyst is whatever drove you to apply for the job in the first place. Lakis's approach not only demonstrates the energy she will bring to the job but also creates an opening for her to show how she will contribute if she is offered the job.

Trials and tribulations: In the standard play, this is the second act. Your character is tested by the interviewers' examination of your past experience, and their sometimes aggressive questioning. Lakis stayed in the role she had created to foreshadow her future job performance. However, she still needed to be ready to improvise, and respond to anything interviewers might throw at her.

*A **turning point:*** In the classical play, this closes the second act. In the interview, it occurs as you approach decision time. Will you get the job, make the shortlist, meet the key decision maker or whatever, or will you be thanked for your time and sent on your way? Lakis anticipated this and sent a clear signal—with a magnifying glass or a baseball—saying she was ready.

*A **resolution:*** This is the third act of the play. In Ibarra and Lineback's words, the protagonist either "succeeds magnificently or fails tragically."[6] You have done your best to understand the script and to demonstrate your ability to play the required part. Your final line is to ask for the job—even if you do so a little less directly than in Lakis's "Put me in, coach!" line.

Lakis's storytelling is interesting because of the creative way she applied her theatrical knowledge. However, the same process underlies any interview situation. You are the protagonist, the job opening is the catalyst.

Your "trials and tribulations" need to cover what you have done before and anticipate how you will perform in the vacant position. You need to cover these in a way that both makes sense and casts you in a favorable light. There will come an inevitable turning point in the interview when your opportunity is over, and after that a subsequent resolution where you will be offered the job or it will be offered to someone else. However you choose to tell your story, the five elements described call out to be covered, and history has deemed them necessary to get the audience on your side.

PROMOTING YOUR PRODUCT

You can also increase the chances of having a successful interview by taking a rigorous look at what you have to offer. Career consultant Pam Lassiter invites you to turn to Philip Kotler's classical "four Ps" of marketing—product, placement, promotion, and pricing—and apply them to yourself. Your product is you, with all the skills and resources that you bring. Your placement reflects the channels through which you communicate with your potential employers. Your promotion is about the content—for example, your resume, or social media posts—through which you inform potential employers about your talents. Finally, your pricing reflects the compensation and benefits you seek for the work you can offer. Table 11.1 summarizes this line of thinking, and adds a column for product *development*. This is especially useful for looking beyond any immediate job offer to the longer-term implications of that offer.

Take the example of a graduating biology student, Kalyn Roche. She differentiated her *product* from others through her earlier investment in emergency medical technician (EMT) training. This led to her initial *placement*—a job with a local biotechnology company. There, she collaborated with other employees on research papers to be delivered at regional and national industry meetings. Soon she volunteered to present those papers, *promoting* herself in front of industry insiders. The skills and visibility she gained, and her investment in an MBA

TABLE 11.1   THE FOUR PS OF THE PRODUCT YOU

The Four Ps	The Product You	Product Strategy	Product Development
Product: The product or service to be offered, and its benefits to consumers.	Mainly your skills, and how you can differentiate yourself (including through your commitment or your network).	Your preferred ways to reach your market.	What product upgrade (e.g., skill- and relationship-building) would you like the job to expose you to?
Placement: Where and through which channels the product or service can reach a customer.	Your immediate channels reflect your personal network and publicly available job information.	Your preferred ways to publicize what you have to offer.	How can you develop your channels—e.g., through greater Web exposure or reputation building?
Promotion: Informing a potential customer about the benefits of the product or service.	Your résumé and related evidence of your abilities, including your presence on the Web.	The initiatives you take to promote "the product you" through, for example, alumni networks.	What can you learn (in terms of market research) from this round of job-seeking?
Pricing: A competitive amount to be charged for the product or service.	The compensation package that you seek (while valuing future learning opportunities).	Doing your homework to value yourself and con-cluding the "right price."	How much do you want to earn, and at what cost to your family and leisure commitments?

program, made her comfortable she would soon earn a higher *price* for her services. This approach led to new job offers. First, she accepted an offer of a more demanding researcher position at a regional (US East Coast) competitor. Later, she accepted a project leader position at a West Coast competitor that would involve a three-thousand-mile move. In her own and her husband's assessment, the price she would be paid and the further *product development* potential she would gain were well worth the move.[7]

DOING YOUR HOMEWORK

Another way of increasing the chances of a successful interview is by doing your homework. journalist Ira Glass once said this about the people he interviews:

> I have this experience when I interview someone, if it's going well and we're really talking in a serious way, and they're telling me these very personal things, I fall in love a little. Man, woman, child, any age, any background, I fall in love a little. They're sharing so much of themselves. If you have half a heart, how can you not?[8]

Although he wasn't talking about job interviews, his remarks are still relevant for our purposes. If you can make the interviewers "fall in love a little," it may well help you to succeed. However, you will need to do more than offer spontaneous responses to their questions. You will need to have done your homework and find ways to show it.

If you are new to the world of work, any interview will call for some fundamental homework in determining the industries and occupations in which you may be interested, the kind of entry-level positions that may be available, the range of positions to be found on job posting websites like monster.com, and how to seek out opportunities in the vast but less publicized worlds of small-to-medium business and not-for-profit organizations. It will also call for some fundamental guidance about dressing and acting the part, and preparing for tough questions, just to give your interviewers the opportunity to "fall in love a little."

Almost all educational institutions have a careers center to get you started in sifting through established sources and guidebooks to help narrow your job search. Many organizations outside the education system, including libraries, offer similar services. Be forewarned, though, that those centers tend to use "career" in a limited sense, focused on helping you to find your first professional job, or to find another job after a layoff. From an intelligent career perspective, though, your career develops over the whole of your working life. So use that careers center, use it for everything it can help you with, and appreciate the exceptional support you may receive. Remember, though, that your career is yours to own, and what you are reading here complements rather than competes with the support a traditional careers center will provide.

Turning to how to prepare for a specific interview, your homework can usefully address all of the industry, the company, its competitors, and the particular department and people involved. Moreover, the emergence of the Web means that expectations of your level of preparation have risen. So use search engines and play with keywords combining company or industry names with qualifiers such as "success" or "crisis," and work especially hard to uncover recent information. Use your own network or your alumni network to try to reach people who may already be employed in the company, or even in the interviewing department. Prepare questions not only for your own interest, but to show what you can do for the company. For example, an applicant for a director of marketing position introduced questions such as:

> "I read your annual report, and I understand you have a problem in the area of research and development. How are you dealing with it?"
> and
> "A competitor has developed and introduced a new teenage acne cream that is more advanced than your leading product. Do you feel threatened by your competitor's new product? What plans do you have for improving your product?"[9]

He got the job.

BEING READY FOR ANYTHING

Homework can also cover the kind of interview to expect. Interviewing expert Ron Fry describes an early experience applying for an editor's job at a major publishing house. The director of personnel went for the jugular: Why had he majored in liberal arts instead of doing something more practical? What in the world made him think he could edit a successful magazine? What did he know anyway that would add anything useful in her house? Changing the subject, what was his fitness routine? What was his favorite movie? Who were his heroes? The interrogation, described by Fry as "worthy of the secret police in a country on Amnesty International's Top Ten List" made him confused, fearful, and hostile. He mumbled monosyllabic replies, avoiding eye contact.[10]

Fry learned later that the interviewer was drawing on an established technique of deliberately putting someone under stress. The *stress interview* is used in situations where jobs involve high emotional demands, sudden emergencies, or a breakneck work pace. The idea is to simulate the kind of pressure you would face. Start to sweat, drop your head, break eye contact, become noisy or sarcastic, and you're gone. Moreover, the interviewer will congratulate him or herself for exposing your inner nature and your obvious lack of suitability for the job in question. Stay in control, and avoid letting the approach get to you, and you may win out.

Other standard interviewing approaches are: the *behavioral interview*, asking questions about how you behaved in past job situations to assess how you'll behave in the job you're interviewing for; the *team interview*, in which the interviewer is a team seeking to find out whether you'll fit in; and the *situational interview*, where you are asked hypothetical questions about work situations that might reveal if you would panic, or avoid seeking help, when the situation demands it. In all of these situations, you need to recognize what's going on and give people what they're looking for.

Then there are those wacky questions, including all of the following that come from established corporations:

> "If you were on an island and could only bring three things, what
>   would you bring?"
> "You're a new addition to the crayon box, what color would you be
>   and why?"
> "Describe to me the process and benefits of wearing a seatbelt."
> "Can you instruct someone how to make an origami 'cootie catcher'
>   with just words?"
> "How many square feet of pizza are eaten in the United States
>   each year?"
> "What is the funniest thing that has happened to you recently?"

These kinds of questions are intended to provide insight into your "thought process, critical thinking skills and overall personality," above and beyond the usual stuff about achievements and lessons learned. As with the different kinds of interview, they call for you to be expecting them, or something similar. If you are, then you—the intelligent career owner—can thrive on the opportunity.[11]

USING YOUR RÉSUMÉ—AND THE ELEVATOR

Let us turn away from the interview to other approaches to sharing your story—your résumé and your "elevator pitch." Most experts on résumé writing focus on helping you to share a good story, rather than fussing over the details. Ibarra and Lineback, whom we met earlier, stress that "everything in the résumé must point to one goal—which is, of course the climax of the story you are telling."[12] Career consultant and author Karen Hansen adds that by letting your résumé tell your story you are helping the decision maker gain a rapid first impression—in between, say, two and twenty seconds—of who you are and what you can bring to the vacant position. Many experts recommend a three-part format, covering your accomplishments, professional experience, and education. Others recommend a preceding section that states your job search objective. Briefly, the purpose of each part is:

1. *Objective:* This gives you an opportunity to state your target market and presents a future orientation rather than focusing on the past.
2. *Qualifications or accomplishments:* Whichever title you choose, your goal is to show the reader what you have done and how this positions you for your target market.
3. *Professional experience:* This talks about the previous jobs you have held, but does so in language that reinforces and highlights the experience you have had.
4. *Education:* As a rule of thumb, start with the most recent and most relevant, and show how your formal learning connects to the job you are applying for.

However, times are changing. Some employers are moving toward standardized forms that are more easily scanned for key terms. Others are having you fill out a form directly on their own website. Moreover, expectations vary with the job market. Academics are encouraged to list their publications—which can run for pages! Graphic artists are encouraged to submit a portfolio. Photographs are either encouraged, discouraged, or banned depending on the country you live in. One website on executive careers says to keep the résumé brief, but to provide "deeper slices of success" or collateral stories in one-to-two-page documents—leadership initiatives brief, achievement summary, career biography, reference dossier, and the like—to fulfill a variety of interview or networking purposes.[13] Our best advice for your intelligent career is to think strategically. Take the time to both reach out to a prospective employer on the one hand, and to represent what you are seeking for your career on the other hand.

A further channel for telling your story is through what has come to be called your *elevator pitch*. Rumor has it that the term was used around

Microsoft's head office in Seattle when founder Bill Gates was still CEO. Job seekers were asked to imagine they walked into an elevator in which Gates was already traveling, and describe how they would use the opportunity. The approach can also be compared to an aspiring politician's getting a TV "sound bite" to promote their campaign, or to speed-dating in a bar. In each case, it helps to have prepared beforehand. Introduce yourself with a smile, say where you work and just a sentence or two about that work, and await a response. If you are stuck, try preparing your résumé and elevator pitch together, knowing that for each you're likely to get no more than half a minute of the target party's attention.

COPING WITH DISAPPOINTMENT

If you don't get the job, or worse, if you don't get any of a series of jobs, there's the issue of coping with disappointment. MIT scholar Ofer Sharone set out to cover job loss and subsequent job search experience in two comparable high-technology districts—Tel Aviv in Israel and Silicon Valley in the United States. What he found were systematic differences, as illustrated by the contrasting reports of Eldad and Beth, as follows. Both were out of work around the same time, facing the same global economic downturn.[14]

Eldad in Tel Aviv was laid off from a marketing position, and shot off the same résumé for every job opening that seemed to match his skills. However, he could not get beyond the preliminary screening interviews that checked the job specifications (specs) against his individual qualifications. He complained that the system meant "you are just a collection of buzzwords," but he kept on sending out résumés commenting there was "nothing to lose" from still doing that. In contrast, Beth lost her job as a technical writer in Silicon Valley, but set out eagerly on her new job search. She crafted personalized cover letters and targeted résumés, and networked extensively. One month later she had her first job interview, but said there was "no chemistry" in it. Four months later she still had no job and appeared overwhelmed by self-doubt. She reported she felt as if she had a "character defect" and was "flawed in some way."

These were not isolated cases. Rather, Eldad and Beth reflected a widespread pattern of differences between struggling Tel Aviv and Silicon Valley job searchers. Tel Aviv searchers blamed the system, and saw their struggles as a challenge for society. Silicon Valley searchers blamed themselves, and saw their struggles as their own problem. Each group was playing a different job-search game, what Sharone characterized as a "specs game" versus a "chemistry game." Each game called for a different strategic focus—on the external job market in the specs game, but on the internal self in the chemistry game. These games brought about different approaches in the way résumés, cover letters, networking, and interviews were handled, as summarized in Table 11.2. In turn, each game gave rise to different experiences that protected the self on the one hand, but rendered it fragile on the other hand (and in one of Sharone's Silicon Valley cases led to suicide).

In a knowledge-driven world, it can be expected that more people will experience job loss at some point in their careers. Sharone's main conclusions are directed at policy makers and call for increased understanding and greater support for people who lose one job and set out to find another. However, you can take away an individual lesson not to get caught up in either the specs or the chemistry game to the exclusion of the other. Both games are relevant, but neither ought to determine your personal narrative. You can also take away a very firm lesson not to be too proud

TABLE 11.2   DIFFERENCES BETWEEN THE SPECS GAME AND
THE CHEMISTRY GAME

Game	Space	Chemistry
Strategic Focus	Market	Self
Resumes	List	Advertisement
Cover Letters	Two-sentence formality	Self-revealing
Networking	Corrupt	Efficient
Interviews	Oral exam	First date

to talk about any job search difficulties, and to seek support from others who understand what you are going through.

CULTIVATING RESILIENCE

A further important topic to bear in mind for your intelligent career is the need for resilience, or more specifically career resilience, which can be seen as "positive adaptation within the context of significant adversity."[15] Career resilience is often seen as a trait, like having the "right stuff" or a "strong character." However, the message from this chapter is that career resilience is something you can cultivate as you develop the narrative of your life. Each of the stories you share can reflect the resilience you have shown so far, in staying the course of your studies or in negotiating a troublesome situation. Each can also project the resilience you will show in a future assignment, and thereby contribute to any contract you make with a new employer, customer, or collaborator. To stay with the gardening metaphor, the variety of your developing career needs to be increasingly nurtured by the career resilience you breed into it.[16]

Cultivating career resilience can be particularly important for career owners in highly innovative work roles. Innovation projects fail "at an astonishing rate," and those failures precipitate setbacks in the lives and careers of project participants.[17] You need to exercise judgment about how well you can perform your assigned job, how much effort you will put into the project, how you will adjust to any setback, how much to let your experiences with previous projects influence your approach, how loyal to remain to the project leader and other project contributors, and finally how to interpret the project episode as you turn to seek further project assignments.

As it goes for innovative role-takers, so it is likely to go for you. You will inevitably be involved with innovation (or its neglect) and its related successes and failures. As you work with other contributors, you can cultivate career resilience directly from your social interactions and the learning you draw from them. In this way, career resilience can become embedded in your personal life narrative, and the stories you tell to extend that narrative. Intelligent career owner that you are, you owe it to yourself to make that happen.

BUILDING YOUR BRAND

We've already covered "you, the product"—but what about "you, the brand"? Marketing specialists will tell you that product marketing differentiates your product from other products, while brand marketing differentiates your customer from other customers. Wikipedia defines personal branding as "the ongoing process of establishing a prescribed image or impression in the mind of others."[18] Suppose you want to set up a small consulting company to sell your expertise in, say, restaurant management. In product marketing, you think about the kind of restaurateurs who want your expertise. However, in product branding you think about getting those same restaurateurs to want *you*. You're looking for an emotional commitment to increase the chances of your getting the kind of work you are looking for.

Throughout your career, you can benefit from both product marketing *and* brand marketing. However, in the digital age, personal branding has become both more challenging and more necessary. Today's social media are global, open, transparent, nonhierarchical, interactive, and—almost literally—viral in the speed at which they can spread images and information. What kind of presence do you wish to have on these social media? Or as Soumitra Dutta, professor at INSEAD in Fontainebleau, France, has framed the question, "What's Your Personal Social Media Strategy?"[19]

Dutta answers his own question by insisting you get involved, since social media provide a low-cost platform on which to build your personal brand. It is a brand that communicates who you are and invites people to respond, from both inside and outside your present company. However, that's only the start. The presence of your brand also allows you to engage rapidly and concurrently with your audience—colleagues, customers, and followers likely to be interested in the work you are doing. In turn, you position yourself to learn from the responses you receive.

A helpful way of thinking about your brand is to know it will be visible to both personal and professional constituencies, and across both public and private space. You need to think about your brand across all four combinations. In the professional and public space, for example, Dutta suggests the generic message, social media, and goals listed in Table 11.3.

Let us return to supposing you are a restaurant consultant. Your *message* would highlight your industry experience and how that has enabled you to develop your expertise on staffing and service management. Your *social media* would involve services like LinkedIn, Twitter, and one or more restaurant-industry-specific Web communities where you could participate in industry conversations. Your *goals* would be something like these:

Brand: to build recognition in the restaurant industry (possibly, but not necessarily, within driving distance of your home).

Engagement: to demonstrate commitment, highlight achievements with client restaurants, and attract new prospective clients to your work.

Learning: to look out for new industry trends in the responses you receive, seize opportunities to recognize new staffing or service problems, and learn from others about particular regulatory challenges.

TABLE 11.3   PERSONAL BRANDING IN THE PROFESSIONAL AND PUBLIC SPHERE

Message	*I am competent and growing as a professional*
Typical Social Media Tools	*LinkedIN, Twitter, and selected industry or occupational groups*
Goals	*Brand: Build peer recognition*
	Engagement: Show commitment; find fresh opportunities
	Learning: Gather industry knowledge; develop your skills

We close this section with a word of caution. The writers for Wikipedia are correct in observing that personal branding is concerned with self-*packaging* rather than self-development. Be authentic in what you claim, and don't confuse self-packaging with self-deception. Personal branding needs to be about building rather than blowing your reputation—and about developing rather than derailing your narrative.

In summary, sharing your story involves seeing the underlying narrative of your career to-date, and then selecting from that narrative to help you move forward. Telling your story to others, for example in a job interview, calls for you to be in control of five key elements—a protagonist (you), a catalyst (why you're here), trials and tribulations (what you've been through), a turning point (as decision time approaches), and a resolution (ideally a job offer). A product-marketing approach can help you explain what you bring to a position and decide whether you want to take it, homework can help you prepare for both formal meetings and chance encounters, and your résumé can reflect the story you want to tell. Never forget that coping with disappointment and cultivating resilience are both fundamental to an intelligent career. Finally, personal branding across both physical and virtual space is essential for potential employers to want to work with *you*, rather than merely with the capabilities that you bring.

Building Your World

Let us make our future now
And let us make our dreams tomorrow's reality

—MALALA YOUSAFZAI

M oses Zulu grew up in a small farming village in east Zambia. His parents left school after the fourth grade, and Zulu began community school with the same expectation. However, by studying in the fields between plowing obligations, he was able to earn a scholarship to attend a government middle school, and in turn gain entrance to a Dutch Mission high school in the same district. He then worked as an "untrained" teacher until he was selected in 1993 to go to Chainama College of Health Sciences, from where he graduated with a degree in environmental health in 1996. The next year, he was appointed as a Ministry of Health technologist in a rural region of Luapula Province in the north, to review the provision and delivery of health services. He quickly concluded that "anyone who needed to make a difference" had to take a developmental view of their work.[1]

In relatively quick succession, he took a course on holistic community health development, facilitated the largest water and sanitation project in his region, worked part-time for the Population Council of Zambia as a

field supervisor, and was recruited to deliver health services for a nongov-
ernment organization (NGO). He picks up the story as follows:

> "I was still working in the Ministry of Health at the community level
> as an environmental health technologist with two friends, Linda (a
> Peace Corps volunteer) and Anderson (a Community Development
> Officer). The three of us used to meet on Saturday and Sunday re-
> viewing our work. In those days, I was seeing an increased number
> of tuberculosis patients and I also provided counseling and testing
> services for HIV. The majority of parents I served became worried
> for their children once the HIV test was positive. . . . I was drawn to
> create community services to give comfort to families affected with
> HIV, to help them not worry for the welfare of their children."

Anderson's specialty was in community development, including in wom-
en's clubs, where there was an opportunity to educate the members about
HIV. Linda worked in a health clinic and witnessed firsthand the struggles of people with HIV diagnoses. The three agreed to work on a grant
proposal to provide afflicted people and families with "education support, food support, psychological support, and economic support." They
established their own NGO called the Luapula Foundation, and sent in
50 grant proposals. Many proposal recipients simply regretted they could
not help, and with one exception the others did not reply at all. However,
that exception involved the Firelight Foundation, based in California.
The people at Firelight also sent their regrets, but added some feedback
on how the grant application might be strengthened. Zulu led the way
through a series of further reapplication and feedback cycles, before finally gaining a $5,000 grant for a pilot project in 2003.

By the end of the partnership with the Firelight Foundation in 2008,
Zulu and his collaborators had new capacity and confidence. With encouragement from Firelight, they next applied for and received a $2.3-
million grant from the New Partnership Initiative, under the US government's program for AIDS relief. With Zulu as its CEO, The Luapula
Foundation is now the primary provider of HIV counseling and testing

in Luapula province. Unfortunately, the success for his friends was short-lived, as Anderson succumbed to kidney failure in 2010, and Linda to colon cancer in 2013. Zulu mourned the loss of each of them, but has carried on the work they helped promote. He has also completed a master's in public health at his own expense at the University of Western Cape, South Africa, and registered for a PhD in sociology at a local Zambian university. He is married with four children, all still in school. His wife is also back in school, while at the same time running a family business.

The focus here is on building your world. We use "world" in a specific way, in what the *Oxford English Dictionary* defines as "a person's normal or habitual sphere of interest, action, or thought."[2] Our focus is on the way you project your intelligent career onto the social world around you, and how in turn your career responds to other people's careers. We use Zulu's story to help us examine some closing ideas—about composing a life, giving and taking, being mindful, being humble, doing "good work," standing up for family, and sustaining your world—that reaffirm an intelligent-career perspective. After that, we close by reconnecting with the principal messages from earlier chapters in this book.

COMPOSING YOUR LIFE

The idea of composing your life involves bringing its different parts into a coherent whole. Writing about this in the late twentieth century, but before the arrival of the World Wide Web, anthropologist Mary Catherine Bateson alerted us to a new reality. Composing a life in a stable society was "somewhat like throwing a pot or building a house in a traditional form." You know the materials, have the skills to work with those materials, and the use of your product is widely understood. In contrast, the new reality is that "the materials and skills from which a life is composed are no longer clear."[3] This means you have to break new ground, rather than follow the paths of previous generations, and face the "recurring riddle of what the parts have in common."[4]

Moses Zulu's life offers an interesting example. He broke new ground in persisting with his education through high school and college. He found a job in the area of his studies, then grappled with the question of how his skills could address the medical realities his people were facing. With his collaborators, he worked on the "recurring riddle" of how to deliver wider services. He persisted when his early calls for help went unanswered, and pressed on when he saw an opportunity to establish a larger program. Over the same period, he established a healthy family and supported his wife, who was also pursuing further education. He's come a long way from the person who once had to study in the fields.

Zulu also illustrates that composing your life is "autobiographical, not biographical."[5] Just as his composing reflected his choices and selective memory, so too will your composing. In later work, Bateson wrote about the reality of interdependence with others, whereby we need "to compose our lives in such a way that we both give and receive."[6] She also wrote that there are only so many hours in the day to practice interdependence, but "the potential value of any hour is variable."[7] Your intelligent career can respond to this prompting in your own distinctive way.

GIVING—AND TAKING

How, though, can you manage the "giving and receiving" to which Bateson refers? In early 2011 *Fortune* magazine set out to find America's best networker, based on the number of connections people had on the popular professional networking site LinkedIn. The answer was a self-described "shy, introverted computer nerd" with two computer science degrees who seemed destined to continue to do backroom work for organizations like NASA and Microsoft. However, when he moved to California's Silicon Valley, his shyness was the key to his later popularity, since it drove him to "try to make a connection and have a relationship that gives you the opportunity to do something with someone else." Trying to make those connections became a pattern, and eventually led to the *Fortune* acclamation. His name is Adam Rifkin.[8]

Adam who? Rifkin is described by University of Pennsylvania professor Adam Grant as a classical *"giver,"* someone who puts more into relationships than he gets back. As a giver, you might not think about the personal costs at all, but "simply strive to be generous with your time, energy, knowledge, skills, ideas and connections with people who can benefit from them." A giver stands in contrast to a *taker*, who seeks to get more than they give, and to a *matcher*, who seeks to balance what they give with what they get. You might expect that financial success goes mainly to the takers, with less to the matchers and least of all to the givers. However, Grant reports a pattern that's surprisingly different. Givers are predominant at both ends of the success spectrum, while takers and matchers are more likely to be stuck in the middle.[9] In our earlier example, Moses Zulu, CEO, has moved to the successful end of the spectrum.

Grant argues that successful givers, like Zulu, can be just as ambitious as their taker or matcher counterparts. However, they have a different approach to pursuing their goals. It's an approach that seeks to "reverse the popular plan of succeeding first and giving back later." Through their behavior, givers can gain privileged access to knowledge, expertise, and influence. Teamwork provides a particular opportunity for givers to show others what they have to offer, and in today's world relationships are both more manageable and more visible.[10] Studies of values across different cultures indicate that most people want to work with and support givers.[11] Moreover, the costs of giving can be managed, by protecting yourself from burnout or from being pushed around.[12]

Grant concludes with a series of "actions for impact," such as introducing more giving in your own or someone else's job, embracing a principle of doing "five-minute favors," joining a community of givers, helping to crowdsource a project, or launching a "thirty day generosity experiment."[13] The reasons for you to remain or become a giver are powerful, and seem a natural extension of your intelligent career contribution. But as Grant cautions, "if you do it only to succeed, it probably won't work."[14]

BEING MINDFUL

Composing your life can also benefit from a "capacity for distraction," an ability to pay attention in a way that is "open, not focused on a single point."[15] In this regard, Harvard psychology professor Ellen Langer once designed a simple experiment. A colleague stood on a busy sidewalk near a drugstore and made a plea for help. He had sprained his knee, so could a passer-by go into the drugstore and ask the pharmacist for an Ace bandage? Langer stood inside, within earshot of the pharmacist she had already briefed to say the store was out of Ace bandages. Twenty-five people responded to her colleague's call for help. All twenty-five were told the store was out of stock. Not one of them thought to ask if the pharmacist could recommend anything else. They all simply returned to tell Langer's colleague he was out of luck. From this and related experiments Langer concluded that for much of our lives we go around being mind*less*. That is, we stay rigidly committed to one predetermined use of the information we receive, rather than being open to other possibilities.[16]

You can take your predictable mindlessness with you everywhere, on or off the sports field when you favor the home team, among family or friends when you fit them to categories that feel comfortable for you, with the colleague who appears to have let everyone down, with the boss who doesn't value the extra work you do, and—not least—in dealing with a crisis. In each case, you're likely to be limiting your responses to what feels familiar, rather than drawing on a wider range of frameworks that allow other responses. And since Langer's early experiment, a wide range of studies have shown how a lack of mindfulness pervades our careers and the organizations to which we contribute. Langer and her followers have developed scales—for example novice, advanced beginner, competence, proficiency, and expertise—to help you identify and build on your existing level of mindfulness.[17]

Yet, a funny thing happens when you get toward the top of the mindfulness scale: your deliberation becomes less detached and role-bound, and more dependent on intuition and a search for fresh patterns. As the scholar-practitioner team Karl Weick and Ted Putnam point out, you are led from a largely Western perspective focusing on what the mind has already learned toward a more Eastern perspective valuing the mind for what it is.[18] With an Eastern perspective you are invited to focus on "reclaiming the present moment" or being a "perpetual beginner" in your approach to life. You participate in regular meditation, where you "just sit not pursuing anything, and insights come up on their own timetable."[19]

Whether you begin with a Western or an Eastern view, you get drawn toward the same place. As Langer herself put it years later, much of the research on mindfulness has been on various forms of meditation, with a focus on preventing stress and negative emotions. The larger point, though, is that meditation is a tool to achieve *post*meditative mindfulness, and that:

> Regardless of how we get there, either through meditation or more directly by paying attention to novelty and questioning assumptions, to be mindful is to be in the present, noticing all the wonders that we didn't realize were right in front of us.[20]

What wonders are right in front of you?

BEING HUMBLE

Management scholar Edgar Schein stopped on his walk to admire a recently arrived troop of mushrooms. A woman walking her dog said in a loud voice, "Some of those are poisonous, you know." He answered, "I know," but the woman persisted, "Some of them can kill you, you know." Schein was offended. Why couldn't the woman have asked a friendly question, and made a better start in relating to him?[21]

Humble inquiry is "the fine art of drawing someone out, of asking questions to which you don't already know the answer." It involves "building a relationship based on curiosity and interest in the other person." However, Schein is troubled by how many conversations involve telling rather than asking as a primary form of communication, and in particular by a neglect of what he calls here-and-now humility, which is needed when you're dependent on someone else to help accomplish a task. Schein points out that the root problem is sociological. Telling puts a person in their place, whereas asking empowers them, as well as signaling your own vulnerability. By asking, you indicate you'd like a sociologically balanced relationship, and project a willingness to trust.[22]

Some kinds of humility are prescribed by society, either by established statuses or recognized achievements. However, Schein focuses on what he calls here-and-now humility, based on "how I feel when I am dependent on you." In turn, humble inquiry involves asking a friendly question such as "What are you working on today?" This stands in contrast to steering the conversation through *diagnostic* inquiry (for example, "What are you trying to achieve?") or inserting your own ideas through *confrontational* inquiry (for example, "Why don't we take a vote?"). There are also *process* inquiries that cover all three kinds above: for example, a humble inquiry—What's happening here?—versus a confrontational one—Why did you get defensive just now? Leaders, both formal and informal, are especially prone to neglect humble inquiry, and "do and tell" cultures—in particular US culture—reinforce that neglect.[23]

Schein concludes with a series of suggestions to overcome your anxiety about humble inquiry by, for example, slowing down and taking stock of the situation, being more reflective about your own behavior, engaging the unexplored "artist" inside you (like an actor taking on a new role), and becoming more mindful (reinforcing the previous section of this chapter). He says most of us have leadership thrust on us from time to time by the situations we find ourselves in. When that happens, you can take charge with humble inquiry.[24]

DOING GOOD WORK

The topic of leadership leads us to the ideas of three popular American psychologists. In 2001, Howard Gardner, Mihalyi Csikszentmihalyi, and William Damon wrote about what they called "good work in difficult times." Good work was "work of expert quality that benefits the broader society," and difficult times involved "people's ability to know the right thing to do and stay in their professions."[25] An example was journalist Ray Suarez, enjoying a promising career with Channel 5 TV station in Chicago, an affiliate of the national network NBC. A family had sued a major video game maker claiming their children would get seizures. Suarez's research indicated the proportion of children who might be affected was only "one-tenth of one-hundredth of one-thousandth" of the population. He said it was irresponsible to suggest video games were dangerous, but his producer insisted on a sensationalist approach. Suarez was about to leave the journalism profession when he received an offer to work for National Public Radio.[26]

But what about less fortunate people—those who want to do good work but can't find another job? Gardner and his colleagues claim that most people will face situations like Suarez did some time in their careers, where their sense of what's right conflicts with what they're told to do. The authors dismiss the ideas of free market economists, and question whether a combination of marketable skills and available jobs will work for everyone.[27] Instead, they urge you to be active in your profession— contributing to its overall social mission and the standards by which it serves its mission—and to regularly perform a straightforward "mirror test" of where and how you fit in.[28]

The three psychologists offer a closing letter to aspiring workers with recommendations that reinforce earlier sections of this chapter: First, respect a sense of tradition while adapting to changing times. This also means finding teachers, mentors, or role models you admire and seeking to "unclutter" your mind as often as needed. Second, find support from others, both inside and outside your job, who share the same purpose as you, and think about collaborating in a new social enterprise if you don't like what's going on. Third, stick by your principles, since knowing what should be done and having the means to do it "are useless without personal commitment." The authors conclude by invoking broadcaster Garrison Keillor's sign-off on his *Writer's Almanac* website: "Be well, do good work, and keep in touch."[29]

STANDING UP FOR FAMILY

Mary Catherine Bateson once wrote:

> Since households must rely more and more on dual incomes, every
> step must be worked out so that each partner can continue produc-
> tive work, and both may have to improvise.... Almost any move
> puts a working couple at risk and reintroduces old inequalities, and
> even commuting is proving less and less workable as the barrier be-
> tween home and work weakens.[30]

You may relate to this message already, from your past experience or in
anticipating your future. Or, you may relate to the message from witnessing the experiences of your parents, friends, or relatives. One way or another, your career will evolve alongside the careers of family members.
Bateson's thinking is premised on the idea of a dual career couple, usually
with children. In this regard, there is evidence that women pay greater
attention to family considerations than men in the career choices they
make.[31] However, we have also become accustomed to a wider range of
family forms involving single-parent households, blended families (where
one or both partners has a child from a previous relationship), intergen-
erational families, same sex couples, and other arrangements.

So how can you do better, either as a parent or as a family-friendly
member of society? Lotte Bailyn of Massachusetts Institute of Technology
has pursued this question for decades. Her key observation is that, in a
knowledge-driven economy, it is more important to tap into all family
members' intelligence than to rely on any assumption of a sole breadwin-
ner. However, a second observation is that this needs to be done without
sacrificing the care and attention you want to provide for children, the
intelligent career owners of the next generation.

Bailyn's pioneering studies of work and family provide a strong foundation for the research on work-life balance.[32] One path to progress here
is for women to advance their own agendas, or to "lean in," as Sheryl
Sandberg, Chief Financial Officer of Facebook recently put it.[33] Another

path is to see that work and family roles are *inter*dependent. There will be times when a worker needs to be home for a sick partner or child. There will be problems if a parent is physically home, but psychologically still at work and inattentive to family members' concerns.[34] As an intelligent career owner, you are on the front lines in dealing with this interdependence, on your own or your colleagues' or your employees' behalf. How much can you stand up for your own family, or for the families of other workers around you?

We are moving beyond the nine-to-five workplace. Arrangements such as flextime (providing flexible work hours), working from home, job-sharing, and results-only work environments (ROWEs) can help you, the career owner, to satisfy your own and your employer's expectations and cater to the needs of family members.[35] These and other initiatives suggest a "paradigm shift" that not only recognizes the challenges of combining paid work and family care but also responds to people's wider commitment to nonwork roles. These include participation in educational, cultural, recreational, and volunteer activities that provide personal meaning and help build social cohesion. Yet, there is evidence that many people are still fearful of asking their employer's help in fulfilling those roles.[36] Don't let fear get in your way, or in other people's way. There's too much at stake.

SUSTAINING YOUR WORLD

"Sustainability" is a popular term these days. It commonly refers to environmental sustainability, which means taking care of the larger world, and its climate, natural resources, human health, and world peace. An extension of this line of thinking is concerned with "sustainable careers," meaning careers that are managed to provide employability over time, while maintaining individual well-being and accommodating family needs.[37] Combining both of the above meanings, sustaining your world means attending not only to the larger environment but also to your career within it.

We can return to Moses Zulu to find examples of both environmental and career sustainability. Through his work with the Luapula Foundation he seeks to provide a more sustainable environment for the families he serves. In doing so he invests in three communities: a regional one with the people needing care, an occupational one with fellow care providers, and a global one with others fighting infectious diseases. Through these he is clearly seeking to improve the quality of life in his province.

Turning to Zulu's career sustainability, he has stayed in charge of his own employability by seeking grant awards and other funding sources for his foundation. He has also consistently worked with others to gain experiential and formal learning, and to become a likable and experienced CEO. He takes pride in his work, appears to be in good health, and has found the time and energy to support his own family over the same period.

Your own world is distinct from Zulu's world, but the same kind of opportunities apply. Building your world can contribute to sustaining the larger world, at the same time as you sustain your career. May it always be so.

ENGAGING IN REFLECTION

Our conducted tour is about to end. We began by introducing you to a simple definition of an intelligent career—one where you apply your intelligence in pursuing your career—and its relevance to both individual and collective efforts. We highlighted the shift toward a global, knowledge-driven economy where your own career—including both its rational and relational sides—is increasingly coveted. We suggested this book could help you to make informed choices in today's changing world of work, and offered two parts concerned with reflection and taking action, respectively.

Regarding Part 1, in chapter 1 we asked, "What is an intelligent career?" and used the Dominique Browning story to illustrate the prospective fragility of success and the need for your loyalty to any employer to be conditional. We also showed how an intelligent career approach can help you adapt, develop your own talent, and pursue a journey toward authenticity in a knowledge-driven world. In Chapter 2 we considered the question "Where do intelligent careers happen?" and used the story of Shamir Palnitkar's movement between India and the United States to illustrate the importance of industry clusters and the related importance of cities and intercluster collaboration. A further set of responses to this question highlights the growth in opportunities for working away from any company office, and for delivering work—including innovative work—to a distant customer or a global team.

In Chapter 3 we asked, "Why do you work?" by opening with the example of Sarah Robinson, to show how a sense of vocation can be thwarted by the work environment. We contrasted putting bread (necessities) versus cake (for self-esteem or personal development) on the table, and explored the application of psychological ideas. We closed by suggesting your identity was a work-in-progress as you pursued fresh experiments and new connections. In Chapter 4 we raised the question "How do you work?" and drew on the Bruce Knight story to urge you to effectively combine formal education with on-the-job experience. We also suggested that development of specialized expertise, social learning, hard and soft skills, company-specific or transferable skills, and the selective use of power can all enhance your work portfolio.

In Chapter 5 we addressed the question "With whom do you work?" by using the distinctive story of Lois Weisberg to draw a contrast between strong and weak ties, and their complementary benefits to one another. Although Weisberg's story is focused on one city, much of your own social networking—with mentors, protégés, alums, volunteers, reference groups, and teams—is likely to be facilitated over the Web. Across all of these, balancing brokerage and closure is important. In Chapter 6 we asked, "When do you change?" and introduced the story of Jean-Luc Brès. We discussed how he has stayed with one company for over thirty years, yet recommends that you need to seek a new position every three years and always be mobile. He illustrates the new, less presumptive, form of employment contracting and the larger relevance of projects, time, risk, and environmental forces. Most importantly, he illustrates how change is reflected by changes in why, how, or with whom you work and in the links between them over time.

FROM REFLECTION TO ACTION

In Part 2 of this book we asked you to turn your attention from reflecting on your situation to taking action. In Chapter 7, we focused on "Making sense," beginning with a story about Barbara Harris, who acted out over-lapping roles that took her from long-serving pancake waiter to a widely publicized foundation leader. In your own intelligent career, you can wit-ness personal themes, life strands, other people's opposition and personal downfalls as you make sense of and contribute to what is going on around you. In Chapter 8, we focused on "Embracing technology" and sug-gested the advertising executive Doug Gould was working hard at that. Technology places a virtual world beside the familiar physical world. It has its critics, but the virtual world nevertheless brings on Moore's Law and a host of new opportunities for your attention. It also has the poten-tial, if you and others wish, to bring about new standards for transpar-ency for your mutual benefit.

In Chapter 9 we turned to "Investing in communities." Here, we looked at Sarah Horowitz and the "Freelancers' Union" she founded as an exam-ple of a new community form. New communities can capture personal, occupational, or entrepreneurial identities and reach deep into—and sometimes rely on—virtual space. Your own position between adjacent communities also contributes to wider intercommunity coordination. In Chapter 10, we explored "Working with employers," and showed how Pierre Albert navigated the changes in his employers' global strategies—and in turn their employment scripts—as he progressed. Understanding your company's culture, crafting your job, crossing boundaries, going up-stream of the human resources department, developing reputation, acting like a contractor, and protecting your intellectual property are all invest-ments you can make to support your side of the employment contract.

In Chapter 11, we explored "Sharing your story" and showed how the once-aspiring actress Mary Lakis leveraged her knowledge of the key elements of a classic story. Within the overall narrative of your life, you have a range of opportunities to promote "the product you" (to signal your competence) and also your personal brand (to get people to want to work with you). Along the way, you need to be able to cope with disappointment as a predictable part of your story-telling endeavors. That brings us to the present chapter on "Building your world." Here, we used the example of Moses Zulu from Zambia to show how your social world can respond to the way you compose your life, practice giving and taking, exercise humility and mindfulness, and stand up for good work and family.

Before our tour ends, we would like to emphasize a point too often neglected in self-help advice. It is that in a very real sense your own and other people's intelligent careers are interconnected. Your investments in work, life, and family are tied up with other people's investments. Your world—your personal sphere of interest, action, or thought—is interwoven with other people's worlds. Moreover, this weaving takes place across all ethnicities, religions, and nations on the planet, in both physical space and virtual space.

You matter, your career matters, your world matters. Maybe Garrison Keillor's "Be well, do good work, and keep in touch" says it better? Anyway, you get the point. We're on your team, and we'd like to hear from you sometime. We wish you well in your future intelligent career journey.

Visit us at: www.anintelligentcareer.com

INTRODUCTION
1. "Intelligence," *Oxford English Dictionary*, online version, 3rd ed. (Oxford: Oxford University Press, 2011).
2. Michael B. Arthur, Douglas T. Hall, and Barbara S. Lawrence, "Generating New Directions in Career Theory: The Case for a Transdisciplinary Approach," in *Handbook of Career Theory*, eds. Michael B. Arthur et al. (New York: Cambridge University Press: 1989), 8.
3. This definition of intelligent careers builds on an earlier one, that of "the fundamental units through which people's and employer firms' competencies evolve over time." Michael B Arthur, Priscilla H. Claman, and Robert J. DeFillippi, "Intelligent Enterprise, Intelligent Careers," *Academy of Management Executive* 9, no. 4 (1995): 9.
4. James Brian Quinn, *Intelligent Enterprise* (New York: Free Press, 1992), 151.
5. OECD, *Education at a Glance 2014: OECD Indicators*, OECD Publishing, 2014. http://dx.doi.org/10.1787/eag-2014-en. Accessed November 18, 2015.
6. *The Economist* has called this phenomenon brainpower, that is, "people's collective ability to solve complex problems." "The Battle for Brainpower," *The Economist*, October 7, 2006, 3–5.

PART 1 TAKING STOCK
1. See, for example, Daron Acemoglu and James Robinson, *Why Nations Fail: The Origins of Power, Prosperity, and Poverty* (New York: Crown Business, 2012); Thomas Piketty, *Capital in the Twenty-First Century* (Cambridge, MA: Belknap/ Harvard University Press, 2014); Joseph E. Stiglitz, *The Price of Inequality* (New York: Norton, 2012).

CHAPTER 1 WHAT DOES AN INTELLIGENT CAREER INVOLVE?
1. See http://www.dominiquebrowning.com/about.html.
2. Dominique Browning, "Losing It." *New York Times Magazine*, March 28, 2010, p. 24.
3. Browning, "Losing It."

4. Dominique Browning, *Slow Love: How I Lost My Job, Put on My Pajamas, and Found Happiness* (New York: Atlas, 2010). The nonprofit website can be found at http://www.momscleanairforce.org. Accessed December 15, 2015.

5. Edgar H. Schein, *Career Dynamics: Matching Individual and Organizational Needs* (Reading, MA: Addison-Wesley, 1978).

6. The information on IBM job reductions is taken from Denis Kneale, "Tough Choices," *Wall Street Journal*, April 8, 1987, p. 1; Michael W. Miller, "IBM's Gerstner, in Public Debut, Vows to Cut More and Emphasize Services," *Wall Street Journal*, April 27, 1993, p. A3, Eastern edition; Laurie Hays, "IBM's Helmsman Indicates That Bulk of Layoffs Is Over—An Upbeat Gerstner Employs Wind-Direction Similes and Hints at Uses for Cash," *Wall Street Journal* January 6, 1995, p. B3, Eastern edition. The IBM internal document of 1984 was at http://www.03. ibm.com/ibm/history/exhibits/watsonjr/watsonjr_leaving.html. It was accessed on December 1, 2012, but has since been removed.

7. See, for example, Alexander M. Danzer and Peter J. Dolton, "Total Reward and Pensions in the UK in the Public and Private Sectors," *Labour Economics* 19 (2012): 584–594; Thom Reilly, "Comparing Public-versus-Private Sector Pay and Benefits: Examining Lifetime Compensation," *Public Personnel Management* 42, no. 4 (2013): 521–544.

8. Alan Feuer, "Bleak Day at the Bar," *New York Times*, June 7, 2009, p. 1. The *American Lawyer* reported that 2009 was a particularly bleak year for US lawyers. See http://www. americanlawyer.com/id=1202425647706/THE-LAYOFF-LIST. As this book goes to press, White & Case has continued to shed lawyers, although its number of partners has stabilized. See Natalie Rodriguez, "White & Case Sees 10% Atty Drop as Profits Come to Focus," *Law360*, March 16, 2015, http://www.law360.com/articles/631164/ white-case-sees-10-atty-drop-as-profits-come-to-focus. Accessed December 15, 2015.

9. Feuer, "Bleak Day at the Bar."

10. Edgar H. Schein, "Foreword: Career Research, Some Personal Perspectives," in *Handbook of Career Studies*, eds. Hugh Gunz and Maury Peiperl (Thousand Oaks, CA: Sage, 2007), ix.

11. Sources: Terry Smith, "A sound visionary," *The Sun Herald* (Sydney, Australia), August 16, 2009, p. 8; Jeff Price, "The Democratization of the Music Industry," *Huffington Post*, March 24, 2008; Elizabeth Lazarowitz, "Brooklyn-Based Web Business Helps Sell Music in the Digital World," *New York Daily News*, November 25, 2007, http://www.nydailynews.com/money/2007/11/26/2007-11-26_brooklynbased_web_business_helps_sell_mu.html.

12. Jeff Price was abruptly fired in August 2012: http://www.digitalmusicnews.com/ permalink/2012/120815price. This link was accessed on December 1, 2012, but has since been removed. Price's latest venture is to help music providers get paid when their work is played on YouTube: http://www.digitalmusicnews.com/per-malink/2014/03/04/audiam2mil. Accessed December 15, 2015.

13. In 2006, the job-posting site monster.com was among the 20 most visited sites in the world. See http://en.wikipedia.org/wiki/Monster.com. Accessed December 15, 2015. Since then, the pecking order of online job search sites has changed, and job search activities have moved on to make greater use of social networking. See, for

example, Arnie Fertig, "10 Emerging Job Search Tips and Tactics," *US News and World Report*, Money, March 4, 2014.

14. Peter F. Drucker, *Landmarks of Tomorrow* (New York: Harper, 1957), 64.

15. See Peter F. Drucker, "The Age of Social Transformation," *Atlantic Weekly*, November 1994, 53–78. In this, Drucker reverses a 1942 argument that the workplace ought to provide lifetime employment and other social benefits.

16. Cited in "The Battle for Brainpower," *The Economist*, October 7, 2006, 3–5.

17. For a US perspective, see Anthony P. Carnevale, Nicole Smith, and Jeff Stroh, *Recovery: Job Growth and Education Requirements through 1920* (Center on Education and the Workforce, Georgetown University, 2013), http://cew.georgetown.edu/recovery2020.

18. The data come from the website http://www.internetworldstats.com/stats.htm. Accessed December 15, 2015. The website reports that the "Internet usage information comes from data published by Nielsen Online, the International Telecommunications Union, GfK, local ICT Regulators and other reliable sources."

19. The quotes are to be found in Thomas L. Friedman, *The World Is Flat* (New York: Farrer Straus & Giroux, 2005), 6–7.

20. Staffan Nilsson and Per-Erik Ellström, "Employability and Talent Management: Challenges for HRD Practices," *European Journal of Training and Development* 36, no. 1 (2012): 26–45.

21. Ed Michaels and Helen Handfield-Jones, *The War for Talent* (Boston: Harvard Business School Publishing, 2001).

22. Stuart Elliott and Richard Pérez-Peña, "Publication to Cease for *House & Garden*," *New York Times*, November 6, 2007, http://www.nytimes.com/2007/11/06/business/media/06mag.html?module=Search&mabReward=relbias%3Aw%2C%7B%221%22%3A%22RI%3A9%22%7D. Accessed December 15, 2015.

23. Kerr E. Inkson, *Understanding Careers: The Metaphors of Working Lives* (Thousand Oaks, CA: Sage, 2007), 202.

24. Adam Bryant, "Google's Quest to Build a Better Boss," *New York Times*, March 12, 2011, http://www.nytimes.com/2011/03/13/business/13hire.html?pagewanted=all&_r=1&.

25. David Clutterbuck, *The Talent Wave: Why Succession Planning Fails and What to Do about It* (London, Kogan Page, 2012), 112.

26. Katharine Mieszkowski, "The Revolt of the Wage Slave," *Salon*, May 31, 2001, http://Www.Salon.Com/2001/05/31/Free_Agent/. Accessed December 15, 2015.

27. Daniel H. Pink, *Free Agent Nation: The Future of Working for Yourself* (New York: Warner Books, 2001).

28. Bernie Trilling and Charles Fadel, *21st Century Skills: Learning for Life in Our Times* (San Francisco: Jossey Bass, 2009).

29. Stefan Stern, "Which Brings Me to the Subject of Casinos" *The Financial Times Magazine*, February 20, 2010, 10.

30. See James B. Stewart, "The Omen: How an Obscure Breton Trader Gamed Oversight Weaknesses in the Banking System," *New Yorker*, October 20, 2008, 54ff. The Kerviel quote in the previous paragraph is from Scheherazade Daneshkhu, "Rogue Trader Reflects on 'banking orgy." *Financial Times*, May

8, 2010, p. 18. The Casino quote is from Stefan Stern, "Which Brings Me to the Subject of Casinos," *Financial Times*, Magazine Section, p. 10.

31. The quote can be found at https://www.w3.org/People/maxf/XSLideMaker/ hamlet.pdf, page 22. Accessed on June 25, 2016.

32. Robert W. Lent, "Career-Life Preparedness: Revisiting Career Planning and Adjustment in the New Workplace," *Career Development Quarterly* 61 (March 2013); Mark L. Savickas, "Life Design: A Paradigm for Career Intervention in the 21st Century," *Journal of Counseling and Development* 90 (January 2012).

33. Source: Julia Richardson and Jelena Zikic, "Unlocking the Careers of Business Professionals Following Job Loss: Sensemaking and Career Exploration of Older Workers," *Canadian Journal of Administrative Sciences* 24, no. 1 (2007): 58–73.

34. ["Authenticity," *Oxford English Dictionary*, online version, 3rd ed. (Oxford: Oxford University Press, 2011. Definition 3.d.).

35. Rebecca R. Ruiz and Victore Mather, "The FIFA Scandal: What's Happened and What's to Come," *New York Times*, September 25, 2015.

36. Source: Andrew Potter, *The Authenticity Hoax* (New York: Harper, 2010). Both quotes are from page 4.

37. Lisa A. Mainero and Sherry E. Sullivan, *The Opt-Out Revolt* (Mountain View, CA: Davis-Black: 2006), 165.

38. Richard A. Peterson, "In Search of Authenticity," *Journal of Management Studies* 42, no. 5 (2005): 1083–1098.

39. Silviya Svejenova, "'The Path with the Heart': Creating the Authentic Career," *Journal of Management Studies* 42, no. 5 (2005): 947–974.

40. Svejenova, "'The Path with the Heart'" 947.

41. Svejenova, "'The Path with the Heart'" 966.

CHAPTER 2   WHERE DO INTELLIGENT CAREERS HAPPEN?

1. Michael Arthur, personal interview with Samir Palnitkar. We deeply appreciate his collaboration. We are also grateful to C. Gopinath and Ashok Benegal for the introduction.

2. Alfred Marshall, *Principles of Economics*, 3rd ed. (London: Macmillan: 1895), 1:352. The use of the masculine pronoun has been edited out. The original text of the final phrase is "and in many ways conducing to the economy of its material."

3. See   http://www.chinasourcingblog.org/Industrial%20Clusters.png.   Accessed December 16, 2015.

4. Michael E. Porter, *The Competitive Advantage of Nations* (New York: Free Press, 1990) and "Clusters and the New Economics of Competition," *Harvard Business Review* 76 (November–December 1998): 77–90; Mercedes Delgado, Michael E. Porter, and Scott Stern, "Clusters and Entrepreneurship," *Journal of Economic Geography* 10, no. 4 (2010): 495–518.

5. Anna Lee Saxenian, *Regional Advantage: Culture and Competition in Silicon Valley and Route 128* (Cambridge, MA: Harvard University Press, 1994).

6. Patti Ryan, "Bangalore Calling," *National: Magazine of the Canadian Bar Association* (April–May 2011): 16–21. http://southsidecommunications.ca/wp-content/uploads/2013/05/Bangalore-Calling-CBA-National-April-May-2011.pdf. Accessed December 16, 2016.

7. International players in the legal process outsourcing field include Mincrest, Quislex, CPA Global, Evalueserve, and Pangea 3.

8. Susan Adams, "The Shrink Wrap King," *Forbes Magazine*, March 15, 2010. http://www.forbes.com/forbes/2010/0315/second-acts-plastic-fast-wrap-franchise-shrink-wrap-king.html.

9. See http://localvox.com/blog/franchise-facts/. Accessed on June 27, 2016.

10. Donna Kelley, Slavicia Singer and Mark Herrington, "Global Entrepreneurship Monitor 2015/16 Gobal Report." Available at http://gemconsortium.org/report/49480. Accessed on June 27, 2016.

11. See, for example, the European Franchising Federation data at http://www.eff-franchise.com/spip.php?rubrique9. Accessed February 18, 2016. See also Alison Notley, "Franchising—An Engine of Economic Growth and Transformation." http://www.realsuccess.net/franchising-an-engine-of-economic-growth-and-transformation/. Accessed December 16, 2015.

12. See, for example, Catherine Waldby, "Singapore Biopolis: Bare Life in the City-State," *East Asian Science, Technology and Society* 3 (2009): 367–383; "G20 Report on Job Creation," 2013, www.g20russia.ru/load/781688793 (accessed December 16, 2015); and Chun Han Wong, "Singapore Tightens Hiring Rules for Foreign Skilled Labor," *Wall Street Journal Asia*, September 23, 2013.

13. This section draws heavily on Anne Lee Saxenian, *The New Argonauts: Regional Advantage in the Global Economy* (Cambridge, MA: Harvard University Press, 2006).

14. Manuel Polèse, *The Wealth and Poverty of Nations: Why Cities Matter* (Chicago: University of Chicago Press, 2009).

15. Peter Hall, "Creative Cities and Economic Development," *Urban Studies* 37, no. 4 (2009): 639.

16. Richard Florida, *The Rise of the Creative Class* (New York, Basic Books, 2002).

17. Jenna Wortham, "Coming Together in New York: Proximity and Variety Contribute to a Revival of City as a Digital Hotbed," *International Herald Tribune*, March 8, 2010: Finance Section, p. 2.

18. See Polèse, *The Wealth*, 17–28, on history and industrial legacies.

19. "Clusters Flustered: Global Competition Seems to Be Weakening the Benefits of Being in a Cluster," *The Economist*, April 14, 2011. http://www.economist.com/node/18560669. Accessed December 16, 2016.

20. The quotes are from Susanne Tietze and Gill Musson, "Identity, Identity Work and the Experience of Working from Home," *Journal of Management Development* 29, no. 2 (2010): 148–156.

21. See also Julia Richardson, "The Manager and the Flexworker: An Interpretive Interactionist Perspective," *Management Revue* 20, no. 1 (2009): 34–52.

22. Diane Palframan, "Europe's Progress in Promoting Work-Life and Diversity in the Workplace," Executive Action Series, Ottawa, ON: The Conference Board of Canada, 2007.

23. Donna S. Lero, Julia Richardson, and Karen Korabik, "A Cost-Benefit Analysis of Work-Life Balance Practices," Canadian Association of Labour Legislation, Toronto, 2009.

24. The story has been told in a variety of places. For a summary, see Robert J. DeFillippi, Michael B. Arthur, and Valerie J. Lindsay, *Knowledge at Work* (Oxford: Blackwell, 2006), 60–61.

25. Gilbert Probst and Stefano Borzillo, "Why Communities of Practice Succeed and Why They Fail," *European Management Journal* 26, no. 5 (2008): 335–347.

26. Brigid Schulte, *Overwhelmed: How to Work, Love, and Play When No One Has the Time* (New York: Picador, 2015).

27. Jenna Goudreau, "Back to the Stone Age? New Yahoo CEO Marissa Mayer Bans Working from Home," *Forbes*, February 25, 2014.

28. The research was performed by Global Workforce Analytics. See http://global-workplaceanalytics.com/telecommuting-statistics. Accessed December 16, 2015

29. Donald Hislop and Caroline Axtell, "To Infinity and Beyond? Workspace and the Multi-Location Worker? *New Technology, Work and Employment* 24, no. 1 (2009): 60–75, and "Mobile Phones during Work and Non-Work Time: A Case Study of Mobile, Non-Managerial Workers," *Information and Organization* 21, no. 1 (2011): 41–56.

30. Flávio Nunes, "Most Relevant Enablers and Constraints Influencing the Spread of Telework in Portugal," *New Technology, Work and Employment* 20, no. 2 (2005): 133–149.

31. Matti Vartiainen and Ursula Hyrkkänen, "Changing Requirements and Mental Workload Factors in Mobile Multi-Locational Work," *New Technology, Work and Employment* 25, no. 2 (2010): 117–135; Ursula Hyrkkänen and Matti Vartiainen, "Looking for People, Places and Connections: Hindrances When Working in Multiple Locations: A Review," *New Technology, Work and Employment* 29, no. 2 (2014): 139–159.

32. This story is drawn from Jeff Howe, *Crowdsourcing* (New York: Three Rivers Press, 2009). Later references to Sgargetta and InnoCentive are from the same source.

33. Henry W. Chesborough, "The Era of Open Innovation," *MIT Sloan Management Review* 44, no. 3 (2003): 38.

34. Frank T. Piller, "Lego Bridges Mass Customization and Open Innovation with Lego-Factory Website." http://mass-customization.blogs.com/mass_customization_open_i/2005/08/lego_factory_ch.html.

35. It is an open question how much the arrangement suits Giorgia Sgargetta or others in her family. Some commentators would criticize the loss of family time, others would celebrate that in this family women's work is taken seriously.

36. See https://automattic.com/work-with-us/. Accesssed on June 25, 2016.

CHAPTER 3 WHY DO YOU WORK?

1. This story is based on an article by Jennifer Sumsion, "Becoming, Being and Unbecoming an Early Childhood Educator: A Phenomenological Case Study of Teacher Attrition," *Teaching and Teacher Education* 18 (2002): 869–885. Sarah Robinson is a pseudonym. On the Reggio Emilia system, see Kathie Ardzejewska and Pamela M. Coutts, "Teachers Who Support Reggio: Exploring Their Understandings of the Philosophy," *Australian Journal of Early Childhood* 29, no. 4 (December 1, 2004): 869–885.

2. Frank Parsons, *Choosing a Vocation* (Boston: Houghton Mifflin, 1909), 3–4.
3. Edwin L. Herr, "Career Development and Vocational Guidance," in *Education and Work*, ed. Harry F. Silberman, Yearbook of the National Society for the Study of Education, vol. 81, part 2 (Chicago, IL: National Society for the Study of Education, 1982).
4. George Packer, "The Talk of the Town," *New Yorker*, July 25, 2011, 23–24.
5. Douglas A. McIntyre et al., "The 15 Highest Unemployment Rates in the World," *Atlantic*, June 29, 2010. http://www.theatlantic.com/business/archive/2010/06/the-15-highest-unemployment-rates-in-the-world/58706/. Accessed on December 15, 2015.
6. See, for example, Lotte Bailyn, *Breaking the Mold: Redesigning Work for Productive and Satisfying Lives*, 2nd ed. (Ithaca, NY: Cornell University Press: 2006).
7. M.T. Magombeyi and N. M. Odhiambo, "Poverty Dynamics in South Africa: Trends, Policies and Challenges," Socioeconomica – The Scientific Journal for Theory and Practice of Socio-economic Development 2015, 4(8): 333-348.
8. Donald H. Blocher, *The Evolution of Counseling Psychology* (New York: Springer, 2000), 15.
9. Herr, "Career Development," 129.
10. *Collins English Dictionary: Complete and Unabridged* (New York: HarperCollins Publishers, 2003), emphasis added.
11. John L. Holland, *Making Vocational Choices: A Theory of Vocational Personalities and Work Environments*, 2nd ed. (Englewood Cliffs, NJ: Prentice Hall, 1985). On international adoption of Holland's and related ideas, see S. Alvin Leung, "The Big Five Career Theories," in *International Handbook of Career Guidance*, ed. James A. Athanasou and R. Van Esbroeck (New York: Springer, 2008), 115–132.
12. Dan P. McAdams and Bradley D. Olson, "Personality Development: Continuity and Change Over the Life Course," *Annual Review of Psychology*, Vol. 61: 517–542.
13. Isabel Briggs Myers with Peter B. Myers, *Gifts Differing: Understanding Personality Type* (Mountain View, CA: Davies-Black, 1980, 1995).
14. As of April 2011, CPP (formerly Consulting Psychologists' Press), the publisher of the MBTI, was claiming it to be "the world's most trusted personality assessment." See https://www.cpp.com/products/mbti/index.aspx. For a more questioning perspective see David J. Pittenger, "Cautionary comments regarding the Myers-Briggs Type Indicator" Consulting Psychology Journal: Practice and Research, Vol 57(3), 2005, 210–221.
15. Edgar H. Schein, *Career Anchors Participant Workbook*, 3rd ed. (San Francisco: Pfeiffer, 2006), 27.
16. Polly Parker, Ilene Wasserman, Kathy E. Kram, and Douglas T. Hall, "A Relational Communication Approach to Peer Coaching," *Journal of Applied Behavioral Science* 51, no. 2 (2015): 231–252.
17. Heather E. P. Cattell and Alan D. Mead, "The Sixteen Personality Factor Questionnaire (16PF)," In *The Sage Handbook of Personality Theory and Assessment*, ed. G. Boyle, G. Matthews, and D. Saklofske (London: Sage, 2010), 2:135–159.

18. These points are covered in Murray R. Barrick and Michael K. Mount, "The Big Five Personality Dimensions and Job Performance: A Meta-Analysis," *Personnel Psychology* 44 (1991): 1–26; Gregory M. Hurtz and John J. Donovan, "Personality and Job Performance: The Big Five Revisited," *Journal of Applied Psychology* 85, no. 6 (2000): 869–879; and Nathan R. Kuncel and Sarah A. Hezlett, "Fact and Fiction in Cognitive Ability: Testing for Admissions and Hiring Decisions," *Current Directions in Psychological Science* 19, no. 6 (2010): 339–345.

19. See Ian Taylor, *The Assessment and Selection Handbook: Tools, Techniques and Exercises for Effective Recruitment and Development* (London: Kogan Page 2008), 4.

20. Sara A. Begley, Julia Y. Trankiem, and Sarah T. Hansel, "Employers Using Personality Tests to Vet Applicants Need Cautious 'Personalities' of Their Own," *Forbes*, October 30, 2014. http://www.forbes.com/sites/theemploymentbeat/2014/10/30/employers-using-personality-tests-to-vet-applicants-need-cautious-personalities-of-their-own/. Accessed December 15, 2015. Or see the advice given by Erica Klein, "Employment Tests: Get an Edge," *Ask the Headhunter*. http://www.asktheheadhunter.com/gv000802.htm. Accessed December 15, 2015.

21. Marcus Buckingham and Curt Coffman, *First, Break All the Rules* (New York: Simon & Schuster, 1999).

22. Marcus Buckingham and Donald O. Clifton, *Now, Discover Your Strengths* (New York: Free Press, 2001); Marcus Buckingham, *Go Put Your Strengths to Work* (New York: Free Press, 2007).

23. Martin E. Seligman, "The President's Address," *American Psychologist* 54 (1999): 559–562.

24. Current information about the center's activities and publications can be found at http://www.centerforpos.org/. Accessed December 15, 2015.

25. The first Harvard course on positive psychology was taught by Tal Ben-Shahar, assisted by Sean Acher. See Tal Ben-Shahar, *Happier* (New York: McGraw-Hill, 2007); Sean Acher, *The Happiness Advantage* (New York: Crown, 2010).

26. Topics in this paragraph are covered in Kristján Kristjánsson, "Positive Psychology and Positive Education: Old Wine in New Bottles?" *Educational Psychologist* 47, no. 2 (2011): 86–105. More extensive coverage is provided in Kristján Kristjánsson, *Virtues and Vices in Positive Psychology: A Philosophical Critique* (Cambridge: Cambridge University Press, 2013). A further vocal critic was a PhD biologist who claimed cited research did not meet established scholarly standards. See Barbara Ehrenreich, *Bright-sided: How the Relentless Promotion of Positive Thinking Has Undermined America* (New York: Metropolitan Books, 2009).

27. Ryan D. Duffy and Bryan J. Dik, "Research on Calling: What Have We Learned and Where Are We Going?" *Journal of Vocational Behavior* 83, no. 3 (2013): 428–436.

28. Douglas "Tim" Hall, *Careers in and out of Organizations* (Thousand Oaks, CA: Sage, 2002).

29. Amy Wrzesniewski, Clark McCauley, Paul Rozin, and Barry Schwartz, "Jobs, Careers, and Callings: People's Relations to Their Work," *Journal of Research In Personality* 31 (1997): 21–33; Peter A. Heslin, "Experiencing Career Success," *Organizational Dynamics* 34, no. 4 (2005): 376–390.

30. J. Stuart Bunderson and Jeffery A. Thompson, "The Call of the Wild: Zookeepers, Callings, and the Double-Edged Sword of Deeply Meaningful Work," *Administrative Science Quarterly* 54 (2009): 32–57.

31. Heslin, "Experiencing Career Success," 385.

32. Jennifer Sumsion, "Bad Days Don't Kill You; They Just Make You Stronger," *International Journal of Early Years Education* 11, no. 2 (2003): 141–154. Natalie Jones is a pseudonym.

33. Jennifer Sumsion, "Workplace Violence in Early Childhood Settings: A Counter-Narrative," *Contemporary Issues in Early Childhood* 2, no. 2 (2001): 195–208.

34. Ardzejewska and Coutts, "Teachers Who Support Reggio."

35. Herminia Ibarra, "How to Stay Stuck in the Wrong Career," *Harvard Business Review*, 80, no. 12 (2002): 40–48, 42.

36. This can include further development as a leader, as Ibarra emphasizes in a later book: Herminia Ibarra, *Act Like a Leader, Think Like a Leader*, Boston, MA: Harvard Business School Press, 2015.

37. Our argument here overlaps with and takes encouragement from the recent work of Swarthmore College psychology professor Barry Schwartz. See Barry Schwartz, *Why We Work*. New York, TED Books, Simon & Schuster, 2015.

CHAPTER 4 HOW DO YOU WORK?

1. Material taken from a personal interview with Michael Arthur. The name has been disguised.

2. Edith T. Penrose, *The Theory of the Growth of the Firm* (Oxford: Basil Blackwell, 1959).

3. Gary S. Becker, "'Bribe' Third World Parents to Keep Their Kids in School," *Business Week*, November 22, 1999, 15.

4. Richard A. Settersten, and Barbara E. Ray, *Not Quite Adults: Why 20-Somethings Are Choosing a Slower Path to Adulthood, and Why It's Good for Everyone* (New York: Bantam, 2010).

5. Settersten and Ray, *Not Quite*, xii.

6. http://www.mytopbusinessideas.com/school-drop-out-billionaires-successful-entrepreneurs/. Accessed December 16, 2015.

7. K. Anders Ericsson, Michael J. Prietula, and Edward T. Cokely, "The Making of an Expert," *Harvard Business Review*, July–August 2007, 115–121, 116.

8. Malcolm Gladwell, *Outliers: The Story of Success* (New York: Little, Brown, 2008), 35–56. Further Beatles information is taken from Philip Norman, *Shout!* (New York: Fireside, 2003).

9. Ericsson, Prietula, and Cokely, "The Making of an Expert," 119.

10. Albert Bandura, *Social Learning Theory* (New York: General Learning Press, 1977).

11. John D. Krumboltz, "Improving Career Development Theory from a Social Learning Perspective," in *Convergence in Career Development Theories*, ed Mark L. Savickas and Robert W. Lent (Palo Alto, CA: CPP Books, 1994), 9–31; Robert W. Lent, Steven D. Brown, and Gail Hackett, "Towards a Unifying Social Cognitive Theory of Career and Academic Interest, Choice and Performance," *Journal of Vocational Behavior* 45, no. 1 (1994): 79–122.

12. William J. Wilson, *The Truly Disadvantaged: The Inner City, the Underclass, and Public Policy* Second Edition. (Chicago: University of Chicago Press, 2012), 60–61.

13. Daniel Goleman, "What Makes a Leader?" *Harvard Business Review*, January 2004, 82–91. (Reprint of *Harvard Business Review*, November-December 1998, 93–102.)

14. Edgar H. Schein, "Career Anchors Revisited," *Academy of Management Executive* 10, no. 4 (1996): 81–89.

15. Goleman, "What Makes a Leader?" 82.

16. Monica Hamori, "Job Hopping to the Top and Other Fallacies," *Harvard Business Review*, July–August 2010, 156.

17. Adapted from Boris Groysberg, Andrew N. McClean, and Nitin Nohria, "Are Leaders Portable?" *Harvard Business Review*, May 2006, 92–100.

18. D. A. Ready, J. A. Conger, and L. A. Hill, "Are You a High Potential?" *Harvard Business Review*, June 2010, 78–84.

19. Schumpeter, "The Tussle for Talent," *The Economist*, January 8, 2011, 68.

20. Jeffrey Pfeffer, "Power Play," *Harvard Business* Review, July–August 2010, 84. Pfeffer keeps up the criticism in a more recent book: Jeffrey Pfeffer, *Leadership BS* (New York, Harper Collins, 2015).

21. Jeffrey Pfeffer, *Power: Why Some People Have It—And Others Don't* (New York: HarperBusiness, 2010), 5.

22. Pfeffer, "Power Play," 86.

23. Subsequent to the publication of Pfeffer's work, the BCCI board reelected none other than Jagmohan Dalmiya, the president Lalit Modi had originally opposed, as acting president in 2013. Dalmiya was elected as president again in 2015, but died in office shortly after. See https://en.wikipedia.org/wiki/List_of_Board_of_Control_for_Cricket_in_India_presidents.

24. Charles Handy, *The Age of Unreason* (London: Hutchinson, 1989), 183.

25. Charles Handy, *Beyond Certainty* (London: Hutchinson, 1995), 27.

26. Handy's latest book anticipates a "second curve" in which the world will needs to correct the excesses signaled by the financial crisis of 2008 and other global disruptions, sees little future value in "big, ageing, bloated and selfish organizations." Consistent with the portfolio approach, he sees a "new curve of work, with formal careers for many finishing earlier and many more people turning to self-employment." Charles Handy, *The Second Curve*, London, Penguin Random House.

27. Barrie Hopson and Katie Ledger, *And What Do You Do? 10 Steps to Creating a Portfolio Career* (London: A & C Black, 2009), 5.

28. Rachel Nelken, "Portfolio Careers in the Arts," *Guardian Professional*, 2003. http://www.theguardian.com/culture-professionals-network/culture-professionals-blog/2013/mar/05/arts-portfolio-careers-top-tips. Accessed December 16, 2016.

29. Hopson and Ledger, *And What Do You Do?*, 104.

CHAPTER 5 WITH WHOM DO YOU WORK?

1. Malcom Gladwell, "Six Degrees of Lois Weisberg," *New Yorker*, January 11, 1999. The preceding quotes are on page 54. An abridged version of the story appears in Malcolm Gladwell, *The Tipping Point* (New York: Little Brown, 2000): 49–53.

Additional material is drawn from "Lois Weisberg talks about life after the Cultural Center" http://www.chicagobusiness.com/article/20120128/ISSUE01/301289970/weisberg-moves-on-wraps-up-her-past. Accessed May10, 2016.

2. Rick Kogan, "City's Culture Guru Leaving amid Rift with Daley," *Chicago Tribune*, January 19, 2011. http://articles.chicagotribune.com/2011-01-19/entertainment/ct-live-0120-weisberg-quits-20110119_1_maggie-daley-lois-weisberg-cultural-affairs. Accessed June 5, 2015.

3. Mark Granovetter, "The Strength of Weak Ties," *American Journal of Sociology* 78, (1973): 1371.

4. Ronald S. Burt, *Brokerage and Closure: An Introduction to Social Capital* (Oxford: Oxford University Press, 2005), 4.

5. Burt, *Brokerage and Closure*, 96.

6. Ronald S. Burt, "Network Strategy," *Advances in Strategic Management* 25 (2008): 315–360.

7. Gernot Grahber, "The Project Ecology of Advertising: Tasks, Talents and Teams," *Regional Studies* 36, no. 3 (2002): 245–262.

8. Pam Lassiter, *The New Job Security: The 5 Best Strategies for Taking Control of Your Career*, rev. ed. (Berkeley, CA: Ten Speed Press, 2010), 123–124.

9. Lassiter, *The New Job Security*, 126–129.

10. Hugang Lijie, "Fired by Passion," *The Straits Times* (Singapore), May 18, 2009.

11. Kathy E. Kram, *Mentoring at Work: Developmental Relationships in Organizational Life* (Glenview, IL: Scott Foresman, 1985); Monica C. Higgins and Kathy E. Kram, "Reconceptualizing Mentoring at Work: A Developmental Network Perspective," *Academy of Management Review* 26, no. 2 (2002): 264–288.

12. Lijie, "Fired by Passion."

13. Kathy E. Kram and Monica C. Higgins, "A New Approach to Mentoring," *Wall Street Journal*, September 22, 2008. http://www.wsj.com/articles/SB122160063875344843. Accessed June 5, 2015.

14. Erin Millar, "Reading, Writing, Networking: An Old Boys' Network? Current Educators See Long-Lasting Personal Links as a Natural Outcome of a Rich Educational Experience," *The Globe and Mail* (Canada), September 17, 2009, p. E3.

15. Polly Parker and Michael B. Arthur, "Careers, Organizing and Community," in *Career Frontiers: New Conceptions of Working Lives*, eds. Maury A. Peiperl, Michael B. Arthur, Rob Goffee, and Tim Morris (Oxford: Oxford University Press, 2000), 99–121.

16. Rebecca F. Taylor, "Extending Conceptual Boundaries: Work, Voluntary Work and Employment," *Work Employment and Society* 18, no. 1 (2004): 29–41.

17. John Raynolds, *The Halo Effect: How Volunteering Can Lead to a More Fulfilling Life—And a Better Career* (New York: Golden Books, 1998).

18. Taylor, "Extending Conceptual Boundaries," 35.

19. Raynolds, *The Halo Effect*.

20. Jeff Howe, *Crowdsourcing: Why the Power of the Crowd Is Driving the Future of Business* (New York: Three Rivers Press, 2008).

21. Gudela Grote and Douglas T. Hall, "Reference Groups: A Missing Link in Career Studies," *Journal of Vocational Behavior* 83 (2013): 265–279.
22. Barbara S. Lawrence, "Organizational Reference Groups: A Missing Perspective on Social Context," *Organization Science* 17, no. 1 (2006): 80–100.
23. Robert K. Merton, *Social Theory and Social Structure* (New York: Free Press, 1957), chapter 12; Alvin W. Gouldner, "Cosmopolitans and Locals: Toward an Analysis of Latent Social Roles. I," *Administrative Science Quarterly* 2 (1957): 281–306, and "Cosmopolitans and Locals: Toward an Analysis of Latent Social Roles. II," *Administrative Science Quarterly* 2 (1958): 444–480.
24. John Van Maanen and Stephen R. Barley, "Occupational Communities: Culture and Control in Organizations," in *Research in Organizational Behavior*, eds. Barry Staw and Larry Cummings (Greenwich, CT: JAI Press, 1984).
25. Noriko Hara and Khe Foon Hew, "Knowledge Sharing in an On-Line Community of Healthcare Professionals," *Information Technology and People* 20, no. 3 (2007): 235–261.
26. See, for example, Jennifer Duncan-Howell, "Teachers Making Connections: Online Communities as a Source of Professional Learning," *British Journal of Educational Technology* 41, no. 2 (2010): 324–340.
27. Amy C. Edmonson, *Teaming: How Organizations Learn, Innovate and Compete in the Knowledge Economy* (New York: Wiley, 2012).
28. Amy Edmondson, *Teaming*, 56–58.
29. Burt, *Brokerage and Closure*, 44–46.

CHAPTER 6   WHEN DO YOU CHANGE?

1. We are deeply grateful to Loic Cadin for providing this story, and to Jean-Luc Brès for allowing his own and his company's name to be used.
2. Denise M. Rousseau, *Psychological Contracts in Organizations: Understanding Written and Unwritten Agreements* (Thousand Oaks, CA: Sage 1995), xiii.
3. Denise M. Rousseau, *I-Deals: Idiosyncratic Deals Employees Bargain for Themselves* (Armonk, NY: M. E. Sharpe, 2005).
4. Rousseau, *I-Deals*, 209.
5. Tom Schuller, Cathie Hammond, and John Preston, "The Benefits of Adult Learning: Quantitative Insights," in *The Benefits of Learning: The Impact of Education on Health, Family Life and Social Capital*, ed. Tom Schuller (Abingdon, Oxford: RoutledgeFarmer, 2004), 190.
6. Kathryn Anne Edwards and Alexander Hertel-Fernandez, "The Kids Aren't Alright: A Labor Market Analysis of Young Workers," EPI Briefing Paper #258, Washington, DC: Economic Policy Institute, 2010.
7. Susan Bisom-Rapp, Andrew Frazer, and Malcolm Sargeant, "Decent Work, Older Workers and Vulnerability in the Economic Recession: A Comparative Study of Australia, the United Kingdom, and the United States," *Employee Rights and Employment Policy Journal* 15, no. 1 (2011): 43–121.
8. Denis Nishi, "A Tale of a Young Boxer's Redemption," *Wall Street Journal*, December 2, 2008, http://www.bizjournals.com/sacramento/stories/2008/05/19/

story13.html (accessed June 5, 2015); and Gloria Young, "Company's Downsizing Impacts Businesses at Airport Industrial Park," *Auburn Journal*, March 23, 2010, http://auburnjournal.com/detail/145467.html. Accessed June 5 2015.

9. Michael Ryval, "I Found Myself. That's What Motivated Me," *The Globe and Mail*, Toronto, January 26, 2008, p. E2.

10. Jelena Zikic and Ute-Christine Klehe, "Job Loss as a Blessing in Disguise: The Role of Career Exploration and Career Planning in Predicting Reemployment Quality," *Journal of Vocational Behavior* 69 (2006): 391–409.

11. Steve Johnson, *Where Good Ideas Come From* (New York: Riverside Books, 2010), 25–42. The three founders of YouTube were Steve Chen, Chad Hurley, and Jawed Karim.

12. Johnson, *Where Good Ideas*, 31.

13. Underlying theory is covered in, for example, Michael B. Arthur, Priscilla H. Claman, and Robert J. DeFillippi, "Intelligent Enterprise, Intelligent Careers," *Academy of Management Executive* 9, no. 4 (1995): 7–22; Kerr Inkson and Michael B. Arthur, "How to Be a Successful Career Capitalist," *Organizational Dynamics* 30, no. 1 (2001): 48–61; and Polly Parker, Svetlana N. Khapova, and Michael B. Arthur, "The Intelligent Career Framework as a Basis for Interdisciplinary Inquiry," *Journal of Vocational Behavior* 75, (2009): 291–302.

14. Michael B. Arthur, Robert J. DeFillippi, and Valerie J Lindsay, "On Being a Knowledge Worker," *Organizational Dynamics* 37, no. 4 (2008): 365–377.

15. Malcolm Gladwell, "Late Bloomers: Why Do We Equate Genius with Precocity?" *The New Yorker*, October 20, 2008, 38. For more on the Picasso versus Cezanne contrast, see David W. Galenson, *Old Masters and Young Geniuses: The Two Life Cycles of Artistic Creativity* (Princeton, NJ: Princeton University Press, 2007).

16. Lassiter, *The New Job Security*, rev. ed. (Berkeley, CA: Ten Speed Press, 2010), 93–94.

17. Herminia Ibarra and Jennifer L. Petriglieri, "Identity Work and Play," *Journal of Organizational Change Management* 23, no. 1 (2010): 10–25.

18. Sources: Plato's *Republic* (Black and White Classics. Edinburgh, 2014): 132–133; and Wikipedia, "Allegory of the Cave," http://en.wikipedia.org/wiki/Allegory_of_the_Cave. Accessed June 15, 2015. For a three-and-a-half-minute movie, see http://platosallegory.com/. Accessed June 5, 2015.

19. One way to do this is by using the *Intelligent Career Card Sort* (ICCS), through which you can work with a career consultant, coach, or instructor to reflect on your own career using the framework from Figure 6.2. This can be done either individually or in a workshop group. More information can be found at http://www.intelligentcareer.net.

20. Lassiter, *The New Job Security*, 93–94.

PART 2 TAKING ACTION

1. Carl Benedikt Frey and Michael A. Osborne, "The Future of Employment: How Susceptible Are Jobs to Computerisation?" Working paper, Oxford Martin program, Oxford University, September 13, 2013.

2. PWC, "People Strategy for the Digital Age: A New Take on Talent—18th Annual Global CEO Survey. http://www.pwc.com/gx/en/services/people-organisation/publications/people-strategy.html. Accessed December 22, 2015.

3. "There's an App for That." *The Economist*, January 3, 2015. http://www.economist.com/news/briefing/21637355-freelance-workers-available-moments-notice-will-reshape-nature-companies-and. Accessed December 22, 2015.

CHAPTER 7 MAKING SENSE

1. "What If There Was No Destiny?" *Radiolab*, Season 11, Episode 2, 2012. http://www.radiolab.org/search/?q=Barbara+Harris#q=Barbara Harris. Accessed May 10, 2016. Other sources for this story were the Project Prevention website www.projectprevention.org/ and Wikipedia https://en.wikipedia.org/wiki/, both accessed on December 18, 2015.

2. "What If There Was No Destiny?"

3. Weick's writing on the subject has culminated in a two-volume set: Karl E. Weick, *Making Sense of the Organization, Volume 1* (Oxford, UK: Blackwell, 2001) and *Making Sense of the Organization: Volume 2* (Chichester, UK: Wiley, 2009).

4. This definition comes from Wikipedia, https://en.wikipedia.org/wiki/Sensemaking. Accessed June 23, 2015.

5. Roxana Barbulescu, Jennifer Tosti-Kharas, and Herminia Ibarra, "Finding the Plot: How Virtuous Self-Narratives Legitimize Career Downfalls," in *The Selected Works of Roxana Barbulescu*, 2012, 3. http://works.bepress.com/roxana_barbulescu/5. Accessed December 18, 2015.

6. This approach draws heavily on John Van Maanen, "Experiencing Organization: Notes on the Meaning of Careers and Socialization. In *Organizational Careers: Some New Perspectives*, ed. John Van Maanen (New York, Wiley, 1977), 32–36.

7. Angela Mazzetti and John Blenkinsop, "Evaluating a Visual Timeline Methodology for Appraisal and Coping Research," *Journal of Occupational and Organizational Psychology* 85 (2012): 649–665.

8. Mary-Dean Lee, Ellen E. Kossek, Douglas T. Hall, and Jean-Baptiste Litrico, "Entangled Strands: A Process Perspective on the Evolution of Careers in the Context of Personal, Family, Work, and Community Life," *Human Relations* 64, no. 12 (2011): 1531–1553.

9. Lee et al., "Entangled Strands," 1545.

10. Ulla Hytti, "Contextualizing Entrepreneurship in the Boundaryless Career," *Gender in Management* 25, no. 1 (2010): 64–81.

11. Hytti, "Contextualizing Entrepreneurship," 70.

12. Barbulescu, Tosti-Kharas, and Ibarra, "Finding the Plot." summary table on page 58. Earlier related work can be found in Jelena Zikic and Ute-Christine Klehe, "Job Loss as a Blessing in Disguise: The Role of Career Exploration and Career Planning in Predicting Reemployment Quality," *Journal of Vocational Behavior* 69, no. 3, (2006); and Jelena Zikic and Julia Richardson, "Unlocking the Careers of Business Professionals Following Job Loss: Sensemaking and Career

Exploration of Older Workers," *Canadian Journal of Administrative Sciences/ Revue Canadienne des Sciences de l'Administration* 24, no. 1 (2007).

13. Sometimes, writing about your downfall can direct you to its cure, as it did for Australian Nigel Marsh through his book on his job loss experience. Nigel Marsh, Fat, Forty, and Fired. Kansas City, MO: AndrewsMcMeel.

14. See, for example, https://en.wikipedia.org/wiki/Sixteen-bar_blues.

15. Michael Humphries, Deniz Ucbasaran, and Andy Lockett, "Sensemaking and Sensegiving Stories of Jazz Leadership," *Human Relations* 65, no. 1 (2011): 41–62.

16. Humphries et al., "Sensemaking and Sensegiving," 47.

17. Humphries et al., "Sensemaking and Sensegiving," 49.

18. Mairi Maclean, Charles Harvey, and Robert Chia, "Sensemaking, Storytelling and the Legitimization of Elite Business Careers," *Human Relations* 65, no. 1 (2011): 17–40.

19. Weick, *Making Sense of the Organization*, 2:204.

20. Jane Beresford, "Should Drug Addicts Be Paid to Get Sterilized?" *BBC News Magazine*, February 8, 2010. http://news.bbc.co.uk/2/hi/uk_news/magazine/8500285.stm. Accessed June 5, 2015.

21. See the articles by Rheana Murray, "Group Pays Drug Addicts to Get Sterilized or Receive Long-Term Birth Control, Sparks Criticism," *New York Daily News*, May 9, 2012, http://www.nydailynews.com/life-style/health/group-pays-drug-addicts-sterilized-receive-long-term-birth-control-sparks-criticism-article-1.1075432 (accessed June 5, 2015); and Anna Clark, "IUDs to Prevent HIV in Kenya?" *The Nation*, May 6, 2011. http://www.thenation.com/article/160485/iuds-prevent-hiv-kenya. Accessed June 5, 2015.

22. Both the British Medical Association and the Dublin director's information are to be found in "Project Prevention," *Wikipedia*. http://en.wikipedia.org/wiki/Project_Prevention. Accessed March 16, 2013.

23. Clark, "IUDs to Prevent HIV in Kenya?"

24. Beresford, "Should Drug Addicts Be Paid to Get Sterilized?"

25. Van Maanen, "Experiencing Organization," 32.

26. You can work on building your own list of themes by looking back over chapters 3–5 and making notes. Then you can look back through chapter 6 and see how your earlier notes are connected, and how living through different phases of employment or projects can help your themes come alive. The exercise included in the notes to chapter 6 also leads you toward developing your themes and subsequent action steps. See www.intelligentcareer.net.

27. See for example Judith Enterkin, Elizabeth Robb, and Susan McLaren, "Clinical Leadership for High-Quality Care: Developing Future Ward Leaders," *Journal of Nursing Management* 21 (2013): 206–216; Steve Darroch and Lorraine Mazerolle, "Intelligence-Led Policing: A Comparative Analysis of Organizational Factors Influencing Innovation Uptake," *Police Quarterly* 16, no. 1 (2012): 3–37; Micha Popper and Ofra Mayseless, "The Building Blocks of Leader Development: A Psychological Conceptual Framework," *Leadership and Organization Development Journal* 28, no. 7 (2007): 664–684.

28. This section draws on Ian Colville, Andrew D. Brown, and Annie Pye, "Simplexity: Sensemaking, Organizing and Storytelling for Our Time," *Human Relations* 65, no. 1 (2011): 5–15: and Karl E. Weick, "Organized Sensemaking: A Commentary on Processes of Interpretive Work," *Human Relations* 65, no. 1 (2012): 141–153.

29. William James, *The Principles of Psychology*, 2 vols. (New York: Dover Publications, 1957 [1890]), 243.

CHAPTER 8 EMBRACING TECHNOLOGY

1. Sue ShellenbArger, "Don't Be the Office Tech Dinosaur," *Wall Street Journal*, April 17, 2013, D1–D2.

2. Doug Gould left Allen & Gerritsen in April 2015, and is now executive creative director at Boston University. Source: https://www.linkedin.com/in/douggould. Accessed March 31, 2016.

3. Manuel Castells, *The Rise of the Network Society*, 2nd ed. (Chichester: Wiley-Blackwell, 2010), xvii.

4. Castells, *The Rise*, xx.

5. Nicholas Carr, *The Shallows: What the Internet Is Doing to Our Brains*. (New York: W.W. Norton & Company, 2010), 6–7.

6. Carr, *The Shallows*, 74.

7. Carr, *The Shallows*, 191.

8. Carr, *The Shallows*, 91.

9. For example see Johan Lehrer, "Our Cluttered Minds," *New York Times*, Sunday Book Review, June 3, 2010. http://www.nytimes.com/2010/06/06/books/review/Lehrer-t.html?_r=0. Accessed December 18, 2015.

10. "Moore's Law," *Wikipedia*. http://en.wikipedia.org/wiki/Moore's_law. Accessed June 3, 2015.

11. Jaron Lanier, *Who Owns the Future?* (New York: Simon & Schuster, 2013), 367.

12. Lanier, *Who Owns the Future?*, 367.

13. See David Laws, "Moore's Law @ 50: "The Most Important Graph in Human History." http://www.computerhistory.org/atchm/moores-law50-the-most-important-graph-in-human-history/; Sam Reynolds, "Gordon Moore: Moore's Law Will Last Another 10 Years." http://vrworld.com/2015/05/13/gordon-moore-moores-law-will-last-another-10-years/.

14. Tim Wu, "If a Time Traveler Saw a Smartphone," *New Yorker*, online blogs, January 10, 2014. http://www.newyorker.com/online/blogs/elements/2014/01/if-a-time-traveller-saw-a-smartphone.html. Accessed June 3, 2015.

15. Erik Brynjolfsson and Andrew McAfee, *The Second Machine Age* (New York: Norton, 2014).

16. Kevin Kelley, *What Technology Wants* (New York, Viking, 2010).

17. Kevin Kelly, "Better Than Human: Why Robots Will—And Must—Take Over Our Jobs," *Wired*, December 14, 2012. http://www.wired.com/2012/12/ff-robots-will-take-our-jobs/. Accessed December 18, 2015. See also *The Economist* special report, "Rise of the Robots," March 29–April 4, 2012. http://www.economist.

com/news/lea.ders/21599762-prepare-robot-invasion-it-will-change-way-people-think-about-technology-rise. Accessed December 18, 2015.

18. Kelly, "Better Than Human."

19. Andrew Butterfield, "Art and Innovation in Ghiberti's Gates of Paradise," in *The Gates of Paradise*, ed. Gary M. Radke (New Haven, CT: Yale University Press, 2007), 17–41.

20. Clive Thompson, *Smarter Than You Think* (New York: Penguin, 2013), 47.

21. Thompson, *Smarter Than You Think*, 116–123.

22. *Online Etymology Dictionary.* http://www.etymonline.com/index.php?allowed_in_frame=0&search=literate&searchmode=none. Accessed March 29, 2014.

23. Vanessa Au, "10 Creative Ways to Use Instagram for Business." http://www.socialmediaexaminer.com/instagram/. Accessed June 5, 2015.

24. See, for example, "Ushahidi," *Wikipedia*, http://en.wikipedia.org/wiki/Ushahidi (accessed June 5, 2015); and Ushahidi's own website at http://www.ushahidi.com/. Accessed June 5, 2015.

25. Goldcorp's story is included in Donald Tapscott and Anthony D. Williams, *Wikinomics* (New York: Portfolio, 2007), 7–10. There is no longer any reference to it on the company website. For Proctor and Gamble and GlaxoSmithKline, see the company websites: http://www.pgconnectdevelop.com/home/pg_open_innovation.html and http://www.gsk.com/research/sharing-our-research/open-innovation.html. Accessed June 5, 2015.

26. Sang M. Lee, Taewon Hwang, and Donghyu Choi, "Open Innovation in the Public Sector of Leading Countries," *Management Decision* 50, no. 1 (2012): 147–162.

27. Michael Lemonick, "Crowdsourcing the Stars," *Newer Yorker*, online blogs May 1, 2013, http://www.newyorker.com/online/blogs/elements/2013/05/crowdsourcing-the-stars.html (accessed June 5, 2015); and Brenna Farrell, "Help Rewrite History," *Radiolab* blogland, June 6 2013. http://www.radiolab.org/story/297250-help-transcribe-ancient-papyri/. Accessed June 5, 2015.

28. Aruba Networks, "Are You Ready for #GenMobile?" http://www.arubanetworks.com/pdf/solutions/GenMobile_Report.pdf (accessed June 5, 2015); and Samuel Mungadze, "Tech-Savvy Employees 'Changing the Workplace,'" *Business Day* (South Africa), January 31, 2014. http://www.bdlive.co.za/business/2014/01/31/tech-savvy-employees-changing-the-workplace. Accessed June 2015.

29. Donald Tapscott and Anthony D. Williams, *Wikinomics: How Mass Collaboration Changes Everything* (New York: Portfolio Penguin, 2010), 3;

30. Donald Tapscott and Anthony D. Williams, *Macrowikinomics: Rebooting Business and the World* (New York: Portfolio Penguin, 2013), 7;

31. Donald Tapscott and Anthony D. Williams, *Radical Openness: Four Unexpected Principles for Success*, Kindle ed. (TED Books), ch. 1. The quotation is from the last sentence of the Epilogue.

32. Tapscott and Williams, *Radical Openness*.

33. Bill Vlasic and Matthew L. Waldmarch, "G.M. Expands Ignition Switch Recall to Later Models," *New York Times*, March 28, 2014. http://www.nytimes.com/2014/

03/29/business/lawmaker-urges-owners-to-stop-driving-their-cobalts.html. Accessed June 5, 2015.

34. See, for example, Frank W. Baker, *Media Literacy in the K-12 Classroom* (Washington, DC: International Society for Technology in Education, 2012); and Lee Crockett, Ian Jukes, and Andrew Churches, *Literacy Is NOT Enough: 21st Century Fluencies for the Digital Age*, The 21st Century Fluency Series (Thousand Oaks, CA: Corwin/Sage, 2011).

CHAPTER 9 INVESTING IN COMMUNITIES

1. Steven Greenhouse, "Going It Alone, Together," *New York Times*, March 24, 2013, BU1. http://www.nytimes.com/2013/03/24/business/freelancers-union-tackles-concerns-of-independent-workers.html?_r=0. Accessed December 19, 2015.
2. https://en.wikipedia.org/wiki/Freelancers_Union. Accessed December 19, 2015.
3. Sara Horowitz, *The Freelancer's Bible*. New York, Workman Publishing
4. Steven Greenhouse, "Going It Alone, Together"
5. Robert D. Putnam, "Bowling Alone: America's Declining Social Capital," *Journal of Democracy* 6, no. 1 (1995): 65–78, 70.
6. Putnam, "Bowling Alone," 73.
7. Putnam, "Bowling Alone," 72.
8. Putnam, "Bowling Alone," 75.
9. Lee Rainie and Barry Wellman, *Networked: The New Social Operating System* (Cambridge, MA: MIT Press, 2012), 121.
10. Deborah Chambers, *New Social Ties: Contemporary Connections in a Fragmented Society* (Basingstoke, UK: Palgrave Macmillan, 2006).
11. Leonard Seabrooke and Elain Tsingou, "Professional Emergence on Transnational Issues: Linked Ecologies on Demographic Change," *Journal of Professions and Organization* 2, no. 1 (2014): 1–18.
12. Philip H. Mirvis, "'Soul Work' in Organizations," *Organization Science* 8, no. 2 (1997): 192–206. Mirvis in turn credits Seymour Sarason, *The Psychological Sense of Community* (San Francisco, CA: Jossey-Bass, 1974).
13. Michael J. Piore and Sean Safford, "Changing Regimes of Workplace Governance, Shifting Axes of Social Mobilization, and the Challenge to Industrial Relations Theory," *Industrial Relations* 45, no. 3 (2006): 299–325.
14. On physical space, see SueAnn Bottoms, Jerine Pegg, Anne Adams, Ke Wu, H. Smith Risser, and Anne L. Kern, "Mentoring from the Outside: The Role of a Peer Mentoring Community in the Development of Early Career Education Faculty," *Mentoring and Tutoring: Partnership in Learning* 21, no. 2 (2013): 195–218. On virtual space, see Darren Good and Kevin Cavanagh, "Dispersed Sensemaking: Online Career Community as a Tool for Proactive Socialization," *Academy of Management Proceedings* 2013, no. 1, Abstract 17523. Academy of Management.
15. John Van Maanen and Stephen R. Barley, "Occupational Communities: Culture and Control in Organizations," In *Research in Organizational Behavior, Volume 6*, eds. Barry M. Staw and Larry L. Cummings (Greenwood, CT: JAI Press,1984), 295.
16. Etienne Wenger, *Communities of Practice: Learning, Meaning and Identity*. Cambridge University Press, 1998, 73-85.

17. Stephen R. Barley and Gideon Kunda, *Gurus, Hired Guns, and Warm Bodies: Itinerant Experts in a Knowledge Economy* (Princeton, NJ: Princeton University Press, 2004), 291.

18. Barley and Kunda, *Gurus*, 301.

19. Steve Casper and Fiona Murray, "Careers and Clusters: Analyzing the Career Network Dynamic of Biotechnology Clusters," *Journal of Engineering and Technology Management* 22, no. 1 (2005): 51–74.

20. Jean-Denis Culie, Svetlana N. Khapova, and Michael B. Arthur, "Careers, Clusters and Employment Mobility: The Influences of Psychological Mobility and Organizational Support," *Journal of Vocational Behavior* 84 (2012): 164–176.

21. Edward Glaeser, *Triumph of the City: How Our Greatest Invention Makes Us Richer, Smarter, Greener, Healthier, and Happier* (New York: Penguin, 2011), 1.

22. Glaeser, *Triumph*, 6.

23. Gernot Grahber, "Switching Ties, Recombining Teams: Avoiding Lock-In through Project Organization?" in *Rethinking Regional Innovation and Change*, eds. Gerhard Fuchs and Philio Shapira (Boston: Springer, 2005), 63–84.

24. Martin Ruef, *The Entrepreneurial Group: Social Identities, Relations, and Collective Action* (Princeton, NJ: Princeton University Press, 2010), 3–16.

25. Regina Schrambling, "How Startup Weekend Got Its Start," *Entrepreneur*, March 2011. http://www.entrepreneur.com/article/21810. Accessed November 18, 2015.

26. See, for example, "Linux," *Wikipedia*. https://en.wikipedia.org/wiki/Linux. Accessed December 19, 2015.

27. Howard Rheingold, *The Virtual Community* (Cambridge, MA: MIT Press, 2000), xix. The original edition was published by Addison Wesley in 1993.

28. Yoachi Benkler, *The Wealth of Networks: How Social Production Transforms Markets and Freedom* (New Haven, CT: Yale University Press, 2006).

29. Marie-Laure Djelic and Sigrid Quack, *Transnational Communities: Shaping Global Economic Governance* (Cambridge: Cambridge University Press, 2010).

30. Jeff Howe, *Crowdsourcing: Why the Power of the Crowd Is Driving the Future of Business* (New York: Three Rivers Press, 2009). William Safire describes the origins of the term in "On Language," *New York Times Magazine*, February 5, 2009.

31. Daren Brabham, "Crowdsourcing as a Model for Problem Solving: An Introduction and Cases," *Convergence: The International Journal of Research into New Media Technologies* 14, no. 1 (2008): 75–90.

32. Ethan Mollick, "The Dynamics of Crowdfunding: Determinants of Success and Failure," *Journal of Business Venturing* 29 (2014): 1–16.

33. Georgia Institute of Technology, "Crowdsourcing Could Lead to Better Water in Rural India," *US Official News*, September 22, 2014.

34. Yenni Tim, Shan L. Pan, Shamshul Bahri, and Ali Fauzi Ahmad Khan, "Social Media as Boundary Objects: A Case of Digitalized Civic Engagement in Malaysia," 25th Australasian Conference on Information Systems, Auckland, New Zealand.

35. Putnam, "Bowling Alone," 72.

36. Jaewon Yang and Jure Leskovec, "Overlapping Communities Explain Core–Periphery Organization of Networks," *Proceedings of the IEEE* 102, no. 12 (2014): 1892–1902.

37. Ronald S. Burt, *Neighbor Networks: Competitive Advantage Local and Personal* (New York: Oxford University Press, 2010).

CHAPTER 10 WORKING WITH EMPLOYERS

1. We are deeply grateful to Tineke Cappellen and Maddy Janssens for providing the Pierre Albert example and related ideas on its interpretation. The names of Albert and his employers have been disguised.
2. Barley, "Careers, Identities, and Institutions."
3. Edgar H. Schein, *The Corporate Culture Survival Guide* (San Francisco: John Wiley & Sons, 2009).
4. Schein, *The Corporate Culture Survival Guide*, 82–87.
5. Larry Smith, *No Fears, No Excuses: What You Need to do to Have a Great Career.* (Boston, Houghton Mifflin Harcourt, 2016), x
6. Justin M. Berg, Jane E. Dutton, and Amy Wrzesniewski, "What Is Job Crafting and Why Does It Matter?" Working paper, Center for Positive Organizational Scholarship, Ross School of Business, University of Michigan, revised August 2008.
7. Justin M. Berg, Adam M. Grant, and Victoria Johnson. "When Callings Are Calling: Crafting Work and Leisure in Pursuit of Unanswered Occupational Callings," *Organization Science* 21, no. 5 (2010): 973–994.
8. Nicholas Kinnie and Juani Swart, "Committed to Whom? Professional Knowledge Worker Commitment in Cross-Boundary Organisations," *Human Resource Management Journal* 22, no. 1 (2012): 21–38.
9. Deepak Somaya, Ian O. Williamson, and Natalia Lorinkova, "Gone But Not Lost: The Different Performance Impacts of Employee Mobility between Cooperators versus Competitors," *Academy of Management Journal* 51, no. 5 (2008): 936–953; Rafael A. Corredoira and Lori Rosenkopf, "Should Auld Acquaintance Be Forgot? The Reverse Transfer of Knowledge through Mobility Ties," *Strategic Management Journal* 31, no. 2 (2010): 159–181; Benjamin A. Campbell, Martin Ganco, April M. Franco, and Rajshree Agarwal, "Who Leaves, Where to, and Why Worry? Employee Mobility, Entrepreneurship and Effects on Source Firm Performance," *Strategic Management Journal* 33, no. 1 (2012): 65–87.
10. Peter Cappelli, *Why Good People Can't Get Jobs* (Philadelphia, PA: Wharton Digital Press, 2011), 59–68.
11. Cappelli, *Why Good People Can't Get Jobs*, 59–68.
12. Ed Michaels, Helen Handfield-Jones, and Beth Axelrod, *The War for Talent* (Boston: Harvard Business School Press, 2001).
13. Susan Cantrell and David Smith, *Workforce of One: Revolutionizing Talent Management through Customization* (Boston: Harvard Business Press, 2010): 1, 41.
14. Individual and company names have been disguised.
15. Mary's and her employers' names have been disguised. We are grateful to Stephanie Flanagan for providing this story.
16. Chris Komisarjevsky, *The Power of Reputation: Strengthen the Asset That Will Make or Break Your Career* (New York: AMACOM, 2012).

17. Vicki Smith and Esther B. Neuwirt, *The Good Temp* (Ithaca, NY: Cornell University Press, 2008); Arne L. Kalleberg, *Good Jobs, Bad Jobs: The Rise of Polarized and Precarious Employment Systems in the United States, 1970s to 2000s* (New York: Russell Sage Foundation, 2011).

18. Debra Osnowitz, *Freelancing Expertise: Contract Professionals in the New Economy* (Ithaca, NY: ILR Press, 2010).

19. Karl E. Weick and Lisa R. Berlinger, "Career Improvisation in Self-Designing Organizations," in *Handbook of Career Theory*, ed. Michael B. Arthur et al. (New York: Cambridge University Press, 1989), 313–328.

20. Stephen R. Barley and Gideon Kunda, *Gurus, Hired Guns, and Warm Bodies: Itinerant Experts in a Knowledge Economy* (Princeton, NJ: Princeton University Press, 2006), 73–90.

21. "Non-Compete Clause," *Wikipedia*. https://en.wikipedia.org/wiki/Non-compete_clause. Accessed November 18, 2015.

22. Orly Lobel, *Talent Wants to Be Free* (New Haven, CT: Yale University Press, 2013), 67.

23. For example, On Amir and Orly Lobel, "Driving Performance: A Growth Theory of Noncompete Law," *Stanford Technology Law Review* 16, no. 3 (2013): 833–874; Matt Marxa, Jasjit Singh, and Lee Fleming, "Regional Disadvantage? Employee Non-Compete Agreements and Brain Drain," *Research Policy* 44 (2015): 394–404.

CHAPTER 11 SHARING YOUR STORY

1. From an interview by Michael Arthur. Sincere thanks to Mary Lakis for her time, and for the permission to use her name.

2. "Narrative," *Oxford English Dictionary*, online version, 3rd ed. (Oxford: Oxford University Press, 2011).

3. Herminia Ibarra and Roxanna Barbulescu, "Identity as Narrative: Prevalence, Effectiveness, and Consequences of Narrative Identity Work in Macro Work Role Transitions," *Academy of Management Review* 35 (2010): 135.

4. Ibarra and Barbulescu, "Identity as Narrative," 139.

5. Mark L. Savickas, "The Theory and Practice of Career Construction," in *Career Development and Counseling*, eds. Steven D. Brown and Robert W. Lent (Hoboken, NJ: Wiley, 2010), 42–70; Jennifer Del Corso and Mark C. Rehfuss, "The Role of Narrative in Career Construction Theory," *Journal of Vocational Behavior* 79 (2011): 334–339.

6. Herminia Ibarra and Kent Lineback, "What's Your Story?" *Harvard Business Review*, January 2005, 65–71. The quotations are on page 67.

7. Interview with Michael Arthur, with thanks to Kalyn, whose name is disguised.

8. Ira Glass, "Introduction," *The New Kings of Fiction*, eds. Michael Lewis and Jack Hitt (New York: Penguin, 2007), 11.

9. John B. Molidor, *Crazy Good Interviewing: How Acting a Little Crazy Can Get You the Job* (New York, Wiley, 2012), 210.

10. Ron Fry, *101 Great Answers to the Toughest Interview Questions*, 4th ed. (Franklin Lakes, NJ: Career Press, 2000).

11. Laura Entis, "25 Wacky Interview Questions That Work," *Entrepreneur*, January 14, 2014. http://www.entrepreneur.com/article/230931#. Accessed December 19, 2015. The questions, in sequence, are attributed to Yahoo (Search Quality Analyst interview), Urban Outfitters (Sales Associate interview), Active Network (Client Applications Specialist interview), LivingSocial (Consumer Advocate interview), Goldman Sachs (Programmer Analyst interview), and Applebee's (Bartender/ Neighborhood Expert Server interview).

12. Ibarra and Lineback, "What's Your Story?," 70.

13. Meg Guiseppi, "Five Top Trends for Executive Resumes," Quint Careers. https://www.quintcareers.com/executive-resume-trends/. Accessed March 2, 2016.

14. Ofer Sharone, *Flawed System/Flawed Self: Job Searching and Unemployment Experiences* (Chicago, University of Chicago Press, 2014).

15. Suniya S. Luthar, Dante Cicchetti, and Bronwyn Becker, "The Construct of Resilience: A Critical Evaluation and Guidelines for Future Work," *Child Development* 71, no. 3 (2000): 543–562.

16. Gisa Moenkemeyer, Martin Hoegl, and Matthias Weiss, "Innovator Resilience Potential: A Process Perspective of Individual Resilience as Influenced by Innovation Project Termination," *Human Relations* 65, no. 5 (2012): 627–655.

17. Moenkemeyer et al., "Innovator Resilience Potential," 627.

18. "Personal Branding," *Wikipedia*. http://en.wikipedia.org/wiki/Personal_branding. Accessed December 19, 2015. The definition is attributed to the personal brand coach Los Ellis from 2009.

19. Soumitra Dutta, "What's Your Personal Social Media Strategy?" *Harvard Business Review*, November 2010, 127–130.

CHAPTER 12 BUILDING YOUR WORLD

1. Julia Richardson, interview with Moses Zulu. We deeply appreciate his collaboration. Related information is taken from the Firelight Foundation website: http://www.firelightfoundation.org/. Accessed December 19, 2015. The individual described here is no relation to another Moses Zulu who created Children's Town in Malambanya, Zambia.

2. "World," *Oxford English Dictionary*, online version, 3rd ed. (Oxford: Oxford University Press, 2011).

3. Mary Catherine Bateson, *Composing a Life* (New York: Atlantic Monthly Press, 1989), 1–2.

4. Bateson, *Composing a Life*, 2, 15.

5. Bateson, *Composing a Life*, 33.

6. Mary Catherine Bateson, *Composing a Further Life* (New York: Knopf, 2010), 6.

7. Bateson, *Composing a Life*, 33, 170.

8. Adam Grant, *Give and Take: Why Helping Others Drives Our Success* (New York: Viking Penguin, 2013), 40–45.

9. Grant, *Give and Take*, 4–7.

10. Grant *Give and Take*, 8–9.

11. Shalmon H. Schwartz and Anat Bardi, "Value Hierarchies across Cultures: Taking a Similarities Perspective," *Journal of Cross-Cultural Psychology* 32 (2001): 268–290.

12. Grant, *Give and Take*, ch. 1.

13. Grant, *Give and Take*, 261–268.

14. Grant *Give and Take*, 26.

15. Bateson, *Composing a Life*, 166.

16. Ellen J. Langer, *Mindfulness: 25th Anniversary Edition* (Boston, MA: Da Capo Press, 2014), 1–18.

17. Hubert L. Dreyfus and Stuart E. Dreyfus, "Peripheral Vision Expertise in Real World Contexts," *Organization Studies* 26, no. 5 (2005): 779–792.

18. Karl E. Weick and Ted Putnam, "Eastern Wisdom and Western Knowledge," *Journal of Management Inquiry* 15, no. 3 (2006): 1–13.

19. Jon Kabat-Zinn, *Mindfulness for Beginners* (Boulder, CO: Sounds True, 2012).

20. Langer, *Mindfulness*, xxv.

21. Edgar H. Schein, *Humble Inquiry: The Gentle art of Asking Instead of Telling* (San Francisco: Berrett- Koehler, 2013), 1.

22. Schein, *Humble Inquiry*, 2–9.

23. Schein, *Humble Inquiry*, 21–51, 53–67.

24. Schein, *Humble Inquiry*, 99–110.

25. Howard Gardner, Mihalyi Csikszentmihalyi, and William Damon, *Good Work: When Excellence and Ethics Meet* (New York: Basic Books, 2001), ix, 5.

26. Gardner et al., *Good Work*, 7–9.

27. Gardner et al., *Good Work*, 14.

28. Gardner et al., *Good Work*, 10–12.

29. Gardner et al., *Good Work*, 249. The *Writer's Almanac* website is at http://writersalmanac.org/. Accessed December 19, 2015. For further ideas and tools about good work, see http://www.thegoodproject.org/.

30. Bateson, *Composing a Life*, 88.

31. Roxana Barbulescu and Matthew Bidwell, "Do Women Choose Different Jobs from Men? Mechanisms of Application Segregation in the Market for Managerial Workers," *Organization Science* 24, no. 3 (2013): 737–756.

32. Lotte Bailyn, *Breaking the Mold: Redesigning Work for Productive and Satisfying Lives*, 2nd ed. (Ithaca, NY: ILR Press, 2006).

33. Sue Shellenbarger, *The Breaking Point: How Today's Women Are Navigating Midlife Crisis* (New York: Henry Holt, 2005); Ella J. Edmondson Bell and Linda Villarosa, *Career GPS: Strategies for Women Navigating the New Corporate Landscape* (New York, Amistad, 2010); Sheryl Sandberg and Nell Scovell, *Lean In: Women, Work, and the Will to Lead* (New York: Knopf, 2013).

34. Jeffrey H. Greenhaus and Gary N. Powell, "When Work and Family Are Allies: A Theory of Work-Family Enrichment," *Academy of Management Review* 31, no. 1 (2006): 72–92.

35. Lotte Bailyn, "Redesigning Work for Gender Equity and Work–Personal Life Integration," *Community, Work and Family* 14, no. 1 (2011): 97–112; Kathleen

Christensen and Barbara Schneider, *Realigning 20th Century Jobs for a 21st Century Workforce* (Ithaca, NY: ILR Press, 2011).

36. Karen Korabik, "The Intersection of Gender and Work–Family Guilt," in *Gender and the Work-Family Experience: An Intersection of Two Domains*, ed. Maura Mills (NewYork: Springer, 2015), 141–157.

37. Ans De Vos and Beatrice I. J. M Van der Heijden, eds., *Handbook of Research on Sustainable Careers* (Cheltenham, UK: Elgar, 2015).

ACKNOWLEDGMENTS

In the preceding pages we promote intelligent careers as essential social projects involving close collaboration and positive working relationships with others. Similarly, our own project—this book—would never have been possible without the unwavering support and contributions of a great many people. There are those we reached out to directly, to share their ideas and experience as the book evolved. There is the global community of scholars and other professionals whose ideas we have drawn on to inform our own thinking. There are our own academic institutions, and the team at Oxford University Press. Last but not least, this book would never have been possible without the consistent encouragement of our families and friends.

Regarding the people who have directly contributed to this book, first and foremost is Lotte Bailyn, an exceptional friend and advisor to each of us. Many other scholars have also been an invaluable source of prolonged support, including Tania Casado, Loic Cadin, Robert DeFillippi, Hugh Gunz, Tim Hall, Kerr Inkson, Barbara Lawrence, Wolfgang Mayrhofer, Polly Parker, Maury Peiperl, Denise Rousseau, Mark Savickas, Edgar Schein, the late Boas Shamir, Svenja Tams, John Van Maanen, Karl Weick, and Celeste Wilderom. Still others have contributed by allowing us to use their own work in the book or simply by joining in conversations. You know who you are, and we very much appreciate counting you as friends. Finally, there are the many students who offered their feedback on early drafts of the chapters. Again, you know who you are, and we are deeply grateful.

Turning to the scholarly communities that have supported us, the Academy of Management, and within it the Careers Division, was a natural home for scholars passionate about understanding working lives and helping people manage them. The European Group for Organizational Studies (EGOS) provided a second home and further opportunity to test our ideas. We also thank those journals that have hosted the kind of interdisciplinary thinking on which this book depends, most notably *Career Development International, Human Relations,* the *Journal of Organizational Behavior,* and the *Journal of Vocational Behavior.*

Next, we thank our respective employers. Michael has been a long-term member of Suffolk University Sawyer Business School, which has always accepted his globe-trotting with good grace. Dean William O'Neill has been particularly supportive, and generous seed money from the school's research committee helped get this project off the ground. Svetlana is in debt to Vrije Universiteit Amsterdam and its Faculty of Economics and Business Administration for supporting and encouraging her research interest in careers with a dedicated chair. Julia thanks her former colleagues at York University, Toronto, for all their encouragement, and her new colleagues at Curtin Business School, Australia, for their warm welcome.

From the outset, our publishers at Oxford University Press have been everything we could have hoped for. Special thanks to Abby Gross, for believing in and helping to shape this project, and to Jonathan Kroberger, Courtney McCarroll, David Musson, Devasena Vedamurthi (at Newgen KnowledgeWorks), and others who have provided extraordinary help along the path to production. Thanks also to Karen Propp, for her timely schooling in the finer points of authoring a "trade" publication.

Finally, there are our families, most importantly our respective others Pat Keck, Igor Popovic, and Steve McKenna. Somewhere along the way each of them came to realize that our book was intruding on established routines, and each of them responded with good grace and firm encouragement. In addition, Michael thanks Victoria, Tom, Jen, Jeffrey, Eva, Jane, and Peter, for being around and being good fun. Svetlana thanks Anastasia, who at 9 years old has contributed creative ideas for the book title and illustrations, and her family—Ludmila, Nikolay, Lilia, Oleg,

Jelica, Vidoje and little Victoria, for their love and support during the project. Julia expresses special thanks to close friends, ever a source of inspiration with their smiling faces and warm hearts.

As protagonists for people taking ownership of their careers, we take ownership of everything included in this book. All of what's here is our own responsibility, including any outstanding mistakes, clumsy wording, or oversights. We will try to learn from them, as we would like our readers to learn from their own experiences.

Boxes

1.1 Silviya Svejenova, "'The Path with the Heart': Creating the Authentic Career," *Journal of Management Studies* 42, no. 5 (2005): 947–974.

4.1 Jeffrey Pfeffer, *Power: Why Some People Have It—And Others Don't* (New York: HarperBusiness, 2010), 5.

9.1 Derived from Etienne Wenger, *Communities of Practice: Learning, Meaning, and Identity* (Cambridge, UK: Cambridge University Press, 1998).

Figures

1.1 Used with permission from John Wiley and Sons.

2.1 Diercke Learning Maps. www.diercke.com/kartenansicht.xtp?artId= 978-3-14-100790-9&stichwort=sunbelt&fs=1. Accessed February 28, 2016. Used with permission from Bildungshaus Schulbuchverlage Westermann Schroedel Diesterweg Schöningh Winklers GmbH.

3.1 John L. Holland, *Making Vocational Choices: A Theory of Vocational Personalities and Work Environments*, 2nd ed. (Englewood Cliffs, NJ: Prentice Hall, 1985), 29. By permission of Pearson Education.

5.1 Ronald S. Burt, *Brokerage and Closure: An Introduction to Social Capital* (Oxford: Oxford University Press, 2005), By permission of Oxford University Press.

5.2 Source: Ronald S. Burt, *Brokerage and Closure: An Introduction to Social Capital* (Oxford: Oxford University Press, 2005), By permission of Oxford University Press.

7.1 Submitted by a contact of one of the authors.

7.2 Mary-Dean Lee, Ellen E. Kossek, Douglas T. Hall, and Jean-Baptiste Litrico, "Entangled Strands: A Process Perspective on the Evolution of Careers in the Context of Personal, Family, Work, and Community Life," *Human Relations* 64, no. 12 (2011): 1547.

8.1 The chart appeared in *The Economist* on April 19, 2015. See http://www.economist.com/blogs/economist-explains/2015/04/economist-explains-17. Accessed February 11, 2016. Used with permission of Intel Corporation. Thanks to Elizabeth Stollings for her help.

8.2 Adapted from Kevin Kelly, "Better Than Human: Why Robots Will—And Must—Take Over Our Jobs," *Wired*, December 14, 2012. http://www.wired.com/2012/12/ff-robots-will-take-our-jobs/. Accessed December 18, 2015.

8.3 http://www.fusioncharts.com/. Accessed February 26, 2016. Used with permission from FusionCharts.

9.1 Source: Used with permission from Martin Ruef, *The Entrepreneurial Group: Social Identities, Relations, and Collective Action* (Princeton, NJ: Princeton University Press, 2010), 3–16.

9.2 Used with permission from IEEE Publications.

10.1 Modified from Stephen R. Barley, "Careers, Identities, and Institutions: The Legacy of the Chicago School of Sociology," in *Handbook of Career Theory*, eds. Michael B. Arthur, Douglas T. Hall, and Barbara S. Lawrence (New York: Cambridge University Press, 1989), 41–65; and Tineke Cappellen and Maddy Janssens. "Enacting Global Careers: Organizational Career Scripts and the Global Economy as Co-existing Career Referents," *Journal of Organizational Behavior* 31, no. 5 (2010): 687–706.

Tables

4.1 Albert Bandura, *Social Foundations of Thought and Action* (Englewood Cliffs, New Jersey, 1986), 51– 80.

4.2 Daniel Goleman, "What Makes a Leader?" *Harvard Business Review*, January 2004, 88. Used with permission of Harvard Business Review.

6.1 Adapted from Pam Lassiter, The New Job Security, rev. ed. (Berkeley, CA: Ten Speed Press, 2010), 93–94.

11.1 Adapted from Pam Lassiter, *The New Job Security*, rev. ed. (New York: Ten Speed Press, 2010), 47–48.

11.2 Ofer Sharone, "Why Do Unemployed Americans Blame Themselves While Israelis Blame the System?" *Social Forces* 91, no. 4 (2013): 1429–1450.

11.3 Adapted from Soumitra Dutta, "What's Your Personal Social Media Strategy?" *Harvard Business Review*, November 2010, 127–130.

Epigraphs

I.1 Rudyard Kipling, *Just So Stories* (London: Macmillan, 2002). A recent reprint by Snowball Publishing shows the verse on page 29. www.snowballpublishing.com. Accessed December 23, 2015.

1.1 Walt Whitman, "Song of Myself," section 46, in *Leaves of Grass* (1855/2008), https://www.gutenberg.org/files/1322/1322-h/1322-h. htm. Accessed December 15, 2015.

2.1 NPWA Words and Music by Billy Bragg, Martyn Baker, Ian Mclagan, Louis Edmonds, Benjamin Norman Mandelson and Simon Edwards. Copyright (c) 2002 Sony/ATV Music Publishing LLC and Union Prod. Ltd. All Rights on behalf of Sony/ATV Music Publishing LLC Administered by Sony/ATV Music Publishing LLC, 424 Church street, Suite 1200, Nashville, TN 37219. All Rights on behalf of Union Prod. Ltd. in the United States Administered by Universal Music - MGB songs. International Copyright Secured. All Rights Reserved. *Reprinted by Permissions of Hal Leonard Corporation.*

3.1 Eve Curie, *Madame Curie* (1937; reissued, Boston: Da Capo Press, 2001): Part 2, 116.

4.1 Karen Blixen, Cited at http://fiveminutehistory.com/out-of-africa-10-inspirational-quotes-from-karen-blixen/. Accessed June 8, 2016.

5.1 Amy Poehler, "You Can't Do It Alone," *Harvard Magazine*, May 25, 2011. http://harvardmagazine.com/2011/05/you-cant-do-it-alone. Accessed January 8, 2016.

6.1 Piet Hein, "PAST PLUPERFECT," in *Grooks* (New York: Doubleday, 1969), 28. Reprinted with kind permission from Piet Hein a/s, DK-5500 Middlefart, Denmark.

7.1 Wislaw Szymborska, 1. Excerpt from "Nothing Twice," in *MAPS: Collected and Lost Poems by Wislawa Szymborksa*, translated from the Polish by Stanislaw Baranczak and Clare Cavanagh. English translation copyright 2015 by Houghton Mifflin Harcourt Publishing Company, Boston, MA. Reprinted by permission of Houghton Mifflin Harcourt Publishing Company. All rights reserved.

8.1 Rush, Digital Man, Words & Music by Neil Peart, Music by Geddy Lee and Alex Lifeson. Copyright © 1982 CORE MUSIC PUBLISHING. All Rights Reserved. Used By Permission of Alfred Music.

9.1 Ruth Reichl, "Teach Your Children Well," *Gourmet Magazine*, March 2007.

10.1 Quoted at http:// www.oprah.com/ spirit/What-Oprah-Knows-for-Sure-About-Always-Saying-Yes. Accessed March 31, 2016.

11.1 Samuel Johnson, *Works* (Oxford edition, 1835) VI:214.

12.1 Malala Yousafzai, quoted in the *Boston Globe*, September 8, 2013. https://www.bostonglobe.com/metro/2013/09/27/malala-yousafzai-pakistani-teen-shot-taliban-tells-harvard-audience-that-education-right-for-all/6cZBan0M4J3cAnmRZLfUmI/story.html. Accessed January 8, 2016.

INDEX